With expert readings and forecasts, you can chart a course to romance, adventure, good health, or career opportunities while gaining valuable insight into yourself and others. Offering a daily outlook for 18 full months, this fascinating guide shows you:

- The important dates in your life
- What to expect from an astrological reading
- How the stars can help you stay healthy and fit And more!

Let this sound advice guide you through a year of heavenly possibilities—for today and for every day of 2012!

SYDNEY OMARR'S® DAY-BY-DAY ASTROLOGICAL GUIDE FOR

ARIES—March 21–April 19
TAURUS—April 20–May 20
GEMINI—May 21–June 20
CANCER—June 21–July 22
LEO—July 23–August 22
VIRGO—August 23–September 22
LIBRA—September 23–October 22
SCORPIO—October 23–November 21
SAGITTARIUS—November 22–December 21
CAPRICORN—December 22–January 19
AQUARIUS—January 20–February 18
PISCES—February 19–March 20

IN 2012

SYDNEY OMARR'S®

DAY-BY-DAY ASTROLOGICAL GUIDE FOR

VIRGO

AUGUST 23–SEPTEMBER 22

2012

by Trish MacGregor
with Rob MacGregor

A SIGNET BOOK

SIGNET
Published by New American Library, a division of
Penguin Group (USA) Inc., 375 Hudson Street,
New York, New York 10014, USA
Penguin Group (Canada), 90 Eglinton Avenue East, Suite 700, Toronto,
Ontario M4P 2Y3, Canada (a division of Pearson Penguin Canada Inc.)
Penguin Books Ltd., 80 Strand, London WC2R 0RL, England
Penguin Ireland, 25 St. Stephen's Green, Dublin 2,
Ireland (a division of Penguin Books Ltd.)
Penguin Group (Australia), 250 Camberwell Road, Camberwell, Victoria 3124,
Australia (a division of Pearson Australia Group Pty. Ltd.)
Penguin Books India Pvt. Ltd., 11 Community Centre, Panchsheel Park,
New Delhi - 110 017, India
Penguin Group (NZ), 67 Apollo Drive, Rosedale, Auckland 0632,
New Zealand (a division of Pearson New Zealand Ltd.)
Penguin Books (South Africa) (Pty.) Ltd., 24 Sturdee Avenue,
Rosebank, Johannesburg 2196, South Africa

Penguin Books Ltd., Registered Offices:
80 Strand, London WC2R 0RL, England

First Printing, June 2011
10 9 8 7 6 5 4 3 2 1

First published by Signet, an imprint of New American Library,
a division of Penguin Group (USA) Inc.

 REGISTERED TRADEMARK—MARCA REGISTRADA

Printed in the United States of America

CONTENTS

CHAPTER 1

Paradigm Shift

There's more hype about December 21, 2012, than there was about the Y2K scare at the turn of the century. Depending on which Web site or book you read, the world will end on that day, the poles will shift, the aliens will land. In fact, there's been so much hype that in March 2007 *USA Today* ran an article titled "Does Maya Calendar Predict 2012 Apocalypse?"

"Maya civilization, known for advanced writing, mathematics and astronomy, flourished for centuries in Mesoamerica, especially between A.D. 300 and 900. Its Long Count calendar, which was discontinued under Spanish colonization, tracks more than 5,000 years, then resets at year zero," wrote G. Jeffrey MacDonald in the *USA Today* article.

It resets on December 21, 2012. It's the day that marks the winter solstice in the northern hemisphere. It's also the day that the sun will be aligned with the center of the Milky Way galaxy for the first time in nearly 26,000 years or, to be exact, in 25,625 years, what the Mayans considered to be a single galactic day. They divided that galactic day into five cycles of 5,125 years, and on December 21, that fifth cycle ends. So, what's that mean for us?

According to Mayan Indian elder Apolinario Chile Pixtum, it definitely doesn't mean the end of the world. He, in fact, says the doomsday theories spring from

Western, not Mayan ideas. "I came back from England last year and man, they had me fed up with this stuff."

Jose Huchin, a Yucatan Mayan archaeologist, says that if he went into Maya-speaking communities and asked people what was going to occur in 2012, they wouldn't have any idea. "That the world is going to end? They wouldn't believe you," he says.

A likely possibility for 2012 is a shift in paradigms. If 2011 was the year of transitions, then 2012 can be viewed as the year when people begin to embrace new ways of thinking about themselves, the society in which they live, and the world. With the meltdown in the financial and housing markets in 2008–2009, the election of the first African-American president, the bailouts of banks, rising foreclosures and unemployment, and the broken health-care system, a shift in belief systems seems inevitable.

As Daniel Pinchbeck wrote in *2012: The Return of Quetzalcoatl*: "If we were to conclude, after careful consideration, that our modern world is based upon fundamentally flawed conceptions of time and mind, that on these fatal defects we had erected a flawed civilization ... then logic might indicate the necessity, as well as the inevitability, of change. Such a shift would not be 'the end of the world,' but the end of a world, and the opening of the next."

How You Can Adapt to the Paradigm Shift

Our lives are marked by transitions. We make the *transition* from adolescence to adulthood, from dependent to independent, from being single to being married, from youth to middle age to old age, from life to death. These transitions are often marked by rituals—diplomas, ceremonies—that recognize our rites of passage.

In astrology, we have similar transitions, but they are triggered by the movement of the outer planets—Jupiter, Saturn, Uranus, Neptune, and Pluto. These planets are the slowest moving, so they exert the most impact on our lives. The lineup in 2011 pushed us toward the paradigm shift that will occur in 2012.

So now you're asking, *How's it going to affect me?* That depends on the angles these slower-moving planets make to your sun sign—and on your attitudes and deepest beliefs. After all, the planets only depict possible patterns that may occur. *We're* the scriptwriters. We have free will, the ability to make choices. Astrology simply provides information that makes those choices easier. To be informed is to be empowered.

The planet to watch in 2012 is Neptune, which enters Pisces on February 3 and remains there until the end of March 2025. Neptune was in Pisces briefly in 2011—from April 5 to August 5—then turned retrograde and slipped back into Aquarius for a final time. Since it takes this planet fourteen years to transit a single sign, it won't be back to Aquarius for another 168 years!

Now let's take a closer look at what Neptune's transit may mean for each of us.

The Role of Neptune in 2012

Neptune is an elusive planet, so far away from the sun that it's one of two planets that can't be seen without a telescope. The temperature of its surface clouds is around -218 degrees Celsius. Its atmosphere is composed of hydrogen and helium, and its interior is mostly ice and rock.

When Voyager 2 flew past Neptune in 1989, it was discovered that Neptune had a dark area composed of gas that swirled violently with the force of a hurricane. They called it the Great Dark Spot and compared it to the Great Red Spot on Jupiter. In 1994, however, the Hubble telescope found that that spot had disappeared. So we know that Neptune, like Jupiter, has weather patterns.

To understand Neptune's influence in our lives and how it will impact us from 2012 to 2026, when it moves through Pisces, let's take a walk through a brief slice of history.

The planet was discovered in 1846—not because it was spotted through a telescope, but due to a disturbing characteristic in the orbit of Uranus. Astronomers suspected the erratic orbit was created by the gravitational pull of another planet. In a sense, then, the way in which Neptune was discovered is a metaphor for its elusive characteristics in astrology. It symbolizes imagination, spiritual and intuitive talents, psychic experiences, artistic inspiration. On the downside, it represents our illusions, our blind spots, and governs alcoholism, drug addiction, confusion, escapism of all kinds. Astrologer Steven Forrest calls Neptune "the planet of consciousness . . . the blank state."

Shortly after Neptune was discovered, the California gold rush began (illusions). The Romantic movement (inspiration) also started, a reaction against intellectualism, materialism, and the rigidity of social structures that protected the wealthy, the privileged. Then in 1848, just two years after Neptune's discovery, the Spiritualist movement was born in a small cottage in Hydesville, New York, where the Fox family lived.

John and Margaret Fox and two of their daughters, Margaret and Kate, had moved into the house in December 1847. The place was reputedly haunted and strange noises and rappings could be heard at night, which kept the family awake. On the night of March 31, about three nights after the family had moved into the house, young Kate heard the noises and responded by snapping her fingers and called out, "Mr. Splitfoot. Do as I do." She then clapped her hands several times.

4

The pattern of her clapping was instantly duplicated. Her sister then joined in and demanded that "Splitfoot" do what she did. Her four claps were immediately answered with four claps. Mrs. Fox asked the invisible guest to rap out the ages of all of her seven children, which it did, with a pause between each one to individualize them.

Mrs. Fox began to question the rapper. Was it a human being? There was no response. She then asked it to rap twice if it was a spirit. It rapped twice—and the spiritualist movement was born.

Twenty-nine years after Neptune's discovery, a medium named George Colby of Iowa was holding a séance at the home of a local resident, a fellow named Wadsworth. Nothing extraordinary had happened so far that night. Colby was already a successful medium, and he'd done the usual things that night—passed on messages from the dead to the living.

Then, suddenly, Colby received a message from his Indian guide, Seneca, instructing him to travel immediately to Eau Claire, Wisconsin, where he was to hook up with T. D. Giddings, a Spiritualist. Once he was in Wisconsin, Seneca said, further instructions would be given. Colby, being a product of a time when the Spiritualist movement was sweeping across the country, did the expected thing. The next morning he packed up and left for Wisconsin. He met up with Giddings, and at a séance shortly afterward Colby and Giddings were given instructions to leave Wisconsin and head to Florida.

Colby was only twenty-seven years old at the time, a single man ready for adventure. Giddings, however, had a family and took them along. Back then, steamboats and trains were the only route south, and this odd little entourage took both. They rode a train to Jacksonville, Florida, then traveled by steamboat down the St. John's River to a place called Blue Springs. This frontier town was supposedly in the general vicinity of their final destination.

Seneca had described the place they were going to settle as having hills and a chain of lakes. The only thing that lay beyond the borders of Blue Springs looked like dense, subtropical forest. But when Seneca made contact and told the two men to begin their trek into the woods and to follow his directions, they did so.

They made their way through dense growth and after several miles arrived at the spot where Seneca said the Spiritualist camp would be created. Everything—from the high bluffs to the lakes and the lay of the land—looked exactly as Seneca had described.

Colby built a house on the shores of Lake Colby, and Giddings and his family built a home nearby. Colby eventually obtained a government deed for seventy-four acres that adjoined the area where he and Giddings had settled. They were apparently the only people for miles around.

For eighteen years, Colby didn't do much of anything about establishing a Spiritualist community in the area. He adopted several orphans, however, and raised them. He also operated a dairy.

In 1893, a Spiritualist named Rowley showed up and decided to establish a Spiritualist center in either De-Leon Springs or Winter Park. He invited a number of prominent Spiritualists from the north to travel to Florida to check out the area. Two of these Spiritualists were women who were prominent in the Lily Dale Spiritualist camp in New York. They didn't particularly care for Rowley, but Colby won them over, and they decided to create a Spiritualist camp on his property.

In October 1894, twelve mediums signed the charter for the Southern Cassadaga Spiritualist Camp. According to the charter, the association was to be a nonprofit organization that would promote the Spiritualist beliefs in the soul's immortality, "the nearness of the Spirit World, the guardianship of Spirit friends, and the possibility of communion with them," as the charter reads.

Seneca, Colby's guide, apparently advised him to remain in the background during this time, so his name doesn't appear on the charter, and he didn't have much to do with the organization of the camp. However, in 1895, he deeded the association thirty-five acres of his land. The first meeting was held in late 1895 and lasted three days. A hundred people attended the event to meet and sit with the mediums who had been invited.

Within three years of that first meeting, eight cottages, a dancing pavilion, a lodging hall, and a library had been built on the association grounds. Wealthy mediums from the north were being enticed to move to Cassadaga on a more or less permanent basis. From the late 1800s to the early part of the twentieth century, not much is written about the town. The camp apparently flourished, however, because the Cassadaga Hotel was built in 1922 and so were most of the cottages that still stand today.

In the century plus since Cassadaga was established, the rest of central Florida has grown up around it. Just thirty minutes south of it on I-4 is a whole other kind of world—Disney World! But as soon as you turn off Interstate 4, memories of Dumbo and Epcot, Universal and MGM, give way to southern pine forests. A kind of presence infuses the still air. You can't help but feel that nothing is what it appears to be.

For years there wasn't even a sign for Cassadaga. It was almost as if the people who are supposed to find their way here did so in spite of the lack of directions. Even today Cassadaga is little more than a black dot on a map, a punctuation point in the vastness of the pine forest. Lake Helen is the nearest town.

But if you blink too fast, Lake Helen is already a memory. Just beyond the outer edge of the town, the road climbs and dips through a series of low hills and shallow valleys. The trees seem thicker and darker here, the Spanish moss sways in the breeze, and shapes eddy across the shadowed road. A hush lingers in the air. Stop your car, lower your windows, and you probably won't hear a sound.

About half a mile outside of Lake Helen, you'll see a sign announcing that you're now in Cassadaga. But it isn't until you come around the next sharp curve that you know you're there. A large two-story stucco building looms in front of you, the Cassadaga Hotel. Its Mediterranean architecture dates back to the 1920s, during the heyday of Spiritualism. Along the right side of the building stretches a wide porch filled with rocking chairs. At dusk some evenings, when the light plays tricks with perception, some of the empty chairs rock, creaking softly in the quiet.

Spirits enjoying the evening? One never knows for sure. But perhaps that's part of the lure and the mystique of Cassadaga.

Given the uncertainty of the times in which we live, it's not surprising that business in Cassadaga is flourishing. On any weekend, the hotel lot is jammed with cars, and everywhere you look, people are walking around in search of the right psychic. Both sides of the main street are lined with small buildings that have signs posted out front advertising the kind of reading available. Unlike the early days of Cassadaga, when it was mainly Spiritualists, today's psychic offerings are vast. You can find everything from astrologers, tarot readers, and Reiki healers. But the mediums are still the draw, the magnet. As one young woman explained to us during a recent trip, "Everything is changing so fast, life is moving at such a rapid clip, that people are turning more and more to spiritual and intuitive insights and guidance."

And that pretty much sums up a large part of what Neptune's transit through Pisces may bring for each of us.

Neptune in Pisces

We had a brief taste of Neptune in Pisces, the sign it rules, between April 3, 2011, and August 4, 2011. Then Neptune turned retrograde and slipped back into Aquarius. But on February 3, 2012, it enters Pisces again. For clues about how this transit may manifest itself for you, look back to those four months in 2011. What was going on in your life then? Did you feel more creative? Did you take up a new artistic hobby? Did your spiritual beliefs undergo some sort of transformation? Were you more intuitive? Were you called upon to give selflessly in some respect? Did you feel your life was confusing, your goals muddled? Did you indulge more frequently in alcohol and drugs?

All of these areas fall under the governance of Neptune. So now let's look specifically at each sign for possible shifts under Neptune's fourteen-year transit through Pisces.

Aries ♈

Cardinal, fire

You're the trailblazer of the zodiac, known for your fearlessness, impulsiveness, and well, yes, sometimes your recklessness. You enjoy anything that induces an adrenaline rush—from extreme sports to love affairs to high-wire creative projects. You think outside the box, aren't known as a team player, and would rather delegate than be delegated to. In love, your passions are often extreme, you can be jealous and possessive, but when you fall, you fall hard, with your entire heart.

You're like an action hero, always on the move, doing, figuring the angles. Even your strong intuition comes through action—mostly impulses and burning hunches

9

on which you act quickly. Your spiritual beliefs probably aren't traditional, i.e., not associated with a particular religion or church. It's more likely that you've pieced together your own beliefs over the years and are still adding to them.

During Neptune's transit of Pisces and your solar twelfth house, your intuition and spirituality will deepen, the scope will broaden, and chances are it will all begin in the privacy of your interior world. Your dream life will be more vivid, and it should be easier to recall your dreams and work with them. You should have greater access to your own unconscious, so that it's easier to recall past lives and understand your own motives and psyche. In fact, the more you work consciously with your intuitive abilities and spiritual beliefs, the easier this paradigm shift will be for you.

Since the twelfth house represents institutions, it's possible that you may have more contact with hospitals, nursing homes, even prisons. You might be an employee or volunteer in one of these organizations. In some way, this experience enables you to reach for the greater good rather than for what is good only for you.

Taurus ♉

Fixed, earth

Your stubbornness, patience, and resoluteness are legendary. You complete whatever you start and often end up completing what other people start as well. In other words, due to your resilience and endurance, you often win where others fail. Where Aries trailblazes, you cultivate—relationships, a beautiful home, a family, a career, a garden. You enjoy being surrounded by beauty but aren't necessarily an extravagant spender.

Some signs need drama to thrive, but you're not one of them. You're a romantic who enjoys a harmonious relationship in which creativity can flourish. You tend to keep things to yourself—not so much secretive as circumspect. You speak when you have something meaningful to say.

Once Neptune enters Pisces, the tide will turn more in your direction. Pisces is a water sign that's compatible with your earth-sign sun, and you'll find that it deepens your innate curiosity about the deeper mysteries in life—telepathy, precognition, psychokinesis, synchronicity, what makes the universe tick, communication with the dead, UFOs, crop circles. You may join groups that support these interests and get involved with charitable organizations that support ideals in which you believe.

The eleventh house symbolizes groups, friends, our wishes, hopes and dreams, the people you hang with, goals, your life plan. So during Neptune's transit through Pisces, groups will be a major theme for you. You may join online groups that support your ideals, interests, and goals. There may be a psychic or intuitive component to these groups. Perhaps you end up in England, investigating crop circles. Or you might join a ghost-hunting group, a writer's group, a theater group. You might teach yoga for meditation to groups. You get the idea. One way or another, through group participation, online or off, you learn to reach for the greater good, the higher inspiration, the greater spiritual ideal.

Gemini ♊

Mutable, air

You're the communicator of the zodiac and can talk circles around anyone, anywhere, at any time, on virtually any subject. Your knowledge may not always be deep, but it's broad. When you don't know something, you research and ask questions incessantly, until your burning curiosity is sated.

Because you're ruled by Mercury, the planet of communication, you tend to use your rational, intellectual mind to explore your world. Your rational analysis of everything—from ideas to relationships—probably drives you nuts at times. But when this characteristic leads you into an exploration of psychic and spiritual realms, you're more grounded. With Neptune's transit through Pisces, you're going to have plenty of opportunities for this kind of exploration.

Neptune will be transiting the career section of your chart for fourteen years, suggesting that your professional life will be the focus of subtle but important change. In some way, psychic and spiritual exploration will become part of your professional endeavors. Opportunities will present themselves in these areas. Your creative ventures during this time will have a deeply psychic and spiritual texture to them. Your own intuition should deepen considerably, and as long as you act upon that inner knowledge, you won't be disappointed.

If you're not satisfied with your profession when this transit starts, then you may change career paths. Don't worry about how this will come about. You'll recognize the choices you should make and will have a strong inner sense about when to make them. During this transit, you'll learn to trust this inner sense and through your profession will learn to reach for inspired creativity and for what is best for the larger good, not just for what is good for you.

Cancer 69

Cardinal, water

You need roots, a place to call home, and it doesn't matter if that place is a camper, a palace, or a state of mind. Home is your harbor, your refuge, your retreat.

As a cardinal water sign, your intuition and perceptions are finely honed. Just about everything for you is filtered through a subjective lens, through your emotions and intuition. You may not always be able to explain to others why you make certain decisions, but you don't have an overpowering need to explain yourself. You do what you do because it feels right to you.

You're affectionate, passionate, and even possessive at times. Emotionally, you act and react the same way that a crab moves—sideways. It's how you avoid confrontation and revealing who you really are, deep within. You're often moody and changeable, but once you trust someone, you trust forever.

With Neptune in fellow water sign Pisces, transiting your solar ninth house, you'll be enjoying a prolonged period of psychic and spiritual development that your Cancer nature will love. Workshops and seminars on intuitive development are a possibility—you take them or teach them! Travel to foreign countries is likely, but it won't be strictly for pleasure. You could be on a spiritual quest of some kind, visiting sacred sites in different countries in search of answers, information, illumination.

In romance and love, any relationship that develops under this transit may have a deeply spiritual component to it. The person could be someone you have been with in past lives and now you're together again for this psychic exploration.

Leo ♌

Fixed, fire

Life is your stage, Leo. Your flamboyance and flair for drama infuse you with great magnetic appeal toward which others gravitate. You seek to succeed in everything you do and undertake, want to make an impact in every situation and usually do. Your generosity and loyalty are legendary, but not without strings! You expect to be the sun around which others spin like planets. Nothing short of center stage suits you. Perhaps this is why so many Leos enter the dramatic and creative arts. It's an area where they excel.

Your leadership abilities, fun-loving nature, and genuine compassion are much appreciated by your friends and loved ones. You bring passion and commitment to everything you do, and it's these qualities that enable you to tackle challenges head on. In love and romance, you're passionate and loyal.

During Neptune's transit through Pisces and your solar eighth house, you may find the boundaries between you and others blurring. It's as if you're being asked to move off center stage for a while so that you can give freely of your time, money, energy, to others. The eighth house represents shared resources—usually with a spouse, but it can be anyone with whom you share expenses, time, energy, expertise. So it's possible that your spouse or partner's income may be muddled or confused during this transit.

Since the eighth house also represents inheritances, there could be some confusion concerning a will. But however this transit unfolds for you in terms of specific events, the point is to heighten your spiritual and intuitive awareness so that you reach first for the greater good.

Virgo ♍

Mutable, earth

You're the perfectionist of the zodiac, something you probably consider both a blessing and curse. Your attention to detail is extraordinary—think Tony Shalhoub in *Monk*. The man walks into a room, and in a single sweeping glance the details leap out at him—the pencil aligned with due north, the faintest smudge of lipstick on a coffee mug, the rug slightly askew. Thanks to this attention to detail, you're able to penetrate deeply into any topic you study, any research you conduct. You dig and dig until you have all the information you need.

Like Gemini, you're ruled by Mercury, so your mind is lightning quick and you communicate your ideas with great authority. Duty and responsibility are important to you, and your focus is on doing your job, whatever it is, efficiently and well. There's no harder worker than you, Virgo.

Neptune's transit through Pisces and your solar seventh house means it will be opposed to your sun for fourteen years. Oppositions are like an itch you can't scratch; you just learn to live with it. During this period, your greatest lessons and challenges will come through business and personal partnerships. You may be called upon to place a partner's interests and well-being before your own. The best way to navigate this opposition is to develop your intuition and learn to rely on your inner guidance.

There may be some confusion around partnerships too. But if you continually strive to associate with upbeat, spiritual individuals, to seek out those of like minds and interests, you should do just fine. Any relationships in which you get involved are likely to have deep past-life connections.

Libra ♎

Cardinal, air

You're the mediator, Libra, the one who sees both sides of an issue because you can step into the other guy's shoes, zip yourself up inside his skin, understand how and why he feels the way he does. You're all about finding harmony and balance, the very quality that often eludes you. But seek it you must, as if it's your prime directive. In love, you're a romantic who flourishes in a committed, enduring relationship. But regardless of how long the relationship lasts, you still need to be shown and told that you are loved.

You excel in any profession that requires a balanced intellect and sensitivities. Music and the arts suit you, but so does the law, teaching, research, investigation. During Neptune's transit through Pisces, your daily work will take a decided turn toward the spiritual and psychic. You may begin to take time each day to meditate, practice yoga, or engage in creative work that develops and enhances your intuition.

You may find that the individuals who enter your daily work life during this transit are people you have known in past lives, and you're coming together again for a specific purpose. Perhaps you're going to join forces for some large-scale project that makes a difference in the world. Or maybe you meet up again simply to support each other. One thing is for sure: it's going to be an intriguing fourteen years. The best way to navigate it, Libra, is to pay close attention to synchronicities. They're your guides.

Scorpio ♏

Fixed, water

Intensely passionate, secretive, and downright psychic, you're one of the most strong-willed signs in the zodiac and certainly one of the most misunderstood. Like your fellow water signs Cancer and Pisces, you live in a world of feeling and intuition, filtering all your experiences through a subjective lens. But you're also vastly different from your brethren water signs. You're basically fearless, with a great capacity for endurance that rivals Taurus, and you don't know the meaning of the word "indifference." You live pretty much in a black and white world, where things are either right or wrong, without nuance.

You're the consummate investigator. Easy answers never suit you, so you dig deeper and deeper, connecting the dots the rest of us miss. You have a rich inner life, glean a lot of information through nontraditional means, i.e., psychically, and never apologize for it.

During Neptune's transit of Pisces and your solar fifth house, you're in for a treat, Scorpio. Your considerable intuition will deepen even more. You'll be so in tune with your muse that your creativity simply flows out of you. Since the fifth house also symbolizes love and romance, you can expect some intense relationships that are madly passionate and perhaps rooted in past lives. If you have a child during this transit, he or she will be intensely creative in some way, with some special talent. It will be up to you to help the child develop and nurture that talent.

Because Neptune blurs the boundaries between us and others, it's possible that you'll be called upon to give of yourself in a selfless way—to a lover, a child, a creative project. If you resist the urge to get lost in escapism—drugs, alcohol, sex—then this transit should prove beneficial in your evolution as a human being.

Sagittarius ♐

Mutable, fire

You're blunt, witty, nomadic. You're the seeker of truth, express what you feel and believe, and don't care if anyone agrees with you. You're after the big picture, the broad canvas of any issue, belief, situation, relationship. Mundane details bore you. Intellectually, you're logical and rational, like Gemini, your polar opposite. But there are some important differences. Gemini is focused on the here and now; you've always got one eye on the future, on the larger family of humanity, the planet, the universe.

You love your freedom, the ability to just take off on a whim, with a pack and your ATM card, and chafe at any restrictions others try to put on you. Yet, in a relationship, you're passionate though rarely possessive; attentive to your partner and yet careful to maintain your freedom.

Once Neptune enters Pisces and your solar fourth house, you may find that your natural interest in mysticism, metaphysics, and things that go bump in the night takes on a whole new meaning. Suddenly, but subtly, your home and family life could become a hub of psychic activity and spiritual exploration. Your quest involves your family, your emotions toward them and vice versa, and you may discover layers of meaning in these relationships that you simply didn't see before.

There can be confusion during this transit too. If you move, there could be confusion about the neighborhood, the house, the contract. Depending on your age, one of your parents may need additional help and support or may move in with you. However this part of the equation unfolds, you may have to give more than you receive. But ultimately, your intuition becomes your compass, and through giving without expectation of compensation, you learn to extend yourself for the greater good.

Capricorn ♑

Cardinal, earth

Any boss worth her job knows that if you give a task to a Capricorn, it gets done with a shocking efficiency, dedication, and understanding of the nuances involved. But it's not just work at which you excel, Capricorn. This is how you conduct everything in your life—you appraise the situation, event, or relationship, figure out a strategy, then set things in motion that are intended to reach the goal, whatever it may be.

You're industrious, disciplined, structured, and have so much common sense it sometimes works against you! When you need intuition, right-brain thinking, your left brain, your rational mind, hurls up blocks and urges you to rely solely on logic. But that's going to change under Neptune's transit through Pisces and your solar third house, Capricorn.

The third house governs communication, and during Neptune's fourteen-year transit through Pisces, your conscious mind becomes more intuitive, psychic, right-brain. It will be easier for you to grasp the larger picture of your goals, daily life, and relationships with siblings, friends, neighbors. Whereas before you might have been intent on a particular course, now you'll be urged to explore other options, to take interesting detours into unexplored realms.

You'll learn to rely more and more frequently on your gut feelings, your hunches, your initial sense about people, situations. Your intimate partnerships will have a richness and depth you haven't experienced before. The spiritual and psychic connections you feel in these relationships will be based on your genuine beliefs and not on something you've learned to believe from parents, peers, friends. You'll be operating on a whole different level and will learn to trust these feelings first and foremost.

Aquarius ♒

Fixed, air

You value freedom and individuality above all else, and it's evident in the way you think, your belief system, your passions, and interests. Others may sometimes see you as eccentric, but in truth you're the visionary of the zodiac. You believe that whatever you can imagine, can become tangible.

You're a conundrum to the people who know you. You're a nonconformist who conforms when it suits you and a passionate advocate for your causes, but from an intellectual rather than an emotional basis. Once you commit in a relationship, you still demand your freedom and space, and this is true for all facets of your life. You work best in avant garde fields—film, electronics, the arts, television, broadcasting.

Neptune's transit through Pisces and your solar second house will impact your finances and your values. For instance, you may become more cognizant of how you spend your money. Do you, for instance, buy products from a company that promotes ideals that are contrary to your own? Do you use your power as a consumer to make statements about your ideals and beliefs? Are you generous toward charities and nonprofit organizations whose causes are in line with your ideals? Is your profession in line with them?

You may find that you begin to value different qualities in your romantic relationships. You may be looking for a deeper spiritual or psychic connection with a partner. You may decide that the area where you live no longer feels right for you. There are many possible ways this transit can unfold for you. But you will certainly discover that you now seek the greater good for the collective—family, friends, community, world.

Pisces)(

Mutable, water

Like Scorpio and Cancer, you live primarily through your emotions and intuition. You also have a fantastic imagination that takes you places denied to the rest of us. Your inner world is rich, textured, alive with arche-typal material, past-life memories, and connections to the collective unconscious. Your empathic nature makes you something of a psychic sponge, so it's important that you associate with positive, upbeat people.

With Neptune in your sign for the next fourteen years, there will be many subtle changes in your life. You may decide to change careers, to pursue a line of work that is more spiritual or psychic in nature. You may find yourself growing away from certain people in your life whose interests and beliefs aren't aligned with your own. It's possible, too, that you take up meditation, yoga, or other mind/body practices that enable you to stay grounded and attuned.

In romance and love, your needs and desires will shift. You'll want a partner whose ideals match your own and will need to feel a deep spiritual connection with anyone with whom you get involved. There can be confusion with this transit—Neptune often fogs the brain!—but as long as you resist escapism, you should do fine.

CHAPTER 2

Astrology 101

On the day you were born, what was the weather like? If you were born at night, had the moon already risen? Was it full or the shape of a Cheshire cat's grin? Was the delivery ward quiet or bustling with activity? Unless your mom or dad has a very good memory, you'll probably never know the full details. But there's one thing you can know for sure: on the day you were born, the sun was located in a particular zone of the zodiac, an imaginary 360-degree belt that circles the earth. The belt is divided into twelve 30-degree portions called signs.

If you were born between July 23 and August 22, then the sun was passing through the sign of Leo, so we say that your sun sign is Leo. Each of the twelve signs has distinct attributes and characteristics. Leos, for instance, love being the center of attention. They're warm, compassionate people with a flair for the dramatic. Virgos, born between August 23 and September 22, are perfectionists with discriminating intellects and a genius for details. Capricorns, born between December 22 and January 19, are the worker bees of the zodiac, serious-minded, ambitious, industrious.

How Signs Are Classified

The twelve signs are categorized according to element and quality or modality. The first category, element, reads like a basic science lesson—fire, earth, air, and water—and describes the general physical characteristics of the signs.

Fire signs—Aries, Leo, Sagittarius—are warm, dynamic individuals who are always passionate about what they do.

Earth signs—Taurus, Virgo, Capricorn—are the builders of the zodiac, practical and efficient, grounded in everything they do.

Air signs—Gemini, Libra, Aquarius—are people who live mostly in the world of ideas. They are terrific communicators.

Water signs—Cancer, Scorpio, Pisces—live through their emotions, imaginations, and intuitions.

The second category describes how each sign operates in the physical world, how adaptable it is to circumstances:

Cardinal signs—Aries, Cancer, Libra, Capricorn—are initiators. These people are active, impatient, restless. They're great at starting things, but unless a project or a relationship holds their attention, they lose interest and may not finish what they start.

Fixed signs—Taurus, Leo, Scorpio, Aquarius—are deliberate, controlled, resolute. These individuals tend to move more slowly than cardinal signs, are often stubborn, and resist change. They seek roots and stability and are always in the game for the long haul. They aren't quitters.

Mutable signs—Gemini, Virgo, Sagittarius, Pisces—are adaptable. These people are flexible, changeable, communicative. They don't get locked into rigid patterns or belief systems.

SUN SIGNS

Sign	Date	Element	Quality
Aries ♈	March 21–April 19	·Fire	Cardinal
Taurus ♉	April 20–May 20	Earth	Fixed
Gemini ♊	May 21–June 21	Air	Mutable
Cancer ♋	June 22–July 22	Water	Cardinal
Leo ♌	July 23–August 22	Fire	Fixed
Virgo ♍	August 23–September 22	Earth	Mutable
Libra ♎	September 23–October 22	Air	Cardinal
Scorpio ♏	October 23–November 21	Water	Fixed
Sagittarius ♐	November 22–December 21	Fire	Mutable
Capricorn ♑	December 22–January 19	Earth	Cardinal
Aquarius ♒	January 20–February 18	Air	Fixed
Pisces ♓	February 19–March 20	Water	Mutable

The Planets

The planets in astrology are the players who make things happen. They're the characters in the story of your life. This story always begins with the sun, the giver of life.

Your sun sign describes your self-expression, your primal energy, the essence of who you are. It's the archetypal pattern of your Self. When you know another person's sun sign, you already have a great deal of information about that person. Let's say you're a Taurus who has just started dating a Gemini. How compatible are you?

On the surface, it wouldn't seem that you have much in common. Taurus is a fixed earth sign; Gemini is a mutable air sign. Taurus is persistent, stubborn, practical, a cultivator as opposed to an initiator. Gemini is a chameleon, a communicator, social, with a mind as quick as lightning. Taurus is ruled by Venus, which governs the arts, money, beauty, love, and romance, and Gemini is ruled by Mercury, which governs communication and travel. There doesn't seem to be much common ground. But before we write off this combination, let's look a little deeper.

Suppose the Taurus has Mercury in Gemini and suppose the Gemini has Venus in Taurus? This would mean that the Taurus and Gemini each have their rulers in the other person's sign. They probably communicate well and enjoy travel and books (Mercury) and would see eye to eye on romance, art, and music (Venus). They might get along so well, in fact, that they collaborate on creative projects.

Each of us is also influenced by the other nine planets (the sun and moon are treated like planets in astrology) and the signs they were transiting when we were born. Suppose our Taurus and Gemini have the same moon sign? The moon rules our inner needs, emotions and intuition, and all that makes us feel secure within ourselves. Quite often, compatible moon signs can overcome even the most glaring difference in sun signs because the two people share similar emotions.

In the section on monthly predictions, your sun sign always takes center stage, and every prediction is based on the movement of the transiting planets in relation to your sun sign. Let's say you're a Sagittarius. Between January 7 and February 4 this year, Venus will be transiting your sign. What's this mean for you? Well, since Venus rules—among other things—romance, you can expect your love life to pick up significantly during these weeks. Other people will find you attractive and be more open to your ideas, and you'll radiate a certain charisma. Your creative endeavors will move full steam ahead.

The planets table provides an overview of the planets and the signs that they rule. Keep in mind that the moon is the swiftest-moving planet, changing signs about every two and a half days, and that Pluto is the snail of the zodiac, taking as long as thirty years to transit a single sign. Although the faster-moving planets—the moon,

Mercury, Venus, and Mars—have an impact on our lives, it's the slow pokes—Uranus, Neptune, and Pluto—that bring about the most profound influence and change. Jupiter and Saturn fall between the others in terms of speed. This year, Jupiter spends the first six months in Taurus, then enters Gemini on June 11 and doesn't leave that sign until late June 2013.

In the section on predictions, the most frequent references are to the transits of Mercury, Venus, and Mars. In the daily predictions for each sign, the predictions are based primarily on the transiting moon.

Now glance through the planets table. When a sign is in parentheses, it means the planet corules that sign. This assignation dates back to when we thought there were only seven planets in the solar system. But since there were still twelve signs, some of the planets had to do double duty!

THE PLANETS

Planet	Rules	Attributes of Planet
Sun ☉	Leo	self-expression, primal energy, creative ability, ego, individuality
Moon ☽	Cancer	emotions, intuition, mother or wife, security
Mercury ☿	Gemini, Virgo	intellect, mental acuity, communication, logic, reasoning, travel, contracts
Venus ♀	Taurus, Libra	love, romance, beauty, artistic instincts, the arts, music, material and financial resources
Mars ♂	Aries (Scorpio)	physical and sexual energy, aggression, drive

Planet	Rules	Attributes of Planet
Jupiter ♃	Sagittarius (Pisces)	luck, expansion, success, prosperity, growth, creativity, spiritual interests, higher education, law
Saturn ♄	Capricorn (Aquarius)	laws of physical universe, discipline, responsibility, structure, karma, authority
Uranus ♅	Aquarius	individuality, genius, eccentricity, originality, science, revolution
Neptune ♆	Pisces	visionary self, illusions, what's hidden, psychic ability, dissolution of ego boundaries, spiritual insights, dreams
Pluto ♀ ♇	Scorpio	the darker side, death, sex, regeneration, rebirth, profound and permanent change, transformation

Houses and Rising Signs

In the instant you drew your first breath, one of the signs of the zodiac was just passing over the eastern horizon. Astrologers refer to this as the rising sign or ascendant. It's what makes your horoscope unique. Think of your ascendant as the front door of your horoscope, the place where you enter into this life and begin your journey.

Your ascendant is based on the exact moment of your birth and the other signs follow counterclockwise. If you have Taurus rising, for example, that is the cusp of your first house. The cusp of the second would be Gemini, of the third Cancer, and so on around the horoscope circle in a counterclockwise direction. Each house governs a particular area of life, which is outlined below.

The best way to find out your rising sign is to have your horoscope drawn up by an astrologer. For those of you with access to the Internet, though, there are several sites that provide free birth horoscopes. www.astro.com and www.cafeastrology.com are two good ones.

In a horoscope, the ascendant (cusp of the first house), IC (cusp of the fourth house), descendant (cusp of the seventh house), and MC (cusp of the tenth house) are considered to be the most critical angles. Any planets that fall close to these angles are extremely important in the overall astrological picture of who you are. By the same token, planets that fall in the first, fourth, seventh, and tenth houses are also considered to be important.

Now here's a rundown on what the houses mean.

Ascendant or Rising: The First of Four Important Critical Angles in a Horoscope

- How other people see you
- How you present yourself to the world
- Your physical appearance

First House, Personality

- Early childhood
- Your ego
- Your body type and how you feel about your body
- General physical health
- Defense mechanisms
- Your creative thrust

Second House, Personal Values

- How you earn and spend your money
- Your personal values
- Your material resources and assets
- Your attitudes and beliefs toward money
- Your possessions and your attitude toward those possessions
- Your self-worth
- Your attitudes about creativity

Third House, Communication and Learning

- Personal expression
- Intellect and mental attitudes and perceptions
- Siblings, neighbors, and relatives
- How you learn
- School until college
- Reading, writing, teaching
- Short trips (the grocery store versus Europe in seven days)
- Earth-bound transportation
- Creativity as a communication device

IC or Fourth House Cusp: The Second Critical Angle in a Horoscope

- Sign on IC describes the qualities and traits of your home during early childhood
- Describes roots of your creative abilities and talents

Fourth House, Your Roots

- Personal environment
- Your home
- Your attitudes toward family

- Early childhood conditioning
- Real estate
- Your nurturing parent

Some astrologers say this house belongs to Mom or her equivalent in your life, others say it belongs to Dad or his equivalent. It makes sense to me that it's Mom because the fourth house is ruled by the moon, which rules mothers. But in this day and age, when parental roles are in flux, the only hard and fast rule is that the fourth belongs to the parent who nurtures you most of the time.

- The conditions at the end of your life
- Early childhood support of your creativity and interests

Fifth House, Children and Creativity

- Kids, your firstborn in particular
- Love affairs, romance
- What you enjoy
- Creative ability
- Gambling and speculation
- Pets

Traditionally, pets belong in the sixth house. But that definition stems from the days when pets were chattel. These days, we don't even refer to them as pets. They are animal companions who bring us pleasure.

Sixth House, Work and Responsibility

- Day-to-day working conditions and environment
- Competence and skills
- Your experience of employees and employers
- Duty to work, to employees
- Health and the daily maintenance of your health

Descendant/Seventh House Cusp: The Third Critical Angle in a Horoscope

- The sign on the house cusp describes the qualities sought in intimate or business relationships
- Describes qualities of creative partnerships

Seventh House, Partnerships and Marriage

- Marriage
- Marriage partner
- Significant others
- Business partnerships
- Close friends
- Open enemies
- Contracts

Eighth House, Transformation

- Sexuality as transformation
- Secrets
- Death, taxes, inheritances, insurance, mortgages, and loans
- Resources shared with others
- Your partner's finances
- The occult (read: astrology, reincarnation, UFOs, everything weird and strange)
- Your hidden talents
- Psychology
- Life-threatening illnesses
- Your creative depths

Ninth House, Worldview

- Philosophy and religion
- The law, courts, judicial system
- Publishing
- Foreign travels and cultures

- College, graduate school
- Spiritual beliefs
- Travel abroad

MC or Cusp of Tenth House: The Fourth Critical Angle in a Horoscope

- Sign on cusp of MC describes qualities you seek in a profession
- Your public image
- Your creative and professional achievements

Tenth House, Profession and Career

- Public image as opposed to a job that merely pays the bills (sixth house)
- Your status and position in the world
- The authoritarian parent and authority in general
- People who hold power over you
- Your public life
- Your career/profession

Eleventh House, Ideals and Dreams

- Peer groups
- Social circles (your writers' group, your mother's bridge club)
- Your dreams and aspirations
- How you can realize your dreams

Twelfth House, Personal Unconscious

- Power you have disowned that must be claimed again
- Institutions—hospitals, prisons, nursing homes—and what is hidden
- What you must confront this time around, your karma, issues brought in from other lives

- Psychic gifts and abilities
- Healing talents
- What you give unconditionally

In the section on predictions, you'll find references to transiting planets moving into certain houses. These houses are actually solar houses that are created by putting your sun sign on the ascendant. This technique is how most predictions are made for the general public rather than for specific individuals.

Lunations

Every year there are twelve new moons and twelve full moons, with some years having thirteen full moons. The extra full moon is called the Blue Moon. New moons are typically when we should begin new projects, set new goals, seek new opportunities. They're times for beginnings. They usher in new opportunities according to house and sign.

Two weeks after each new moon, there's a full moon. This is the time of harvest, fruition, when we reap what we've sown.

Whenever a new moon falls in your sign, take time to brainstorm what you would like to achieve during the weeks and months until the full moon falls in your sign. These goals can be in any area of your life. Or, you can simply take the time on each new moon to set up goals and strategies for what you would like to achieve or manifest during the next two weeks—until the full moon—or until the next new moon.

Here's a list of all the new moons and full moons during 2012. The asterisk beside any new moon entry indicates a solar eclipse; the asterisk next to a full moon entry indicates a lunar eclipse.

LUNATIONS OF 2012

New Moons	Full Moons
January 23—Aquarius	January 9—Cancer
February 21—Pisces	February 7—Leo
March 22—Aries	March 8—Virgo
April 21—Taurus	April 6—Libra
*May 20—Gemini	May 5—Scorpio
June 19—Gemini	*June 4—Sagittarius
July 19—Cancer	July 3—Capricorn
August 17—Leo	August 1—Aquarius
September 15—Virgo	August 31—Pisces
October 15—Libra	September 29—Aries
*November 13—Scorpio	October 29—Taurus
December 13—Sagittarius	*November 28—Gemini
	December 28—Cancer

Every year there are two lunar and two solar eclipses, separated from each other by about two weeks. Lunar eclipses tend to deal with emotional issues and our internal world and often bring an emotional issue to the surface related to the sign and house in which the eclipse falls. Solar eclipses deal with events and often enable us to see something that has eluded us. They also symbolize beginnings and endings.

Read more about eclipses in the Big Picture for your sign for 2012. I also recommend Celeste Teal's excellent book, *Eclipses*.

Mercury Retrograde

Every year, Mercury—the planet that symbolizes communication and travel—turns retrograde three times. During these periods, our travel plans often go awry, communication breaks down, computers go berserk, cars or appliances develop problems. You get the idea. Things in our daily lives don't work as smoothly as we would like.

Here are some guidelines to follow for Mercury retrogrades:

- Try not to travel. But if you have to, be flexible and think of it as an adventure. If you're stuck overnight in an airport in Houston or Atlanta, though, the adventure part of this could be a stretch.
- Don't sign contracts—unless you don't mind revisiting them when Mercury is direct again.
- Communicate as succinctly and clearly as possible.
- Back up all computer files. Use an external hard drive and/or a flash drive. If you've had a computer crash, you already know how frustrating it can be to reconstruct your files.
- Don't buy expensive electronics. Expensive anything.
- Don't submit manuscripts or screenplays, pitch ideas, or launch new projects.
- Revise, rewrite, rethink, review.

In the Big Picture for each sign, check out the dates for this year's Mercury retrogrades and how these retrogrades are likely to impact you. Do the same for eclipses.

CHAPTER 3

Matters of the Heart in 2012

When you're in the throes of a paradigm shift, every area of your life may feel more vulnerable. You may notice a distinct change in what you want and expect in a romantic partnership. You may find yourself attracted to people who are different from people to whom you've been attracted in the past. Whether you're in a new or long-term relationship or are just looking, it's important to keep the channels of communication wide open.

There are, however, some constants to keep in mind with romance and love—which sun signs are most compatible with your own.

Astrology and Carl Jung

In 1950, Swiss psychologist Carl Jung undertook an astrological study about the compatibility of 180 married couples and used 50 aspects—or angles that planets make to each other. This was in the days before personal computers and astrology software that can erect a natal chart and compare several charts in just seconds. The study took several years, and the results were intriguing.

He found three aspects to be the best indicators for compatibility: a sun/moon conjunction, where one partner's sun sign is the same as the sign of the other person's moon; a moon/moon conjunction, where both individuals have their moons in the same sign; and a moon/ascendant conjunction, when one partner's moon is in the same sign as the other person's ascendant. In his book *Synchronicity, An Acausal Connecting Principle,* Jung noted that the first two aspects "have long been mentioned in the old literature as marriage characteristics, and they therefore represent the oldest tradition."

The sun/moon conjunction makes perfect sense astrologically. Your sun sign describes your overall personality; the sign of your moon describes your inner world, your emotions, what makes you feel secure. So if you're a Pisces involved with someone who has a Pisces moon, for example, then there's a beautiful give and take between you. You understand each other. If you have different sun signs, but your moons are in the same sign, then the emotional and intuitive connection is so strong you probably finish each other's sentences.

What about that third aspect, with the moon and ascendant in the same sign? This one also makes perfect sense. The ascendant is the doorway to your chart and describes, among other things, the persona you project to the outside world. So an individual with his or her moon in the same sign as your ascendant feels emotionally secure in your presence and sees the person behind the mask you wear.

Another compatibility aspect includes Venus, the planet that symbolizes love and romance. The most common I've seen are: Venus/sun, Venus/moon, Venus/ascendant; Venus/descendant cusp (cusp of the seventh house of partnerships); and Venus/Mars in the same sign. Another interesting connection I've noted is among couples who have "mirror" charts, where the sign of one partner's ascendant is the same as the other person's descendant. In other words, let's say you have Scorpio rising and your partner has Scorpio on the cusp of his or her seventh house. This aspect brings balance to the relationship.

But because one size doesn't fit all, you and your partner may have other aspects in your charts that make you compatible. For the purpose of this book, we're going to be looking only at sun-sign combinations for compatibility.

Your Best Matches

Aries

Your freedom and independence are paramount to your happiness, so you need a partner who understands and respects your space. But because you're a stranger to compromise, a vital part of any relationship, you may find intimate relationships challenging. Once you're involved, your passions are fierce and can easily topple into the dark extremes of jealousy, possessiveness, suspicion.

Your entrepreneurial and fearless spirit enjoys a partner who can compete with you on any level—on those long hikes into the wilderness, in the boardroom, in the classroom, in the garage out back where you're building your newest invention. You get the idea here, right, Aries? Boredom is your nemesis. So, which signs are good matches for you? Let's take a closer look at some of the possibilities.

Sagittarius. This fellow fire sign will give you all the freedom you crave—and then some. She'll match you joke for joke, drink for drink. If she's the physical type, and many of them are, she'll match you on those hikes. But for a Sadge, those hikes may be in some far-flung spot like Tibet. Like you, Sadge pushes herself, but she's more adaptable than you are. Sometimes she may come off like a know-it-all. But overall, this combination holds great promise.

Gemini. This air sign's wit, versatility, and ability to talk about virtually anything appeal to you. He's generally not possessive, either, a major plus when you're in one of your darker moods. His mind is sharp and lightning quick, and he probably has a vast, complicated network of friends and acquaintances. Also appealing. So what're the negatives? Gemini generally isn't as independent as you are and may spend more time with his friends than he does with you. But overall, this combination is lively, fun, and never boring.

Leo. Another fire sign. On the surface, it looks like a good match. Leo possesses an infinite capacity for enjoyment, which appeals to you. But she also loves having center stage—not just sometimes, but most of the time—and that can be a major turnoff for you.

Libra, Aquarius. Libra is your opposite sign. The match could be fantastic because you balance each other. Where you're the loner, she's the social butterfly. You're independent, she's a networker with more friends than a hive has bees. Whether this works or not depends on the signs of your natal moons, ascendants, and Venus. You and Aquarius could be a winning combination. His independence matches yours, he's as sharp as the proverbial tack, and he pulls no punches in expressing what he wants, when he wants it. Downside? He may not be as physical or competitive and lives much of his life in his head.

What about another *Aries*? Depends on the signs of your moons. Strictly on the basis of sun signs, you're both so independent the relationship may never get off the ground!

Taurus

Stable, dependable, patient. You bring these qualities to any close relationship, and once you commit it's usually for keeps. You aren't into drama, artifice, flamboyance—not for yourself and not in a partner, either. But you en-

39

joy a partner who is physically attractive or who has a particular artistic gift that you appreciate—music, art, a way with words, anything that appeals to your senses.

If you're a Taurus who is into sports and health, and many of them are, then a health-conscious partner is a major plus. But there's another side to you, too, an inner mystic, a quiet, observant Buddha who remains calm and centered, in tune with unseen forces. You would do well with a partner who possesses that quality as well.

Leo, Sagittarius, Aries. Unless you have a moon, rising, or Venus in one of those signs, the fire signs probably won't work for you. Too much drama, boisterous behavior, and anger to suit your tastes.

Virgo, Capricorn. Fellow earth signs. Virgo could be the ticket. She's as practical as you are and, in many instances, just as mystical. Capricorn is focused, as physical as you are, but may not be as mystically inclined.

Scorpio. Your opposite sign, so there may be a good balance. She's secretive and can be vengeful, but she's just as mystical as you are.

Gemini

In a romantic relationship, conversation and discussion top your list. In fact, any potential partner must seduce your mind first—with ideas, information, books, theories that connect seemingly disparate bits of whatever it is that rushes through your head 24/7. You're up front about what you feel, but those feelings could change at a moment's notice, a dichotomy that can be confusing to a partner. And to everyone else around you, for that matter. No wonder your sign is represented by the twins.

For you, everything starts with a single burning question: *Why?* You then set about to find out why, and in the course of your quest you may be distracted by a million other pieces of information that are eventually integrated into your journey. This means, of course, that your journey toward the why of the original question may not end in *this* lifetime! So you need a partner whose curiosity matches your own.

Sagittarius, Aries. Sadge is your opposite sign. He matches you in curiosity, but may not be up to snuff in other areas. With Aries, there's never a dull moment. She's a match for your quickness and wit, but may not have the curiosity you do about other people.

Libra and Aquarius. Usually compatible in that both signs value information and communication.

Water signs. Oddly, Pisces might be a good match because it's the only other sign represented by two of something, and his imagination will appeal to you.

Cancer

In romance, it's always about feelings first—not the mind, not even the body, but *emotions*. Your partner has to be as dedicated to her inner world as you are to yours, so that your inner worlds can, well, *merge*. That's the ideal. Yet, because you're a cardinal sign, like Aries, Libra, and Capricorn, there's a certain independence in you that demands emotional space. Contradictory, but not to you.

Despite your emotional depth, you tend to avoid confrontations. Like the crab that symbolizes your sign, you retreat into your shell at the first sign of trouble. Yet, how can you smooth out anything in a relationship if you can't discuss disagreements? It's as if you expect disagreements to be ironed out telepathically. So if that's true, then your best matches romantically are probably other water signs. Let's take a deeper look.

Pisces, Scorpio. Both signs are as psychic as you are, but in different ways. Pisces is the softer of the two signs, dreamier. Scorpio might overwhelm you, but gives you the emotional space you need.

Taurus. A good match. This earth sign helps you to ground yourself in the real world and gives you emotional space—maybe more than you need!

Capricorn, Virgo. Cappy is your opposite sign, so the possibility of balance is there. Virgo might be too picky for your tastes, but shows you how to communicate verbally.

Air signs? Fire signs? Not so good, unless you have a moon, ascendant, Venus, or Mars in one of those signs.

Leo

You've got enough passion for all the other signs in the zodiac—and then some. That passion is often linked to the attention of others, which probably explains why so many actors and actresses have a Leo sun, moon, or ascendant. Your life is about drama, and the higher the drama, the deeper your passion. But it's that passion that busts through obstacles, that burns a path toward where you want to go in both life and love.

Your compassion extends to anyone in a tough situation—or to any creature that needs love and reassurance that we humans aren't heartless. So, let's be real here. Your partner, whoever he or she is, probably has to love animals the way you do. Even if there are twenty strays in your back yard, your partner must be amenable to the idea that you feed the multitudes. Not an easy request, says the universe. But there are some strong possibilities.

Sagittarius, Aries, fellow fire signs. Sadge, symbolized by a creature that is half human and half horse, usually has animal companions—not pets, but *companions.* There's a big difference. She's your match in the compassion area. She understands your need to connect to an audience. But she may not stick around to be a part of that audience. The energy match with Aries is great. But unless you've got the moon, ascendant, or Venus in Aries, she may not shower you—or your animal companions—with enough attention.

Gemini, Libra. These two air signs could be excellent matches for you, Leo. You'll enjoy Gemini's lively intellect and Libra's artistic sensibilities.

Virgo

You're the absolute master of details. You collect massive amounts of information, sift through it all with an eye for what works and what doesn't, and toss out everything that is extraneous. Your quest for perfection is never compromised, and it's evident in the inner work you do, honing your own psyche, and in everything you take on in the external world. These qualities can make a romantic partnership somewhat challenging because your partner goes under the same microscope that everything else does.

You're a layered individual and benefit from a partner who understands that and knows how to peel away those layers without making you feel vulnerable or exposed. A partner who enjoys every single one of those layers. So who's your best match?

Taurus and Capricorn. Fellow earth signs. Taurus takes all the time the relationship needs to peel away the layers of your personality so she can find the gold at your core. She's patient, resolute, determined. Capricorn might consider the relationship as just one more challenge to be conquered, but could be a nice balance to your penchant for details.

Cancer, Scorpio. These two water signs complement you. Cancer grasps who you are emotionally, but may not be as willing as you are to discuss elements of the relationship. Since your sign is ruled by Mercury, the planet of communication, that could be a drawback. Scorpio's emotional intensity could be overwhelming, but he'll be delighted to peel away the layers of your personality!

Gemini. Even though air and earth aren't usually compatible, Gemini and Virgo share Mercury as a ruler. Communication in this combination is likely to be strong and fluid, with a constant exchange of ideas.

Libra

There's a certain duality in your psychological makeup that isn't mentioned very often. It's not due to a penchant for secrecy or deviousness, but to a reluctance to hurt anyone's feelings. As a result, you often find yourself paralyzed by indecision. *Who do I really love? A or B?* Since you don't want to hurt either person, you maintain both relationships and make yourself and everyone around you absolutely nuts.

You have a need for harmony and balance in relationships. You dislike confrontation and dissension, so all too often you surrender to your partner's wants at your own expense. So which signs are good matches for you?

Gemini, Aquarius. Fellow air signs understand your psychological makeup. Gemini experiences some of the same duality that you do, but for different reasons. He isn't bothered by dichotomies, since his own life is predicated on them. He appeals to that part of you who needs to communicate honestly. Aquarius may be a bit too rigid for you, insisting that you bend to his desires, but the depth and breadth of his vision attract you at a visceral level.

Sagittarius, Leo, Aries. Any of the fire signs could be an excellent match. Sagittarius never bores you and enjoys you for *who you are.* Leo may want more attention than you're willing to give, but her warmth and compassion will delight you. You and Aries, your opposite sign, balance each other.

Taurus, Virgo, Capricorn. Of the three earth signs, Taurus is probably the best match because you share Venus as a ruler. That means you have similar tastes in music and art and probably share some of the same attitudes and beliefs about money.

Scorpio

As the most emotionally intense sign of the zodiac and one of the most psychic, your powerful and magnetic personality can intimidate even heads of state. Your life patterns are about breaking taboos, digging deeper, looking for the absolute bottom line in whatever you do, in any relationship in which you become involved. You feel and intuit your way through life, and your partner must understand that.

All of this brooding and mulling takes place in the privacy of your own head. The side you show others is light and funny, with a dry wit that can charm, seduce, or spar with the best of them. Yet inside you're always asking, *What motivates him? What secrets does he have?* Given the complexities of your personality, which signs are most compatible with yours?

Pisces, Cancer. Of these two water signs, Pisces matches you in raw intuitive ability, but may be too indecisive to suit you long term. Cancer can be just as secretive as you, but unless you've got a moon or rising in Cancer, this sign could be too clingy.

Taurus, Virgo, Capricorn. The earth signs are compatible matches. Taurus, your opposite sign, brings sensuality to your sexuality and helps to dispel your suspicions about other people's motives. Her earthiness grounds your psychic ability. Virgo's discerning and gentle nature mitigates your emotional intensity. Capricorn's determination appeals to that same quality in you.

Fire signs? *Leos* and Scorpios are both fixed signs, and there seems to be something between them that is powerful. Look at Leo Bill Clinton and Scorpio Hillary.

Sagittarius

You're so multifaceted, with so many different talents, that a relationship presents certain dilemmas—namely, commitment to another person. It's so much easier to commit to, well, your own interests! Also, there's that little ole thing called personal freedom, which you value every bit as much as Aries.

Like Libra, there's a curious duality in your makeup,

best explained, perhaps, by the symbol for your sign—the mythological centaur. Half-horse, half-human, this figure might be defined as the wild woman (or man) versus the conformist. A part of you operates from gut instinct and the other part of you is acculturated. Which signs are your best matches?

Aries, Leo, Sagittarius. As remarked under the Aries section, a relationship with this sign may not go anywhere because you're both so independent. Aries might want to be in charge all the time, and you get fed up and hit the open road. Leo could be a terrific choice, particularly if one of you has a moon in the other's sun sign. Another Sadge would be intriguing.

Taurus, Virgo, Capricorn. Of these three earth signs, Capricorn is the best match. Even if she lacks your intuitive gifts, her focus, direction, and resolute determination equal yours. Taurus, your opposite sign, could also be a good match. You share a fascination with the paranormal, and your energies would balance each other.

Air signs? Water signs? Probably not, unless you have a moon, rising, or some other prominent planet in those signs.

Capricorn

You build relationships in the same careful way that you build everything else in your life—a brick at a time. A conversation here, a dinner there, a movie, a moonlit walk, an exchange of beliefs: you're methodical, consistent, disciplined. Pretty soon, the foundation is solid, the chemistry is exactly right, and you know exactly what you want.

A relationship, of course, involves the human heart—not mortar and bricks—and that's where it may get tricky. You could discover that your methodical approach doesn't work as well in a relationship as it does with your career. Your success will depend, to a certain extent, on your compatibility with your partner.

Taurus, Virgo, Capricorn. Taurus's solidity and dependability appeal to you, and he's as private as you are. But his still waters run deep, and he may not express his emotions as readily as you would like. Yet the match would be a good one. Virgo understands what drives you. Another Capricorn, i.e., type A personality, would wear you out!

Scorpio, Pisces. While either of these water signs is compatible with your earth-sign sun, Pisces may too ambivalent for you, too indecisive. Scorpio, though, is a strong match. All that intensity appeals to you at a visceral level, your sex lives would be fantastic, and you share a similar determination. *Cancer*, your opposite sign, might work if the Cancer has a moon or rising in your sign.

Fire signs? Air signs? Again, it depends on the distribution of fire- and air-sign planets in your natal chart.

Aquarius

In love and romance, as in life, your mind is your haven, your sanctuary, your sacred place. It's where everything begins for you. From your visionary, cutting-edge ideas to your humanitarian causes and interests in esoterica, you're a wild card, not easily pigeonholed. It doesn't make any difference to you whether your partner shares these interests, as long as he or she recognizes your right to pursue them.

There's a rebel in you that pushes against the status quo, and that's something your partner has to understand too. Your connections to people and to the world aren't easily grasped by others. Too weird, they think. Too out there. But that's fine. You understand who and what you are, and in the end, that's all you need. So, which signs are your best matches?

Gemini, Libra. Your air sign *compadres* are excellent matches. Gemini suits your prodigious intellect, causes, and ideas. Good communication usually is a hallmark of this relationship, and Gemini is supportive of your causes. With Libra, the focus is on relationships—yours and Libra's connection to five million others. But the right mix exists for a strong partnership. A relationship with another *Aquarius* could be challenging since you'll both insist you're right. But if you can move past that, you'll do fine. Another Aquarius may be like looking in the mirror 24/7. Not for the faint-hearted.

Aries, Leo, Sagittarius. With these fire signs, you enjoy the freedom to be your own person. Life with Aries is never boring and the conversation and adventures are stimulating, but he may not share your humanitarian and esoteric interests. Sagittarius loves your mind and insights, your idealism and rebellion against the establishment. Great compatibility overall. Leo is your opposite sign, suggesting a good balance between your head and his heart.

Earth or water signs? Only if you have prominent planets in either of those elements.

Pisces

It's true that your inner world is often more real and genuine to you than anything in the external world. The richness of your imagination, the breadth of your intuition . . . these qualities create a kind of seductive atmosphere that's tough to move beyond. But because you're a physical being, in a physical world, who has to eat and sleep, work and function, who loves and triumphs and yearns, you have to move beyond it. So you do.

But always there's an inner tension, a kind of bewilderment, a constant questioning. *Where am I going? What am I doing? Do I really want to do this or that?* Your head and your heart are forever at odds, so no wonder your sign is symbolized by two fish moving in opposite directions. In romance and love, this indecisiveness can be problematic. So which signs are most compatible for you?

Scorpio, Cancer. Scorpio's emotional intensity could overwhelm you, but he balances your indecisiveness with his unwavering commitment to a particular path. Intuitively, you're on the same page, a major plus. Cancer's innate gentleness appeals to you, and she appreciates you exactly as you are.

Taurus, Capricorn. These two earth signs appeal to you at a visceral level. Taurus's solid, grounded personality comforts that part of you that is so often torn between one direction and another. Her sensuality is also a major plus. Capricorn's singular vision and direction are a mystery to you, but there's much to learn from her. *Virgo*, your opposite sign, can bring balance.

Fire signs probably won't work for you unless you have a moon or rising in a fire sign. Of the air signs, *Gemini* is probably the most compatible for you. Since you're both symbolized by two of something—two fish, the twins—he understands your dichotomies.

CHAPTER 4

Your Career Choices in 2012

Despite how things may look in the job market, despite the grim statistics about the economy, the housing market, the banks, the plunging dollar, and all the rest of the depressing news that flows into our lives 24/7, many people flourish in economically difficult times. In fact, if you've been laid off from your job, the first thing you can do to turn things around is to look at it as an opportunity. The more positive and upbeat your attitude, the more frequently you view every challenge as an opportunity, the greater the chances that you'll turn things around.

Several years ago friends of ours, a married couple who are both writers, had pretty much hit rock bottom. The wife admitted that she was ready to start cleaning pools just to have a steady income. Then practically overnight everything turned around. Her husband sold a novel that became a popular cable TV show, a producer commissioned her to write a script, and suddenly their bank account fattened, they bought a second home, a new car and a boat, and the world opened up for them. It can open up for you, too.

We create our realities from the inside out. Everything you see around you is a manifestation of a belief that you hold. Some of our beliefs have been passed down to us by well-meaning family members, mentors, teachers, or friends, and we adopt those beliefs because we respect the people who handed them to us. But what do *you* believe about your abilities and talents and your ability to earn your living doing what you love? How do you handle stress? Change?

In 2012, when so much of the world seems to be shifting beneath our feet, we have a chance to delve into those beliefs and get rid of the ones we have adopted out of convenience. We can either go with the flow, change with the times, or we can offer up resistance. The more we resist, the more pain we experience. The more we go with the flow, the greater our capacity to discover where we should be. Which path will you take?

Inventory

One way to prosper professionally during good *and* bad times is to know what you want. So let's take an inventory.

1. Describe your dream job/profession

_____

_____

_____

2. Lay out a strategy for finding/attaining this dream job/profession. Do you need more education, time, additional skills? If so, include those things, and set a goal for attaining them.

_____

_____

_____

3. Set realistic professional goals. Choose a time frame—a month, six months, a year—whatever feels right to you. Ask yourself what you would like to be doing a year from now. Describe it in detail. Make it real!

_____

_____

_____

4. What kind of inner work can you do to make these goals a reality more quickly? Visualization? Take workshops or seminars? Develop your intuition? Describe in detail.

_____

_____

_____

5. What are your greatest strengths? Describe them. Then focus on the strengths you have—not your weaknesses.

_____

_____

_____

Using Synchronicity in 2012

The Swiss psychologist Carl Jung coined the term. It means: the coming together of inner and outer events in a way that can't be explained by cause and effect and that is meaningful to the observer. Or, it's a meaningful coincidence. When it happens to you, don't dismiss it as a random curiosity. A synchronicity can be a navigational tool, a confirmation, warning, or guidance.

For Frank Morgan, an actor who played five different parts in *The Wizard of Oz*, a stunning synchronicity served as confirmation that he was on the right professional track by accepting parts in the movie.

One of the parts he played was the disreputable Professor Marvel. For that role, the director and wardrobe man wanted him dressed in a "nice-looking coat, but tattered," said Mary Mayer, a unit publicist on the film. So they traipsed down to a second-hand clothing store and purchased a rack of coats. Then Frank, the director, and the wardrobe guy all got together and selected one of the coats.

Imagine his surprise when he turned the pocket of the coat inside out and found a name sewn into the lining of the coat: L. Frank Baum, the author of *The Wizard of Oz*. The additional synchronicity here is that both men who wore the coat were named Frank.

In times of stress or major transitions—marriage, divorce, birth, a move, career change or change in employment and income—synchronicities may occur more frequently. Decipher the message if you can, and know that synchronicities indicate we're in the flow, exactly where we're supposed to be.

Your Career Path in 2012

Regardless of what you do for a living, whether you love or detest it or merely tolerate it, you can maximize your strengths and talents to enhance your professional opportunities.

Aries

As a cardinal fire sign, your entire life is about movement, action, doing. You're the pioneer, the entrepreneur, the one who really does march to the beat of a different drummer. Your pioneering spirit is your most valuable asset for navigating any professional changes you encounter this year.

There is no such thing as a challenge for you. You simply rise to the occasion and banish the challenge. You also refuse to recognize defeat. What someone else might see as a setback, you view as an opportunity. In 2011, you learned to follow your passions, wherever they led, and in 2012 that faith starts paying off. Whenever a negative thought enters your mind, change it immediately to something upbeat and positive. Follow the methods that feel right to you.

Taurus

Your senses are so finely tuned that you hear the music of the spheres, poetry flows through your dreams, you have the heart and soul of a mystic. You're the most enduring, taciturn, and physical of the twelve signs. You always finish what you start unless it's just unbearable! In 2011, you learned that your resolute determination is your greatest asset for navigating professional changes. In 2012, you learn to trust your intuition.

Until June 11 this year, Jupiter remains in your sign, a positive and lucky transit that you should take advantage of. Jupiter expands whatever it touches, and every twelve years it touches your sun. You're in the right place at the right time with this transit, so take full advantage of it. Don't shy away from new opportunities that broaden your life.

You already know your own value. In 2012, everyone around you learns it as well, and you keep moving forward and never look back.

Gemini

You're the communicator, your mind buzzing constantly with information that you eagerly share with others.

Some people say you never shut up, that you talk just to fill the silence. Not true. Beneath your chatter lies an insatiable curiosity.

Your ability to multitask and your curiosity are your greatest assets for navigating any professional changes this year. In fact, in 2011 you learned to follow the impulses of your curiosity to see where they might lead, and they led some mighty strange places. But you were in the right place, at the right time. In 2012, your versatility and communication abilities enable you to navigate the paradigm shift that's underway.

Cancer

You're completely attuned to emotions—yours and everyone else's. It's easy for you to slip into someone else's skin and feel what they feel. You hurt as they hurt. You weep as they weep. You laugh as they laugh. Like fellow water sign Pisces, you're a psychic sponge, an empath. Your extraordinary memory is intimately linked to your emotions, and your intuition is remarkable. All of these traits helped you to successfully navigate the transitions of 2011. During the first six months of 2012, when Jupiter is in compatible earth sign Taurus, your hard work last year really begins to pay off. You meet people who not only share your interests, but who are helpful in some way professionally. Your professional options expand. Perhaps you launch a business, write a novel, have a photography exhibit. One way or another, you begin to achieve your dreams, Taurus.

Embrace whatever change comes your way, and trust that the universe works for your highest good.

Leo

You were born to express your creativity through performance. You love the applause, the recognition, the immediate gratification and feedback. Of course, not every

Leo is an actor or actress, but every Leo loves drama. So whether you're on the stage, in front of a classroom, or counseling a patient in therapy, your creative flair moves through you like a force of nature. In 2011, you learned how valuable this asset was in helping you to navigate any professional changes you experienced.

Now, in 2012, especially from June 11, 2012, to late June 2013, you're well positioned for seeing your dreams unfold. Jupiter will be in compatible air sign Gemini, and things should expand explosively for you. Join groups, engage your friends, and offer zero resistance to whatever comes your way.

Virgo

Your gift is details. Whether it's your own life that you're honing, sculpting, and shining like some fine gem, or a particular project or relationship, you can see the finished product in a way that others can't. You also have a particular gift or ability that you're always willing to provide to others, without thought of compensation. These traits carried you through professional changes you may have experienced in 2011.

The first six months of 2012, when Jupiter is in fellow earth sign Taurus, should be fantastic for you, regardless of any doom and gloom around you. Your worldview expands, you may have a chance to travel overseas, perhaps even a publishing opportunity presents itself. It's all preparation for Jupiter's transit through Gemini and your career sector from June 11, 2012, to late June 2013. Now *that* period, Virgo, is going to blow your mind. So prepare yourself for a wild, wonderful career ride.

Libra

You can work a room like a seasoned politician, spreading peace and harmony even among people who can't agree on anything. That's your magic. Yet the very qualities that you can instill in others often elude you. Not that any of us could tell by looking at you. Libra is a master of social camouflage. It seems that nothing ruffles you. But within, you're struggling to maintain harmony without compromising your principles. Your sphere is relationships. More than any other sign, you can see the many sides of an issue and understand that your truth may not be everyone's truth. But you can live with the paradox. It's your gift.

Any professional challenges you encountered in 2011 were undoubtedly overcome by your ability to connect with people. You're in for a real treat from June 11, 2012, to late June 2013, when expansive Jupiter transits fellow air sign Gemini. During this period, your professional opportunities should abound, taking you into new areas and new creative venues and bringing opportunities for foreign travel.

Scorpio

You're the emotional vortex of the zodiac, a spinning whirlwind of contradictions. You aren't like the rest of us, and that's the way you prefer it. You dig deeply into everything you do, looking for the absolute bottom line, the most fundamental truth, and then you excavate everything at the discovery site just to make sure you've gotten it all.

Professional challenges that you encountered last year were met with the fortitude and resilience for which you're known. In 2012, your best bet is to team up with a professional or romantic partner and launch a business or some other endeavor you've always wanted to try. The best time for this is from January 1 to June 11, when expansive Jupiter is in Taurus, your solar seventh house. Your intuition will be spot on during this period. Listen to it.

Sagittarius

You're the life of the party, just like your fellow fire sign Leo. But your approaches are different. Where Leo seeks recognition and applause, you're after the big picture, and it doesn't matter how far you have to travel to find it, how many people you have to talk to, how many books or blogs you must read. When your passion is seized, you're as doggedly relentless as Taurus. One part of you operates from raw instinct; the other part of you is acculturated, aware of how to work the system.

In 2011, the year of transition, you realized that you don't recognize professional challenges. You learned that any bump in a road simply means you take an alternate path to get to where you want to go. Between June 11, 2012, and late June 2013, expansive Jupiter will be in Gemini, in your solar seventh house. To maximize this beautiful transit—and to get the most out of it professionally—team up with a partner, romantic or professional, and try some entrepreneurial venture that suits your soul, Sadge.

Capricorn

You're the achiever, the builder, the classic type A personality whose focus is so tight that everything and everyone becomes part of your journey toward . . . well, the top of the hill, the pinnacle of whatever you're attempting to reach. You can build anything, anywhere. A fictional world, a belief system, an invention, a concept, a family, a video world. Name it, and you can build it.

Any professional challenges you encountered in 2011 were undoubtedly tackled the same way that you have tackled any other challenge in your life—by finding a way around it. Or through it. As a cardinal earth sign, you value what is tangible, practical, efficient, and your journey through any obstacle reflects it. In 2011, you learned how not to fear, and that got you through every professional challenge you encountered. In 2012, particularly until June 11, when Jupiter is in fellow earth sign Taurus, your muse is so up close and personal that your creativity soars. Use it to navigate the shifting sands in your world.

Aquarius

You're not easy to pigeonhole. Sometimes you seem to be the paragon of independence. Yet you enjoy the company of groups who share your passions. You're the one who thinks so far outside the box that people close to you may accuse you of communication with aliens, ghosts, goblins, elves. Even if it's true, you just laugh and continue on your journey into the strange, the unknown, on into the heart of the universe.

Any challenges you encountered professionally in 2011 were no major thing for you. You always managed to work your way around the challenge by continuing to explore what interests you. Between June 11, 2012, and late June 2013, Jupiter transits fellow air sign Gemini and your solar fifth house. This should be a huge bonus for you, Aquarius. Your creativity becomes your most valued asset for navigating the paradigm shift. And regardless of how out of the box your professional ideas are this year, you come through it all in great shape.

Pisces

Dreamer, healer, mystic: all these adjectives fit you, Pisces. You live within a rich, inner world that is both a buffer and a conduit to deeper experiences. You don't need anyone else to tell you this. At some level you already know it, appreciate it, embrace it. While it's true that you're a sucker for a sob story, an attribute that can turn you from hero to martyr in the space of a single breath, there's no concrete evidence that you're more of a victim than any other sun sign.

Any professional challenges that came your way during 2011 were met with your powerful intuition, your prodigious imagination, and your unique way of dealing with adversity through faith in your role in the larger scheme of things. The tentacles of your psychic abilities were active 24/7, at your disposal, and awaited your instructions. In 2012, especially until June 11 when Jupiter transits compatible earth sign Taurus, your communication abilities shine. Everything that swirls through your head, in your imagination, can be expressed in ways that others understand. Professionally, this talent alone puts you well ahead of the pack.

CHAPTER 5

Family Stuff

Our birth family is like a mini world. It's with them that we develop psychologically, emotionally, spiritually and intellectually. It's with them that we develop our defenses, needs, expectations, belief systems. They encourage certain behaviors and discourage others. We learn to rebel or conform or just fit in. Family, then, is where it all begins, which is probably why many books and movies deal with dysfunctional or eccentric families.

The paragon of dysfunctional families is probably the Corleones, in the *Godfather* movies. So much drama, violence, and emotion. The emotion is equally intense in *My Big Fat Greek Wedding*, where a young Greek woman falls in love with a non-Greek man. She tries to convince her family to accept him while she struggles to come to terms with her cultural identity. And it's all couched in comedy.

Jeanette Walls, in her memoir, *The Glass Castle,* recalls her bizarre childhood with an alcoholic father and a mother who abhorred domesticity. Jeanette and her siblings gradually made their way to New York. Their parents followed them but chose to be homeless.

Brokeback Mountain, based on a short story by Annie Proulx, is about a forbidden passion between two cowboys in the early sixties and how their love for each other impacts their families.

Your Family

Take a look at your own family. What are the dynamics? Does everyone get along? Are there certain issues that surface time and again? If you have siblings, do they each seem to have different roles in the family? One might be the rebel, for instance, and the other might be the intellectual. What about your parents, partner, and your own kids? If you're an only child, what is your relationship with your parents like?

Families often have commonalities in their respective charts that illustrate the deep connections among them. The parents might have opposing signs, like Taurus/Scorpio, Gemini/Sagittarius, so there's a kind of balance. Then one child might have a moon in Sadge, and the other child has a Gemini sun. There's an infinite number of combinations, and some aren't as obvious as sun or moon signs. But for the purpose of this chapter, let's keep things simple.

Your Style as a Parent

Aries

Your parenting style isn't like anyone else's, that's for sure. Man or woman, you encourage independence in your children from a very young age. You're no control freak. Or, if you are, then it may be due to the sign of your moon. You may be one of those parents who keeps close tabs on your child's growth progress: *7 months, crawling; 9 months, utters first word; age 2, a puzzle prodigy!* Any rules you lay down are in the name of safety rather than an attempt to control your child's every move and decision.

Some Aries wing it as parents. They don't have a clue, really, about what they're doing, so they fine-tune their parenting style at every stage of their child's growth. But even for you, Aries, there are certain constants that probably won't change. In addition to the emphasis on independence, you have a finely honed sense of privacy and probably won't violate your child's unless you have a reasonable suspicion that you should. That's more likely to happen during the turbulent teen years. You give your child plenty of freedom to make his own choices. However, when you do offer guidance or advice, you may blurt it out, which could create some major tension if your child is an adult.

An *Aries mom* can be brash, funny, exciting, unpredictable. Kids enjoy her company because everything with her is an adventure. But she can be fiercely protective—that's the ram who symbolizes her sign—ready to defend her child's turf at the slightest provocation. She isn't nurturing in the traditional sense of the word, i.e., you won't find her slaving over a hot stove preparing the evening meals. She's more likely to have a pizza delivered. But when her child's in need, she's there in a flash.

When an *Aries dad* hangs out with the kids, there's an air of impatience, brashness, restlessness, a kind of *let's get this show on the road!* If he encourages his child to take risks—in sports, love, life—it's because he himself is so fearless. He's terrific at organizing activities, but they happen on the fly. *In ten minutes, we're going on a picnic,* he announces, and then everyone scrambles around grabbing stuff they need. He usually has great pride in and passion for his kids.

In 2012, with Uranus in your sign all year (until March 2019, actually), there may be sudden, unexpected events that impact your parenting style. If you've fallen into a personal rut (unlikely for an Aries, but it does happen now and then), then Uranus whips into your life, turns everything upside down, shakes out what is no longer needed or useful. Your temperament may be erratic, you may be more impatient than usual, your blood pressure could soar at the slightest provocation. Best advice? Sign up for yoga classes with your kids. Meditate with them. Hike with them. Engage them.

Taurus

Your parenting style reflects your stability, determination, and patience. You enjoy your children immensely and strive to nurture their talents, strengths, and gifts. You try to create a beautiful home environment, a place in which everyone delights, where your kids feel comfortable bringing their friends. HOME. In caps.

You probably enjoy music, art, books, movies, and politics, and these interests are reflected in your environment—and are passed on to your kids through a kind of osmosis. So don't be surprised when your son or daughter cranks up the music so loudly it threatens to shatter crystal or when the weekly allowance is blown at the local bookstore!

Since you're the most stubborn sign in the zodiac, that stubbornness certainly surfaces in your parenting. Your child says *yes*. You shake your head *no*. The child keeps saying yes, yes, his voice growing louder and louder until your patience snaps, and the legendary bull's rush seizes you. *No,* you shout, and slam your door. End of story, end of argument, end of struggle.

Since Venus rules your sign, though, your bull's rush usually passes quickly and peace and tranquillity are restored. But you still refuse to change your mind!

A *Taurus mom* is loyal and dedicated to her role as a mother. It won't be her *only* role, but she's likely to consider it her most important role. She's in the line for school drop-offs in the morning, in that same line for pickup in the afternoon. In between she's in court, defending someone like you or me, or she's writing the great American novel, or teaching English to recalcitrant seventh-graders. Or she's selling real estate or jewelry or scooping the next big political story.

The *Taurus dad* works hard and patiently at whatever he does. He finishes everything he starts—and that includes the projects his kids begin for their science classes! He, like his female counterpart, is usually health conscious and watches his diet, exercises regularly, and takes good care of himself. Part of this could be vanity, but whatever it is, his kids pick up on it and sometimes take up the same sports in which dad indulges.

In 2012, Uranus in Aries is transiting your solar twelfth house, that place in your chart that is most hidden and secretive. With Uranus here until 2019, your inner world is shaken up, elements of your unconscious surface abruptly and inexplicably. It's as if you're confronted with psychological archetypes in yourself that you haven't seen before. This kind of turmoil certainly will affect your family and kids—*if* you let it. The bottom line here is that Taurus rarely shows anyone the face of that inner world. The best way to navigate whatever stuff is surfacing is to deal with it and move on.

Gemini

Ideas and communication. That's what you're about, and it's evident in your parenting style. From the time your child is very young, you read to her, talk to her, encourage her to express herself verbally. You buy her puzzles, coloring books, picture books, anything that expands her knowledge and creativity. Your fascination with information and relationships is found in the way you encourage her to reach out to other people, to make friends, to invite them to her house. Don't be surprised, then, if by the time your child is a teen, she has several thousand friends on Facebook!

You're a voracious reader, and it's likely that your home has hundreds—if not thousands—of books. This love of reading is something you pass on to your child, and by the time she's preparing for college, her facility with language and ideas is a major plus. It's said that a typical Gemini is actually two people—the twins are the symbol for your sign—so you're comfortable with duality. This can be confusing to a young child, particularly if you vacillate about what's allowed and what isn't.

With Mercury ruling your sign, any connections between the Mercury in your chart and the sun, moon, rising, or Mercury in your child's chart portend strong communication.

A *Gemini mom* is the supreme multitasker. She can simultaneously pack school lunches, talk on the phone, and be writing a novel in her head. At times she may appear scattered to her kids, but then she suddenly comes out with a zinger of logic or insight that stops them in their tracks. Glances are exchanged, eyebrows shoot up. She's a fount of information and eagerly passes on what she knows to her kids—and their friends and the friends of their friends. If anything, when her kids are with their friends, she must learn to back off and give them space.

A *Gemini dad* is quick, witty, enigmatic. Just when his kids think they've got him figured out, he does or says something that makes him impossible to peg. His intellect is as finely honed as a Gemini woman's, but takes him in different directions. He might be an avid sports fan, for example, a master at chess, a general aviation pilot, or an animal lover. His interests and passions are passed on to his kids.

One thing is certain: a home with at least one Gemini parent in it is never boring!

In 2012, you have several fantastic things going for you astrologically that are sure to bolster your parenting style. First, Uranus in Aries is transiting your solar eleventh house, so you're going to be more involved with friends and groups that support your parenting style. These groups will be kid friendly, too, so it's not as if you have to find a sitter or drop the kids at someone else's place. These group associations may begin and end suddenly, but that's fine with you. They bring an excitement and unpredictability that suit you.

The second transit is fantastic—Jupiter moving

through your sign from June 11, 2012, to late June 2013. This transit enhances all the Gemini qualities of your parenting style—emphasis on communication, books, writing, travel. It will be a period your kids remember as pure fun and enjoyment.

Cancer

You're the nurturer of the zodiac, the one who needs roots, a home, a place or state of mind and spirit that you can call your own. You're a gentle, kind person who takes everything to heart—and this is certainly reflected in your parenting style. Through your example, your kids learn to respect all forms of life, to never hurt others, to treat them as he would like to be treated.

You can be overprotective, for sure, and before your child hits his teens, you'll have to come to grips with how to handle those feelings. Emotionally, you rarely reveal yourself. Like the crab that represents your sign, you tend to move sideways, skirting unpleasant issues, anxious to avoid confrontation, reluctant to discuss the heart of the matter. Your exceptional intuition keeps you in tune with your children, alerting you when they're in danger or happy. You forgive easily, but rarely forget. So if one of your kids hurts your feelings, you'll remember it thirty years from now.

A *Cancer mom* is the prototypical nurturer—always there for her kids, supportive of their wishes and dreams. Yes, if she cooks, you'll find her whipping up delectable dishes that include everyone's favorite foods, whatever they are. Her home is her palace—but it could be the cabin of a boat, a tent in the wilderness, an RV. No matter where she is, she tends to the creature comforts of her family. As a parent, she has rules, but they're emotionally based, just like everything else in her life, so they won't change unless the emotions behind them change first.

A *Cancer dad,* like his female counterpart, is kind,

affectionate, and nurturing, but only to a point. When he feels his personal space is being violated in any way, he backs off, scurries into his crab's shell, and retreats quickly. For a child, he's hard to figure out. Sometimes he's the hero of the child's latest adventure story; other times he's the wet blanket at the party. If he's into metaphysics and alternative healing, then chances are he's in deep, and his kids will pick up on this interest and explore on their own.

In 2012, the period from the beginning of the year to June 11 should be wonderful for you and your kids. You get involved with new groups, your friends become more integral to your life, and in some way, shape, or form you begin to realize your dreams. Your children and family are part of the process. The other transit to watch is Neptune's through Pisces, which begins on February 3 and continues for the next fourteen years. This one brings an emphasis on spirituality and intuitive development that you pass on to your kids. You and your family may travel internationally, but it won't be strictly for pleasure. You'll be on a spiritual quest of some kind. Stonehenge? An ashram in India? Crop circles?

Leo

You love being the center of attention, often surround yourself with admirers, and the world is your stage. But that's just the beginning of your story! You strive to succeed—to shine—at everything you do and to make an impact in every situation. Your personal magnetism draws admirers who are willing to help your cause, whatever it is. You prefer to hang with people whose beliefs are similar to your own, but can get along with just about everyone—as long as no one steals your thunder. Your kindness, generosity, and compassion are nearly legendary.

As a parent, you love unconditionally and fiercely. You tend to instill certain qualities into your children—optimism, loyalty, integrity, honor. When they're toddlers, you enjoy their company and watching them progress to each stage, from crib to crawling to kindergarten. Once they're off to school, particularly by the time they reach middle school and then high school, you may feel marginalized in some way. You really shouldn't. You've got enough interests and passions to fill your next five lives, and your ambitions keep propelling you forward. Generally, you delight in seeing your children fly off into the world, doing what they love.

The *Leo mom* is usually up front about everything—what she feels, why, and for how long. She's definitely disappointed when her kids aren't as forthright, but she gets over it! She likes being at the helm—at home, at work, while traveling—and can be a bit bossy at times. *You and you, do this and that.* Her kids quickly learn to either fall in line or stand up to her. Mom enjoys nice clothes and probably dresses with a flair and style all her own. She's clever at creating impressions and moods through the way she looks and acts (it's the actress in her), but her kids undoubtedly learn to see through it to the gem beneath.

The *Leo dad* is easy to get along with as long as you keep a couple of rules in mind. Never tell *him* what to do, and let him have center stage. If both of your parents are Leos, then the one thing you can count on in your household is plenty of drama! The Leo dad is fun, outgoing, and full of magic. He snaps his fingers and things happen. He has great leadership ability (and not just as a dad), and his energy and frankness endear him to children of any age.

In 2012, two transits will affect your parenting style. Uranus, the planet of sudden, unexpected change, is transiting fellow fire sign Aries, in your solar ninth house. This suggests that your belief system, your worldview, your spiritual beliefs are undergoing radical change. It will be an exciting, unpredictable time, and the whirlwind of events will sweep you and your kids and partner up into a vortex of unpredictable adventures.

The second transit, Jupiter's through Gemini, goes from June 11, 2012, to late June 2013, and emphasizes foreign travel, friends, mental stimulation. Suddenly everything in your life expands, you feel lucky, like you're in the right time and place, and this expansiveness is passed on to your kids.

Virgo

Your mind is lightning quick, just like Gemini's, and you're so mentally dexterous and agile that the competition can't keep pace with you. Due to your attention to detail, to the discerning turn of your intellect, you tend to delve more deeply into subjects than Gemini, and when you gather information it usually has a purpose. You pass this ability on to your children, and it serves you well as a parent, i.e., not much escapes your notice. Your kids will never be able to put anything over on you! Since you're Mercury ruled, like Gemini, you need sufficient outlets for all your mental energy.

You're an attentive parent who does all the expected things—for school, health, your child's happiness—but who may not play by the book. In other words, you probably won't raise your children the way you were raised. If you were brought up in a religious household, for instance, your child won't be. If your parents stressed school over fun, you may do the opposite. If your parents were inordinately strict, you won't be. It's not that you have the heart of a rebel (although you might!) but that your finely honed intellect connects all the dots, and you grasp what's needed for your children to evolve and to achieve their full potential.

The *Virgo mom* is vibrant, upbeat, conscientious, loving. Even though she never *tries* to project a particular image, others sense something different about her, perhaps her softness, her caring. Deep down, she can be a worry wart, fretting about the smallest details, the inconsistencies in life, in her kids, her family. It's part of her insecurity. When she's in that mode, she can be critical—of her kids, her husband, herself. But she can be cajoled out of that mood by lively discussions about ideas, books, travel, any kind of information that seizes her passions. She's generous with her kids and strives to enrich their world through her own wisdom.

The *Virgo dad* is as intellectually curious as his female counterpart. He's a hard worker, detail oriented, with a biting humor that is rarely malicious. He may take his role as dad a bit too seriously at times, but his kids quickly learn how to loosen him up, how to make him laugh. He's an attentive father, the kind who reads to his kids at night, who listens to their dramas and woes as teens, who applauds loudly when they graduate from college. Always with him—and with the Virgo mom— there is tremendous pride in his children, as if he can't quite believe his extreme good fortune.

In 2012, the first six months of the year will be magnificent for you as a parent, for your kids, your family generally. Jupiter will be transiting fellow earth sign Taurus, your solar ninth house. This transit promises international traveling, dealings with publishers and educators, perhaps even living abroad for a while. The living abroad may last longer than the transit because for a year—from June 11, 2012, to late June 2013—Jupiter will be moving through Gemini and your career area. This transit suggests that one possible manifestation is working abroad, and you'll take your loved ones with you.

Libra

You're one of the gentlest souls in the zodiac, usually soft spoken and treading lightly in all matters. You're also deeply romantic about your family and kids. They're your beacons. You love beauty in every shape and form, and when there's no obvious beauty, you find it in what you can imagine. You're an excellent strategist, a natural diplomat, and you often mitigate chaos and drama, dissension and disagreement. Sometimes you assume these roles to your own detriment, just to keep the peace.

As a parent, this tendency to keep the peace at your own expense could be thankless. So strive not to be a martyr, okay? Strive not to bend over backward to please . . . well, everyone. Once you can do that, your natural artistic tendencies take over in your parenting. You nurture your children's passions and interests, their gifts and talents as they emerge. You're tuned in to who they are on a soul level and understand how to help them bring that soul into their conscious awareness. Your love of art, music, literature, and every other creative talent is passed on to your kids. Your grasp of the complexities of relationships is translated into language they speak. Facebook, Myspace, and every other social networking group become their community. In short, you usher your children into the finer beauties of the twenty-first century.

The *Libra mom* creates a domestic environment in which her children flourish. But she also has her career, friends, passions, and interests that get mixed up in this collective soup called life and which, in turn, affect her kids. She brings in music, art, gardens, books, and people. Lots of interesting people. She creates moods and atmospheres and invites her children to participate. The lessons they learn, the insights they carry away from these encounters influence them for life. There's no pinning down the Libra mom. Just when you think you've got her figured out, she surprises you. Boring? Never. Not a chance.

The *Libra dad* loves having a team—wife, kids, friends of kids, neighbors, even stray animals, it doesn't matter. Everyone and everything is part of this team. Membership is open. He's an excellent organizer, supportive of his children's endeavors and dreams. But his high ideals can be problematic once his kids are adults, making choices that don't measure up—in his mind—to those ideals. Like the Libra mom, he rarely loses his temper.

Between June 11, 2012, and late June 2013, Jupiter will be transiting fellow air sign Gemini, in your solar ninth house. This transit will lead to an expansion in your educational opportunities, worldview, even in foreign travel. Until October, Saturn will be in your sign. The combination of these two transits should have positive benefits for you as a parent, your family, and kids. Even if you run into restrictions and delays in your personal life or experience sudden events related to your daily work, you come through this period with a stronger grasp of what it means to be a parent.

Scorpio

You're intense, passionate, and strong willed. You often try to impose your will on others, a trait that may serve your children when they're young, but can prove to be problematic as they get older. Like Aries, you're fearless, but you possess an endurance that Aries lacks and can plow your way through virtually any obstacle, any challenge. This trait serves as an example to your children to never give up in their pursuit of what they want.

Your passions are such that you're never *indifferent*. You live in a world of either/or, approval or disapproval, agreement or disagreement, right or wrong. While this trait drives home the importance of values and purpose, it can be challenging for children whose lives are more nuanced. Your ability to dig deeply for the bottom-line answers indicates that you will usually know what's going on in your children's lives.

The *Scorpio mom* places a high value on honesty. It's the foundation of who she is. So it's no surprise that she expects honesty from her children. Even though she herself is secretive, she won't tolerate secrets from her child. She respects their privacy, certainly, but if she suspects something is going on that needs parental intervention, she investigates until she uncovers the truth. She is a loving, devoted mother who is very protective of her kids. At times she may be too protective and strive to shield them from the outside world.

The *Scorpio dad* is as intense as the Scorpio mom. Unless he has a moon or rising in an air or fire sign, he may be just as much of a control freak too. He often has a magnificent talent or interest that he pursues because he's passionate about it and not because he expects to make money at it. He's a nurturing parent, particularly when it comes to his children's talents and abilities and the educational training that helps them navigate life successfully.

In 2012, your role as a parent may shift in unexpected directions. Due to Uranus's transit through fire sign Aries, your work situation may be somewhat erratic at times—or, at the least, unpredictable. This may actually give you more time to spend with your kids, or you may decide to launch a home-based business or to enter a field that gives you more control over your time. With your ruler, Pluto, in compatible earth sign Capricorn until 2024, you're in the power seat when it comes to communication, Scorpio, so start talking to your kids about everything that interests you.

Sagittarius

You're a wild card. There's a part of you who is always looking for the larger picture, the broader perspective, another part who believes you're always right, and yet another part who focuses on the future and the larger family of humanity. You can be very logical, but there's also a mystical element in your psyche that enables you to glimpse the future.

You dislike having your freedom restricted in any way, so you probably don't have a roll call of rules and regulations for your children. You're a loving parent, but expect your kids to find their own way, their own path.

Yet when they make mistakes, you may offer advice that makes you sound like a know-it-all. Your versatility and natural optimism are hallmarks of your parenting style.

The *Sagittarius mom* thinks big. When she suggests a family outing, it isn't just a trip to the next town for a picnic. It's a trip across country or to some far-flung corner of the world, and who cares if it's beyond the family budget? She wears many hats and excels in everything she does as long as she doesn't feel confined, limited, penned in. Her independent spirit radiates from her every pore, and her kids quickly learn to honor it. She offers her children broad guidelines and her own wisdom, but doesn't force her opinions on them.

The *Sagittarius dad* has a broad, sweeping vision about life, love, and the universe. He talks about it freely with his kids, never holding back. He is loving and devoted to his children, but because he expects big things from them may not be satisfied with what they achieve. He enjoys foreign travel and, given his financial situation, exposes his children to foreign places whenever he can. This man is always moving and has dozens of projects going on simultaneously, and his children learn early on that goals are attained through action.

In 2012, Uranus will be moving through Aries and the children area of your chart (which also governs creativity, romance, and enjoyment). This transit will bring about sudden, unexpected events—exciting, unpredictable events—concerning your kids. You'll have to think more outside the box to keep pace with them, but with your vivid imagination and ability to see the broader picture, it'll be a piece of cake for you.

Capricorn

You're the worker bee of the zodiac, industrious, disciplined, efficient, focused. You dislike inertia in others, so it's likely that your children aren't couch potatoes! You probably get them involved in sports when they're young and nurture whatever athletic abilities they have. They learn their work ethic from you and develop common sense, a trait they witness constantly in you.

Even when you were a kid, you had a mature air about you, and as you get older, that maturity is a kind of calm presence, a rock-solid dependability that your children come to expect. Never mind that you're a worrier, that even when you've prepared long and hard and have all the bases covered, you're certain you've forgotten something. Your kids rarely see that side of you. You love them unconditionally—that's what they see.

The *Capricorn mom* always seems to know what she's doing, when, with whom, and what route she's going to take to get there. She appears to be self-confident, certain about who she is, tough as nails. But as her children come to know her as a person separate from her role as mother, they discover she's not tough at all. She simply runs her home and family life as though it's a business and she's the CEO. Even if she has a career—and many Capricorn women do—she's totally devoted to her kids. She might be a little rigid with rules and regulations, but if so, learns that such excessive control results in outright rebellion.

The *Capricorn dad* is as diligent a worker as the Capricorn mom. He's got work ethic written all over him. He prides himself on being well prepared for just about anything, including being a parent. He either has the answers or will find them—for himself, for his children, or their friends. He excels at problem-solving. He can be dictatorial and bossy, but if his kids call him on it, he backs off. For a while, anyway. He's as completely devoted to his kids as he is to his career goals. In fact, one mirrors the other.

In 2012, the period from January 1 to June 11 should be spectacular for you and your kids. Expansive Jupiter is transiting fellow earth sign Taurus then, and everything you and your kids engage in together turns to gold. The Midas touch, Capricorn. In addition, Uranus's transit through Aries and your solar fourth house brings surprising, unexpected events into your home life. A move, perhaps? The birth of another child? Once Jupiter enters Gemini on June 11, where it will be until late June 2013, your daily work schedule will expand and change, and it may be a bit tougher to accommodate your kids. Make time.

Aquarius

You're such an original thinker, a visionary, that of course you apply these talents to parenting. Your household is really atypical. You might live on a boat, in a commune, in the suburbs, in an RV, or hey, maybe even on the space station. Your family structure isn't business as usual, either. But you aren't interested in typical. Everything you do is *different* from the status quo. You think in unique ways, way outside the box, and rarely if ever trust what authority tells you to believe. This ability to think and perceive in new ways is passed on to your children.

Your interests are vastly varied, and any causes in which you get involved are discussed with and communicated to your children. They learn early in life that mom or dad's interests and causes don't have to become theirs, but deserve respect. There probably aren't many rules in your family. Individuality is honored, encouraged, and thrives.

The *Aquarius mom* is a complete paradox. She's a peace-loving rebel who moves against the tide of the status quo, yet conforms when it suits her. She has the patience of a saint—until she doesn't—and can be more stubborn than Taurus unless it suits her purpose to bend with the wind. If her children are as eccentric as she is, then they have learned the value of individuality and probably share mom's love of freedom as well. Mom allows her kids the freedom to make their own decisions, revels in their achievements, and never lets them down.

The *Aquarius dad* considers his family—partner, kids, animals and orphans of all sizes and shapes—to be his sanctuary. Even if he seems undemonstrative and emotionally remote at times, his love for his kids runs deep. He takes every opportunity to expose them to everything that interests him, from ancient sites like Stonehenge and the Nazca lines to books on what the future may look like in a century. If he's a movie buff, his children are exposed to movies at a young age. If he's a traveler, his kids will be well traveled. He's terrific at sharing his knowledge, expertise, and curiosity.

From June 11 to late June 2013, you're in for a treat as a parent. You'll be watching your children's lives expand in unprecedented ways. Whether they're toddlers or adults, you'll delight in what they're learning about themselves and their world. With Uranus transiting compatible fire sign Aries, your communication skills will be sharp, and your conscious mind will be innovative.

Pisces

Your wonderful imagination and remarkable intuition prove valuable in your parenting style. Your imagination enables you to enter the world of your children with ease and playful joy. Your intuition enables you to stay attuned to their emotions even if they don't discuss what they're feeling. Pisces individuals with highly developed gifts—psychics—may have to take a break now and then from parenting just to find their own centers. It's too easy for this type to be overwhelmed with what their kids are feeling.

At times you fluctuate between rigid left-brain logic and that softer intuitive certainty that you're doing the right thing. Try not to set down rules and restrictions when you're feeling like this. Moodiness and ambivalence can cause you to backtrack from your own rules. Guard against being a sucker for a sob story.

The *Pisces mom* often has a strong psychic connection to her children. If they have been together in past lives, chances are she has a grasp on which lives and how everyone's respective roles played out then. She's able to understand what they're feeling even when they're clueless. She is rarely dogmatic with her children, and any household rules she lays down are probably for the sake of safety—and her own peace of mind. Her love for her kids is bottomless. They're her greatest joy, and she just keeps on giving and giving.

The *Pisces dad* is a great listener. His self-containment, gentleness, quiet strength, and the full attention he gives his kids are enviable qualities that enable him to forge tight bonds with his offspring. He encourages and supports his children's artistic interests and may have artistic or musical talent himself. Like his female counterpart, he must learn to balance the demands of his inner life with his responsibilities in the outer world.

2012 should bring some surprises in how you parent and how you view your children. With Neptune in your sign from February 3 onward, your whole parenting approach may become more spiritual, creative, imaginative. Your own intuition is enhanced too during this fourteen-year transit, so you'll be in closer communication with your kids on an unspoken level, able to grasp their personal issues and concerns in a deeper way.

Kids of the Zodiac

Now that we've looked at adults and their parenting styles, let's explore the kids of the zodiac.

Aries

She's the kid who is off by herself, exploring fields and meadows for unusual bugs. Or she's the fearless teen who leaps into a rushing river to rescue a kitten stranded on a rock. Or on the family camping trip where the matches and lighter fluid have been left behind, she's the one who makes a fire by rubbing sticks together or using a magnifying glass to amplify the sunlight. Inventive, independent, entrepreneurial: welcome to the world of the Aries child. And whether she's a toddler or an adult, high drama and action swirl around her.

Taurus

He's the loner. Or he has a small group of friends with whom he hangs out. But whether it's his friends or his family, no one really knows him. Like an iceberg, nine tenths of his personality is hidden. He only shows what he wants you to know. Yes, these still waters run deep. So much goes on inside his head as he figures out where he belongs in the scheme of things that he wouldn't have a clue where to begin verbalizing any of it. So he nurtures his creative gifts, enjoys the sensual pleasures of physical existence, and moves forward at his own pace, patient, certain that the answers will come to him, from somewhere, when he needs them.

Gemini

If Taurus is the loner, she's the social butterfly, flitting from one person to another, one event to the next, and along the way she's passing on what she has learned, what she suspects, what she believes. She's impatient, quick, dexterous. Her life is propelled by a single burning question: *why?* Everything she does, every connection she makes, everyone she knows and loves serves to answer that question. Somehow. In some way. Forget trying to pigeonhole your Gemini child. It just won't happen. When she's young, provide her with an environment where she can learn and explore at her own pace. Nurture her self-confidence and her belief in herself. With those tools, she's well equipped for her journey out into the larger world.

Cancer

She's a tough one to figure out. She feels her way through life, but you may never know about it. She'll talk if she's in the mood, but otherwise nothing and no one will prod her into an explanation about her feelings. As a parent, you sort of have to divine your way through this kid's childhood and beyond. She needs roots. She needs to feel she's an integral part of the family and is appreciated. Much of her life as an adult is based on her childhood memories—the smells and sights and emotions she was feeling at a particular time. If her childhood is happy and secure, then she grows into a happy, secure adult.

Leo

The Leo child is like his own tribe. From the time he's very young, he has dozens of friends and they all hang out at his place. Even as he gets older, his friends are eager to spend time with him, and some of them are orphans and strays attracted by his innate generosity and compassion. Like fellow fire sign Aries, the Leo child is basically fearless. He accepts every dare and takes risks that would leave other kids gasping in awe. Most Leo kids enjoy the company of animals, and their homes tend to have a lot of pets.

Virgo

She's impatient, wants everything yesterday, and is graced with abundant energy. She has questions about everything and is so eager to learn that in the right environment, she explores until she drops from exhaustion. Like Cancer, she can be moody, but these swings usually occur when she doesn't understand something. Her restless mind gnaws away at the puzzle, dissecting it, scrutinizing the details, the minutiae, until she gets it. She has enormous compassion, a quality that is evident at a very young age, and her ability to connect with people is as easy for her as connecting disparate bits of information is for a Gemini. Even when young, Virgo kids show discernment. They may be picky about what they eat, read, or watch on TV.

Libra

The Libra child can be found listening to music in the comfort of his own room, connecting with friends on Facebook and MySpace, or hanging out with friends in some familiar and pretty spot. He isn't the type to play touch football (unless he's got a lot of fire or earth in his chart) or hunt for bugs under rocks or dissect frogs in the lab. As a youngster, the Libra child may have an imaginary playmate or one special friend in whom he confides. He's loyal to his friends, sometimes to a fault, so any friends he has as a youngster are probably going to be friends for life.

Scorpio

She's distinctive in some way—physically, mentally, intuitively. She has fixed opinions even as a youngster, as if she came into life with a particular agenda or belief system. She feels deeply, of course, one of the trademarks of this sign, and the intensity of her emotions may lead to sudden outbursts if her feelings are hurt or she doesn't get what she wants. She flourishes in an environment that is varied and rich, where she can explore her creative abilities. She won't always be forthright about what's going on inside of her, but if you simply come out and ask her, her response may surprise you. She's wiser than her years.

Sagittarius

This kid is Mr. Popularity, and it's evident from the time he's old enough to crawl and interact. He's vivacious and optimistic and makes other people feel good about themselves. It makes him a people magnet. He can be opinionated, though, and blunt. He doesn't think about what he's going to say before he says it. He just blurts it out, a tendency that can be disconcerting to people who aren't accustomed to it. But he needs the freedom to express himself and to know it's okay to defend what he believes. Rules and structure are a good idea as he's growing up. He probably has a fondness for animals, not surprising for a sign symbolized by a figure that is half human, half horse!

Capricorn

From the time she utters her first word, she's as comfortable being and conversing with adults as she is with her peers. Sometimes she has a seriousness about her that is usually evident in her eyes, in the way she watches and appraises you, sizing you up for who knows what reason. Other times, she can be as wild and playful as any other child. Even then, though, her organizational skills are evident, and she can be bossy, no question about it. She is infinitely patient, intent on achieving her goal, whatever it might be.

Aquarius

To this kid, all people truly are equal, so his friends span the racial and socio-economic spectrum. He's an extrovert, eager to know what makes other people tick, what motivates them, but he's also perfectly happy when he's by himself. His mind is as busy as a Gemini's, but in a much different way. Where a Gemini child collects trivia and information, the Aquarian child is immersed in the stuff of the universe. Although he enjoys people and gets involved in all sorts of groups, he's not a follower and will always defend not only his opinions, but his right to have those opinions.

Pisces

She doesn't need many rules. She's so sensitive to her environment and to the people who inhabit it that a cross look from mom or dad keeps her in line. She's a dreamer, this one, whose imagination soars through time and space with the ease of a bird through sunlight. If her intuitive gifts are allowed to develop, this child can become a genuine medium, clairvoyant, mystic, healer. Her strong creative drive manifests itself early.

CHAPTER 6

Your Finances in 2012

Beliefs

Money and relationships are probably the trickiest areas for most of us to navigate successfully. But if we create our realities from the inside out, then in these two areas it's vitally important that we understand our beliefs.

Let's take a closer look. Here are some commonly held negative beliefs about money and relationships. Do you hold any of these?

- Money is the root of all evil
- My relationships never turn out
- Money is nonspiritual
- True love is rare
- The rich have major problems in their lives
- Marriage is a joke
- Money corrupts
- I'm not worthy of (fill in the blank)
- If you have too much money, you have to worry about losing it

You get the idea here. Many of these beliefs we've adopted from family and peers and have held on to them because they're comfortable, we believe they're true, or because we don't even realize we believe them!

So if you're not satisfied with what you're earning, start monitoring how you think about money. Any time you find yourself thinking a negative thought about money, turn the thought around by thinking something more positive. Also, read *Money and the Law of Attraction* by Esther and Jerry Hicks and *You Can Heal Your Life* by Louise Hay.

Now let's take a look at how you can maximize your earning potential in 2012.

Jupiter

From chapter 2, we know that Jupiter represents luck, expansion, success, prosperity, growth, creativity, spiritual interests, higher education, and the law. It also governs publishing, overseas travel, and foreign countries and any of our dealings with them. But for the purpose of this chapter, we're going to focus on Jupiter's impact on our money for 2012.

This year, Jupiter transits two signs. From January 1 to June 11, it's moving through earth sign Taurus. From June 11, 2012, to June 25, 2013, it's moving through air sign Gemini. It will be retrograde in Gemini between October 14, 2012, and January 30, 2013. A Jupiter retrograde simply means that planet isn't functioning at full capacity.

Let's see how these two Jupiter transits this year impact your sun sign.

Jupiter in 2012 and Its Impact on Your Sun Sign

Aries

Jupiter's transit of Taurus, through your solar second house, began in early June 2011, and initially you may have been spending more money than usual. But as the transit stabilized, your income is likely to have expanded in some way. That trend will continue this year, until June 11.

Your second house doesn't just govern your income, but also your values, personal debt, giving and receiving, jewelry, possessions (particularly those that are valuable), reverses in finances, your earning and spending capacity. And with Jupiter in this house, in stable, dependable Taurus, you may be looking for long-term stable investments that will increase your profit and minimize your risk.

If you dislike your job, i.e., the way you earn your daily bread, then Jupiter should bring plenty of new options and opportunities for expansion. You may decide to return to school to update your skills and knowledge, may decide to go to college or graduate school, or may expand your earning possibilities to overseas markets. Since Jupiter governs publishing, law, and higher education, any of these areas are possibilities for increasing your earning capacity.

Once Jupiter enters Gemini for a year-long transit, you'll feel more comfortable because Gemini is compatible with your fire-sign sun. In fact, this transit should be terrific for you, expanding all the areas governed by the third house and Gemini: communication, your conscious mind, daily activities, siblings, short-distance travel. You may write that book you've had in your head for years, build a Web site, start a blog. More frequent travel could be part of your daily activities—car pools, a longer commute. However this transit manifests for you, Jupiter brings luck and expansion, and you, ever innovative, turn it into a potential cash cow.

Taurus

In early June of 2011, Jupiter entered your sign, Taurus, and suddenly life took on a whole new dimension. The trend of expansion and luck that started with that transit continues until June 11 of this year. Whenever Jupiter transits your sign, the ramifications are big—you're in the right place at the right time, luck is your new best friend, your options and opportunities broaden.

Sometimes when Jupiter initially enters your sign, it seems that more money is going out than is coming in. But eventually your net worth rises, you land the dream job, your investments begin to pay off. You tend to be conservative with money, but if there's something you really want, don't hesitate to buy it if you can pay cash for it. You want to avoid credit-card debt during this transit and the one coming up between June 11, 2011, and June 25, 2013. Conserve your resources, but don't be stingy and don't do it out of fear.

When Jupiter enters Gemini on June 11, you're in for another treat. It will be transiting your solar second house of money, so it's likely that your earning capacity will rise, your values will broaden, your opportunities for self-improvement will increase. Jupiter's transits are nearly always fortunate, but there's a risk with excess in some area. When you see a sharp increase in your income, follow your parents' advice—sock some of it away. But again, don't do it out of fear. Any action taken from a basis of fear is likely to attract circumstances that will cause real fear.

Gemini

During Jupiter's transit of Taurus between January 1 and June 11, your unconscious is easier for you to delve into. Dream work, meditation, yoga, or some other kind of mind/body activity benefits you. In fact, you may discover that your dreams hold important information that will help you with issues or concerns that you have. Ideas come to you through dreams and meditations. Consider a past-life regression with a qualified therapist. Everything you learn during this transit is creative fodder, Gemini, and is preparing the way for Jupiter's transit through your sign between June 11, 2012, and June 25, 2013.

Jupiter transits your sign just once every twelve years. So look back to 2000 for hints about what sorts of experiences you may have during this year-long transit. What were your finances like that year? Did you land a new job that paid more? Did you move into a better neighborhood, a larger house? Did you take unnecessary financial risks? All of these areas are possibilities this year.

One thing you definitely want to avoid during this transit is gambling or speculating with your money. Because Jupiter can be excessive, you may feel cocky, as if you can do no wrong. It's smarter to save and to invest in things that further your education, skills, and future.

Cancer

Since last June, Jupiter has been moving through Taurus and your solar eleventh house, a transit that continues until June 11 of this year. This brings an expansion to your social contacts, your wishes and dreams, and opportunities to promote and publicize your work or product or that of your company. Since this transit forms a beautiful angle to your sun sign, other areas of your life will benefit as well, and one of them is your finances.

You might decide, for example, to join an investment group that shares ideas about which stocks or bonds to buy. Or you and a group of friends may invest in rental property or even buy a place together, fix it up, and then sell it for a handsome profit. Any dealing with real estate and homes is a nonbrainer for you, Cancer. It's what you enjoy doing.

Between June 11, 2012, and June 25, 2013, Jupiter will transit Gemini, through your solar twelfth house. It makes it easier for you to delve into your own unconscious, to recall your dreams. If you don't meditate yet, then this transit presents the opportunity to do so. You may discover moneymaking ideas through meditations and dream recall. You may start a blog or build a Web site and find an innovative technique for making money in this way. Use this transit to find out who you are, Cancer. Self-knowledge can lead to a greater understanding about how the universe works, and such knowledge can lead to greater financial stability and more money.

Leo

Jupiter entered Taurus and your career area in June 2011 and won't leave it until June 11, 2012. That gives you six months this year to enjoy the professional expansion—and thus, the financial expansion—of this transit. The last time Jupiter touched this area of your chart was twelve years ago, so look back to 2000 for clues about how the last six months of this transit may unfold for you.

If you would like to change jobs or careers, then it could happen during this transit. Equally possible? Your responsibilities, job description, and salary increase substantially, you launch your own business, sell a book, work overseas. Regardless of the specifics, you will have plenty of opportunities to do what you do best, Leo—shine!

Between June 11, 2012, and June 25, 2013, Jupiter transits compatible air sign Gemini and your solar eleventh house. This transit not only stimulates your social life, but brings you into a whole new sphere of individuals who help you to attain your dreams, whatever they may be. Any groups you join may also prove to be helpful financially.

With Jupiter in Gemini, your communication skills—which aren't too shabby to begin with!—really sharpen. Your mind becomes a steel trap, and you're able to snap out facts, figures, statistics that astound even you. You learn to make money using your ability to communicate and connect with others.

Virgo

When Jupiter entered fellow earth sign Taurus last June, your income probably increased, and that trend will continue until June 11 of this year. It's possible that your work or a quest of some sort takes you overseas, and whatever you learn and experience changes your fundamental beliefs about money. You may suddenly realize, for example, that you're worthy of being rich. Or that your book is just as good as anything on the market and will find the right publisher. In other words, your inner world is shifting, becoming more certain, stronger. As that happens, your life in the outer world will change accordingly.

If you're a writer, this transit expands your publishing opportunities, could bring about significant foreign sales, and makes it easier, generally, to sell what you write. Regardless of what profession you're in, your business could expand to overseas markets. Other possibilities: you head off to college or graduate school, go to law school, or even move overseas.

Once Jupiter enters Gemini and the career area of your chart, you're in for an exciting time. The specifics of this transit vary for each of us, but here are some possibilities: you switch jobs/careers and land something with a larger salary; you work overseas; you sell your novel or screenplay. One way or another, the professional and financial payoff for you is excellent.

Libra

With Jupiter in Taurus until June 11, you and/or your partner may be accruing items like art and jewelry for investments, could delve more deeply into esoteric subjects like ghosts, past lives, communication with the dead, or may combine your resources in some way. Whatever it is, it pays off financially. Let's say that you and your partner have separate homes, then during this transit you may decide to sell one place and move in together. This transit should bring breaks with mortgages, loans, taxes, and insurance.

When Jupiter transits fellow air sign Gemini between June 11, 2012, and June 25, 2013, you have a wonderful opportunity to explore your worldview and spiritual beliefs and to divest yourself of any that are holding you back from achieving your financial goals. The exploration may come through opportunities for foreign travel, to write a book on whatever seizes your passions, or to even go to graduate school to further your skills.

Scorpio

With Jupiter transiting Taurus, your opposite sign, for six months this year, you and your partner may launch a business together, or you may find a business partner for a venture you've had in mind. By combining talents and resources, your income increases, your self-confidence benefits, and you discover that in order to live the way you want, it's important to do what you love.

Air signs aren't compatible with your water-sign sun. However, there's much to learn from this transit—namely, never hesitate to communicate what you believe and why. Don't hide your wisdom; share it with others. On a mundane level, this transit may increase your partner's income, and the two of you may find investments with large payoffs. Your joint finances benefit tremendously.

The trick with this transit is to share—not just money, but resources, time, energy. If you do that, if you go with Jupiter's flow, you'll benefit greatly from everything this planet has to offer.

Sagittarius

Since Jupiter started transiting Taurus in June 2011, your daily work schedule has been exploding like crazy. So much to do, so little time, but yes, you're having fun! Expect that trend to continue until June 11 of this year. If you work out of your home, then it's possible you add a room onto the house or expand your home to accommodate your office. If you work a regular job, then your schedule keeps growing by leaps and bounds until you feel as if you're all over the place. But it suits you. If you own your own business, then you may add more employees or expand your product/services to overseas markets.

Between June 11, 2012, and June 25, 2013, Jupiter transits Gemini, your opposite sign. This transit augurs well for any joint business venture—with your romantic partner or a business partner or both! By pooling talents and resources, anything done in partnership can pay off handsomely. If you're reading this and thinking that you don't have a partner—either romantic or business—don't fret about it. Chances are good that before this transit ends, you'll have both!

Capricorn

Since June 2011, you've been enjoying Jupiter's transit through fellow earth sign Taurus, in your solar fifth house. It is expanding all your creative ventures, your muse is undoubtedly in attendance 24/7, and some days the ideas flow so fast you forget them before you can find a pen or get to your computer to write them down. This trend continues until June 11. So enjoy it while it lasts, and have faith that your creativity is going to increase your bank account!

Jupiter's transit through Gemini and your solar sixth house lasts from June 11, 2012, to June 25, 2013. Buckle up for the wild ride, Capricorn. This transit should expand your daily work routine and schedule to the point where it's bursting at the proverbial seams. You'll have to be more organized than usual during this transit, but the potential benefits in terms of income can be great. With greater responsibility comes a salary boost. With a salary boost comes greater security for you. Even more important, though, is that with this expansion you can build stronger professional goals.

Aquarius

Jupiter has been transiting Taurus and your solar fourth house since June of 2011 and will be there until June 11 of this year. This transit should expand everything to do with your home, family, and the fundamentals of your life. A birth is a possibility. Or you may move into a larger home or expand the home where you currently live. One of your parents may move in with you. Since the fourth house also governs real estate, it's possible that you buy property as an investment.

Between June 11, 2012, and June 25, 2013, Jupiter transits fellow air sign Gemini in the creativity sector of your chart. It's your ticket, Aquarius. The more creative you are, the greater your earning capacity. You may get involved in a creative venture with one of your kids or a new romantic interest, and because it's done from a basis of pure joy, it has a positive effect on your finances.

Pisces

Since June 2011, Jupiter in Taurus, an earth sign compatible with your water-sign sun, has been transiting your solar third house, and it continues this year until June 11. During this period, your communication skills sharpen your conscious mind expands. You suddenly understand how to make money from, well, talking and writing. A blog, your Web site, magazine articles, a book: any of these venues is possible. The Taurus part of the equation helps to ground your imagination, to bring your ideas into the practical daily world.

From June 11, 2012, to June 25, 2013, Jupiter transits your solar fourth house and Gemini. This transit brings luck and expansion to your home life. In terms of finances, you may start working out of your home, doing something you love, and the money follows. Or perhaps you move to a different city or area where your opportunities for employment are better, where your family is happier, where conditions are more conducive to an increase in your income. Since Jupiter is coruler of your sun sign, its transits are nearly always significant for you in some way.

CHAPTER 7

The Structures in Our Lives

Saturn takes two and a half years to go through a sign, so its effects tend to unfold more slowly than those of the moon, which changes signs about every two and a half days. This planet governs the rules and parameters of physical life and represents responsibility, structure, discipline, limitations and delays, obedience, authority, the building of foundations. So by its transit we are confronted, challenged, or helped by Saturn, depending on the angle it makes to our sun signs.

With Saturn occupying two signs this year, the end of Libra and the beginning of Scorpio (which lasts until December 2014), we're all called upon this year to meet our obligations and responsibilities in two different areas. So let's take a closer look at how Saturn's transits in 2012 impact your sun sign.

Aries

Saturn has been opposite your sun sign since October 2009 and finally leaves Libra on October 5 of this year. During this transit, you're learning to structure your personal and professional partnerships and are deepening your understanding of team work and cooperative living. This last part may not be an easy lesson for a spirit as independent as yours, but learn you will. Chances are that your partner—business or romantic—may have met with some restrictions or delays during this transit that have in turn impacted you in some way.

The Saturn opposition to your sun can be a discouraging time—if you let it. You may feel drained physically, so it's important to have a regular exercise routine. It's also important to maintain contact with friends, family, and other people you love. Try not to resist things that are happening to you. Learn to go with the flow.

Once Saturn enters Scorpio, you feel a distinct relief. A weight has been lifted. During this transit, which lasts until December 2014, you'll learn how to accept other people's values, even when those values aren't in line with your own. It may be more difficult to obtain mortgages and loans during this transit, or sources of income you have depended on may dry up. So it's important that you become as self-sufficient as possible before this transit begins.

Taurus

During Saturn's transit through Libra and your solar sixth house, your daily work responsibility has undoubtedly increased. You may be working longer hours, too, but if you're doing something you love and are getting paid more for your efforts, then it certainly isn't a burden. Due to other demands on your time, you're probably learning how to maximize the time you have and are becoming more organized about your daily work schedule. If you're self-employed, then organization and good time use are vital tools.

Once Saturn enters Scorpio and your solar seventh house, you may be dealing with some of the same issues that Aries dealt with during Saturn's transit through Libra. If you allow this transit—an opposition to your sun—to discourage you, if you resist change, then the transit becomes much more difficult. The important lessons with this transit are about learning to cooperate with partners—business and romantic—and to allow relationships that no longer work to fall out of your experience.

Gemini

Saturn's transit through fellow air sign Libra should be quite productive for you, Gemini. Saturn is now forming a harmonious angle with your sun, strengthening your assets, enabling you to find the proper structures for your creative projects, relationships, your life! This transit may bring professional recognition of some kind and a solid boost in your career and creative output. During this transit, it's smart to establish and/or maintain an exercise routine. Although your health should be fine during this transit, you're building up stamina for times when you may have more stress in your life—like during the Saturn opposition to your sun. This transit also helps you to build solid relationships with your children and to find grounded venues of enjoyment.

Once Saturn enters Scorpio and your solar sixth house, your daily work schedule may have to be revamped. More responsibility will bring a greater need for organization and efficient use of your time. If you're self-employed, Saturn in Scorpio will prompt you to always look at the absolute bottom line—costs in terms of money, time, energy, and resources. Be sure to tend to your health during this transit too. Keep exercising and eating responsibly, and stay away from fad diets.

Cancer

As Saturn transits Libra and your solar fourth house, you're learning to balance responsibilities of home and career. This requires you to be more organized and use your time more efficiently. You may have to cubbyhole your life, with an emphasis on family on certain days and an emphasis on career/work on other days. You tend to go with the flow more than other signs, so it's important that you keep doing that. Any time you feel yourself resisting something that's happening, try to understand why and correct it. If you don't know why you feel resistance, then simply reach for a better thought and feeling.

Once Saturn enters fellow water sign Scorpio and forms a beneficial angle to your sun, you're a much happier camper. This transit helps you to solidify all creative projects. Instead of just writing screenplays, for instance, you begin selling what you write. You discover great depth in your own creativity, your relationship with your children, in romance, and in what you do for fun and enjoyment. Maintain an exercise program during this transit, so that when Saturn enters Sagittarius in late December 2014, your physical strength is at a peak.

Leo

Saturn in Libra forms a beneficial angle to your sun, so you're benefiting from this transit. Your communication skills find a proper venue for expression. A book? Blog? Web site? Radio or TV? Whatever it is, you dazzle with your language skills and win accolades from friends, family, peers. If you move during this transit, the place has to be exactly right for you—and your family. Preferably, it should be in the thick of things—theater, restaurants, bookstores. During this transit, you're enormously productive too and enjoy the work.

Once Saturn enters Scorpio and your fourth house, Saturn is opposed to your career area. This transit indicates that you'll have to learn how to reasonably balance your home and work responsibilities. You'll be aware of the absolute bottom line too, in just about everything—with your family, kids, parents, your family's budget. Your intuition should deepen appreciably, and it will be wise to follow any hunches you have.

Virgo

During Saturn's transit through Libra and your solar second house, your financial earnings may be restricted in some way. Or you find the proper structure for your finances through investments, for example, or a pension plan. You may feel that your values are somehow holding you back, preventing you from doing something or going somewhere. The truth is that you're the only one holding you back. During this transit, you're supposed to learn how to conserve your financial resources and to live within a budget.

When Saturn enters compatible water sign Scorpio on October 5, your relief will be palpable. During this transit, with Saturn forming a beneficial angle to your sun, you'll be in a very good position to bolster your communication skills, find a neighborhood that fits your specific criteria, return to school to enhance your skills. Your conscious mind will be able to take abstract ideas and turn them into practical tools. This transit lasts until December 2014.

Libra

Whenever Saturn conjuncts or opposes your sun sign, it's considered to be a major transit—challenging, but filled with potential. During this transit, you divest yourself of relationships and situations that no longer work or which aren't in your best interest. You may change jobs, get divorced or married, or have to provide support for one of your parents. There can be delays, or your freedom is restricted in some way, but the purpose is to slow down your life so that you tend to what is personal and immediate.

Sometimes Saturn conjunct your sun brings about external events that turn your life in a different direction. The more resistance you offer, the more difficult it is. So it's important to learn to go with the flow.

With Saturn's transit through Scorpio and your solar second house from October 5, 2012, to late December 2014, you learn how to conserve your financial resources, how to budget, how to save. If there's a decrease in your earnings during this transit, try not to fret about it. Your intuition should increase. It's the small voice whispering in the back of your mind to go here, do that, try this. Follow its guidance.

Scorpio

During Saturn's transit through Libra and your solar twelfth house, you're being asked to funnel your discoveries about your own psyche and unconscious into some sort of structure. This transit would be a great time to go through therapy, to take up yoga or some other mind/body discipline, and to start meditating, if you don't already. The twelfth house governs not only the personal unconscious, but past lives, institutions, and everything that is hidden. So with Saturn here, you may run into people you have known in previous lives, will have greater access to your dreams and information that comes to you through meditation, and may have contact with institutions like hospitals and nursing homes, even prisons. This doesn't mean *you* will be institutionalized, but that someone you know may be.

Once Saturn enters your sign, you may feel that your freedom of movement is restricted in some way. It could be due to increased responsibility in some area of your life—career, family, work, no telling. The last time Saturn conjuncted your sun was about twenty-nine to thirty years ago. If you're old enough, look back to that time and remember what was going on in your life. Big changes? How? In what areas? One thing you'll have to do is divest yourself of relationships and situations that aren't in your best interest. You may change jobs, move, get married or divorced. Regardless of the specifics, offer no resistance to events. Go with the flow.

Sagittarius

Saturn's transit through Libra forms a beneficial angle to your sun. It brings structure and solidity to your friendships and wishes and dreams. It actually should be easier to attain your dreams during this transit, particularly if you have laid the groundwork and met your obligations and responsibilities to others. If you don't attain your dreams during this transit, then before it ends you'll have a clearer grasp of what you need to clear out of your life to make room for the attainment of these dreams. Saturn's transit through Scorpio and your solar twelfth house should give you the opportunity to do that.

Saturn transits Scorpio from October 5, 2012, to late December 2014. During this period, you benefit from therapy, meditation, yoga, or any other mind/body discipline. Your dreams can be a source of information and insights. Since the twelfth house represents institutions—prisons, hospitals, nursing homes—it's possible that you have more contact than usual with these places. Basically, this transit enables you to clear your life of what no longer works—relationships, situations, belief systems.

Capricorn

Saturn's transit through Libra and your career area is a major transit that could solidify your professional life and bring recognition from peers and bosses. You may assume more responsibility during this period and work longer hours, and there could be some delays or restrictions on your freedom to come and go as you please. Hard work has never bothered you, especially if you're compensated fairly for it. If you're self-employed, then this transit enables you to solidify your business, client base and income.

During Saturn's transit through compatible water sign

Scorpio and your solar eleventh house, you'll be more in your element. Your friendships and any groups to which you belong will be helpful in achieving your dreams and goals. It's important that you learn how to work with groups and to grasp what group dynamics are in a work situation.

Aquarius

During Saturn's transit through fellow air sign Libra and your solar ninth house, you benefit in a major way. This transit solidifies your worldview and spiritual beliefs and enables you to find the right structure for expressing these beliefs. The ninth house also governs higher education, overseas travel, and foreign cultures, countries, and people, so any foreign travel you do will be structured in some way to fit your goals or needs. If you're in a business that sells products overseas, this transit helps to create a good foundation in overseas markets.

Saturn's transit through Scorpio and your solar tenth house brings increased responsibility in your career, longer hours, perhaps recognition by peers and bosses. It could bring about a promotion, or you may decide to launch your own business. If it's the latter, you're going to love the freedom even if it means a lot of hard work and long hours.

Pisces

During Saturn's transit through Libra and your solar eighth house, your access to funds that have been available previously may be restricted or denied you. If you apply for a mortgage or loan, for example, it may be difficult obtaining it. Your partner's income may take a hit. With Saturn here, you're urged to conserve your resources—money, time, energy. This transit helps you to channel your enormous imagination and intuitive ability.

During Saturn's transit through fellow water sign Scorpio and your solar ninth house, you'll benefit from a positive angle that Saturn makes to your sun. This transit should enable you to explore your worldview and spiritual beliefs in a structured way. You may, for instance, travel overseas to various sacred sites on some sort of spiritual quest. Or you may take courses or workshops in metaphysical areas to explore your intuition or alternative healing methods. This transit lasts from October 5, 2012, to late December 2014.

Saturn in Your Birth Chart

Wherever Saturn appears in your birth chart indicates an area where you will learn lessons in this lifetime. It also indicates life issues you may have brought in from previous lives. Saturn's lessons can be harsh, but it teaches us through experience what we need in order to grow and evolve and what our souls intend to accomplish in this life. It shows us our limitations, teaches us the rules of the game. Without it, our lives would be chaos. Individuals with well-aspected Saturns in their birth charts—the angles other planets make to it—have a practical outlook. With a poorly aspect Saturn, growth may be restricted or limited in some way, and the person's outlook could be rigid.

The sign that Saturn occupies shows how we handle obstacles in our lives, deal with authority, and cope with serious issues. The house placement in your natal chart indicates the area of your life that's affected. If you have Saturn in your tenth house, for example, then your career ambition is one of the driving forces in your life, and you'll work tirelessly to succeed. If your Saturn is in Leo, you may need to learn that it isn't all about just *you* and your career.

Every twenty-eight to thirty years, we experience a Saturn return, when transiting Saturn returns to the place it occupied at our birth. The first return, around the age of twenty-nine, brings major life transitions—we get married or divorced, start a family, move, begin a career. The second return, between the ages of fifty-eight and sixty, is considered to be the harvest. We experience major events—retirement, our kids have left home, we downsize, move, inherit money.

Whenever a Saturn transit hits a natal planet, that period should be navigated carefully, with understanding of what's required of you. Saturn takes about twenty-nine years to circle the zodiac. It entered Libra in late October 2009, retrograded from January 13 to May 29, 2010, then entered Libra again on July 22, 2010, and will be there until October 5, 2012. Then it enters Scorpio for a run of about two and a half years.

Natal Saturn in Aries

Your impetuosity and rashness need to be tempered somewhat, so that you think before you act. You consistently encounter circumstances that force you to develop patience and initiative. If you push against these circumstances, then setbacks occur. With Saturn, you can't take shortcuts. This position of Saturn urges you to develop resourcefulness and discipline and to complete what you start. Once you learn these lessons, you're capable of innovative and unique creations.

The downside with this placement is that you're prone to defensiveness and a kind of self-centered attitude that puts people off. Tact and diplomacy will take you farther and, in the end, may be one of the lessons you're here to learn.

Natal Saturn in Taurus

One of your lessons in this lifetime is to develop persistence and resoluteness, an unshakeable belief in yourself and your talents. This belief helps you to win material security and comfort through hard work, discipline, and perseverance. You may not be the fastest-moving person in the world, but you hang in there long after the competition has bitten the dust.

It behooves you to learn how to handle money and your finances. You tend to be frugal even when you don't have to be, but this frugality may become one of your hobbies. You might, for example, hit garage sales, flea markets, any spot where secondhand goods are sold, and could develop a business around it. On the other hand, if this frugality turns to miserliness, you may want to rethink your attitudes and beliefs about money. The downside is a preoccupation with materialism.

Natal Saturn in Gemini

Since Saturn corules air sign Aquarius and is exalted in air sign Libra, it's pretty comfortable in air sign Gemini. It brings discipline and structure to your mental process and suggests that part of what you're here to learn is how to think through problems logically, working them out in detail so that your solutions are practical. Saturn here may restrict a free flowing expression of ideas, but once you've learned to channel your ideas in a pragmatic way, perhaps through writing or some sort of group activity, you reap the benefits. In other words, it's not enough to have a great idea. How can the idea be put into practice to benefit not only you, but others?

Communication is important to you, but it has to be organized, structured in some way, honest, and dependable. That may be one of the lessons you're here to learn. Downside? If you don't do the grunt work this placement demands, your obstacles multiply.

Natal Saturn in Cancer

This placement may restrict your intuitive gifts and your emotions. Or it could provide the proper structure for expressing both. It depends on how you use your conscious desires and intent to create your life. It depends, too, on your deepest beliefs. Do you believe we have free will or that life is somehow scripted, destined? Are events random, or do they rise from some hidden quantum order? While your crablike tenacity helps you to navigate successfully through obstacles, Saturn here urges you to confront obstacles head on, to reveal what's in your heart, and to channel your intuitive talents in a practical, focused way.

Your home and family are important to you. But strive not to impose so many restrictions in this area that the people who are closest to you—and you yourself—feel suffocated.

Natal Saturn in Leo

This placement is all about power and recognition. The desire for both, however, takes many forms. At one extreme, it results in a need to control your environment and everyone inside of it and a hungry ambition that blinds you to everything else. At the other extreme, this placement results in structures that help you to channel your ambition in a constructive, directed way. This placement also suggests that your ego and need for recognition can be your worst enemies, so be aware of that tendency and do whatever you can to mitigate it.

For Boomers born with this configuration, there can be multiple setbacks that prompt you to work harder, put in longer hours, meet all your obligations—and then some. Eventually, though, if you learn patience and resilience, you succeed. You achieve your goals. Cooperative endeavors are beneficial with this placement, i.e., anything in the professional arena in which you have partners, where you're a team player, where your voice is just one among many.

Natal Saturn in Virgo

The tendency with this placement is that you're such a perfectionist you get bogged down in details. You walk into someone else's house, for example, and immediately notice streaks on the cabinets that scream for a dose of Pledge. Or you enter your son's apartment and are overwhelmed by the disorder and chaos. But if you can direct this tendency toward your work and career, you can handle anything, manifest anything, and perform a service that helps many people understand their roles in this lifetime. It's simply a matter of separating the essential from the inconsequential.

Your intuition is highly developed, just waiting for you to pay attention, to connect all the dots. Find humor in everything you do. Take breaks from work. Treat yourself to a trip to Paris or some other far-flung corner of the globe. Learn to revel in your experiences.

Natal Saturn in Libra

Your lesson this time around is to learn the value of cooperation. The success of any partnership, personal or business, involves the ability to compromise. What can you live with to keep the peace? How much can you surrender without giving away your personal power? Your values? Karma is part and parcel of your most intimate relationships, and the sooner you recognize that, the better off you are. The question, though, is how do you recognize which relationships are karmic and which ones are just the luck (or misfortune) of the draw? Well, bottom line, it's about what you feel when in the presence of another person. It comes down to resonance.

The dark side of this placement is a tendency to surrender too much in the hope that you can keep the peace. The real key here is the ability to forgive and forget and move on.

Natal Saturn in Scorpio

In your work, you're as much of a perfectionist as Saturn in Virgo. But in everything else, you're pure Scorpio—after the bottom line, the absolute truth, the real deal. You're secretive in the way you handle stress and difficulties of any kind and must learn how to deal with this stuff in a calm, centered manner. Allow your intuition to guide you. It's an infallible tool. Your persistence, resilience, and determination are among your greatest assets.

That said, there's a proclivity here for incredible discipline in achieving your goals, but you may need help, and help won't be forthcoming unless you ask for it. *Can* you ask for it? Is a request for help even in your lexicon? Check out the sign of your moon. If it's in a water or earth sign, chances are good that you realize you are part of a collective of like-minded individuals. Start there. You won't be disappointed.

Natal Saturn in Sagittarius

Your pursuit of philosophy and/or religious and spiritual beliefs is one of the primary driving forces in your life. You may have a desire to be recognized as an authority in one of the above areas or in higher education, publishing, politics, or the law. You probably have a strict moral code that guides you, but which could stifle creative thinking. Any kind of rigid approach to problem-solving complicates your challenges and problems. It's best to loosen up, to allow yourself the freedom to explore your ideals free of political or religious restraints.

You're happiest if you can structure your life by incorporating your ideals into your daily life in a practical way. Your professional reputation is vitally important to you, but try not to obsess about every little detail, every little word. You're after the big picture. The darker side of this placement is self-righteousness.

Natal Saturn in Capricorn

Saturn rules this sign, so it's very happy here and functions at optimum capacity. Your ambitions are powerful, and from the time you're old enough to understand what a career is, you are pursuing your own. Your talents are varied, and you may be able to integrate all of them in some unique way to achieve what you desire. Your goals are specific; your discipline is astounding.

The usual description about this placement is that the person may appear cold, detached, remote. But I've found this isn't necessarily true. My daughter and her friends, all of them born in 1989 when Saturn was in the early degrees of Capricorn, are among the most joyful group of people I've ever known. But they're also incredibly focused in their pursuit of educational goals, which certainly fits this placement.

Natal Saturn in Aquarius

Saturn, as the coruler of Aquarius, is pretty comfortable here. Your visionary qualities are channeled and expressed in practical ways that benefit others. Your intellect is organized, focused, objective, and capable of innovative discoveries and solutions. With this placement, there's usually mathematical and scientific ability and the ability to conceptualize. The challenge is to integrate your abilities into your daily life and to ground them. You benefit from regular physical exercise that serves to remind you there's more to life than the mind! Yoga, tai chi, or any other mind/body discipline would be a good place to start.

The downside of this placement can be a lack of feeling, intellectual pride, and impersonal relationships.

Natal Saturn in Pisces

The consensus about this placement is that it's difficult. But any challenges can be overcome by channeling your intuitive ability through a structure that Saturn provides. Instead of letting your memories of the past trap you, use memories of past triumphs as a springboard to achieve what you desire. Your psychic ability is the doorway to spiritual and creative development and to higher spiritual truths.

There can be an inordinate amount of worrying that accompanies this placement, so be sure you always allow yourself solitude, a refuge where you can kick back and relax. It helps to practice yoga, meditate, nurture yourself first.

CHAPTER 8

Health and Fitness Tips for the Paradigm Shift

When paradigms shift, it's not just belief systems that are impacted. Our minds, spirits, and physical bodies are also affected. The slowest-moving outer planets exert the most influence over our lives, so let's take a look at the areas of the body these planets rule for hints about how we can take better care of ourselves in 2012.

Saturn

This planet rules bones, teeth, joints, knees, and spine. So during Saturn transits, these are the areas in your body that are most likely to be affected. With Saturn in Libra until October 5, 2011, your lower back, kidneys, ovaries, and sugar levels—all governed by Libra—could be impacted too. Between October 5 and late December, Saturn transits Scorpio, which rules the endocrine system, menstruation, sex organs, and blood, so these areas could be affected too.

Uranus

This planet rules ankles, nervous ailments, miscarriages, reflexes, and sprains. With Uranus in Aries all year, other areas that could be affected are: adrenals, head, insomnia, retinas, scalp.

Neptune

With Neptune in Pisces, the sign that it rules, from February 3, 2012, for the next fourteen years, areas of the body that can be affected are: feet, glandular swellings, eyes, addictions, parathyroid, pituitary, hard to diagnose diseases.

Pluto

Pluto will be in Capricorn until 2024. Possible trouble areas include: enzyme levels, reproductive organs, hemorrhoids. Capricorn rules pretty much the same areas that Saturn does: bones, joints, knees and kneecaps, gout, rheumatism, sprains.

So when you know that one of these outer planets will be forming an angle to one of your natal planets—your sun, moon, and rising in particular—then you can take extra care with the parts of your body that may be more vulnerable. If Saturn is forming a difficult angle to your sun sign, for example, then it would be smart to take yoga regularly to keep your spine and joints flexible.

Your General Health

If you were an alien watching the evening news and the drug commercials that sponsor it, you might get the impression that Americans are a sickly lot in search of the quickest fix. While drugs certainly have their place, more and more Americans are seeking alternative treatments for whatever ails them. From acupuncture to yoga and homeopathy, from vitamin regimens to nutritional programs, we're seeking control over our own health and bodies.

Health and fitness is more than just eating right and getting sufficient exercise. It's also about our emotions, our inner worlds, our belief systems. How happy are you in your job? Your closest partnerships? Your friendships? Are you generally happy with the money you earn? What would you change about your life? Do you believe you have free will or that everything is destined? Is your mood generally upbeat? Do you feel you have choices? Do you feel empowered? By asking yourself these kinds of questions, you can glean a sense of your emotional state at any given time. The state of your emotions may tell you a great deal about the state of your health.

Louise Hay, author of *You Can Heal Your Life* and founder of Hay House Publishing, is a living testament to the impact of emotions on health. As a young woman, she was diagnosed with vaginal cancer. The doctors wanted to operate, but Hay bought herself time—three months—by telling them she didn't have the money. She then took control of her treatment.

As a battered child who had been raped at the age of five, it wasn't surprising to her that the cancer had shown up where it had. She knew that cancer was "a disease of deep resentment that has been held for a long period of time until it literally eats away at the body." She felt that if she could change the mental pattern that had created the cancer, if she could release the patterns of resentment, then she could cure herself.

She set out a program for her treatment—and forgiveness was at the top of her list. She also knew she had to "love and approve" of herself more. In addition, she found a good therapist, a nutritionist, a foot reflexologist, had colonics three times a week, exercised. Her treatment is spelled out in her book. The end result? Within six months, the doctors pronounced her free of cancer.

In her book, there's an invaluable list: next to every ailment and disease is the probable emotional cause and the new thought pattern that will lead to healing. Her techniques may not be for everyone, but when dealing with health and fitness issues, remember that medical science doesn't have all the answers, and you, in fact, may be your own best healer.

The Physical You

These descriptions fit both sun and rising signs. For a more complete look at the physical you, of course, your entire natal chart should be taken into account, with a particularly close look at the sign of your moon—the root of your emotions, the cradle of your inner world.

Aries

Rules: head and face

What You Look Like

Physically these people tend to have ruddy complexions, narrow chins, and arched eyebrows. Sometimes they have a scar or mole on the head or face. Aries men often have profuse body hair, and in both men and women the hair is sometimes tinged with red.

Health and Fitness Tips

Aries rules the head and face, so these areas are often the most vulnerable physically. Headaches, dizziness, and skin eruptions can be common. If you're an athletic Aries, then do more of whatever it is that you enjoy. Competitive sports? Great, go for it. Long-distance runner? Run farther. Gym? Double your time and your workout. Yoga once a week? Do it three times a week. One way or another, you need to burn off your excessive energy, so that it doesn't turn inward and short-circuit your body!

As a cardinal fire sign, you're an active person who gravitates toward daring, risky sports—mountain climbing, rappelling, bungee jumping, trekking through high mountainous regions, leaping out of airplanes. It's probably a great idea to have good health insurance or to have a Louise Hay attitude toward your health—*I'm attracting only magnificent experiences into my life.*

For maximum benefit, you probably should try to eliminate red meat from your diet. Chicken and fish are fine, but a vegan diet would be best. Herbs like mustard, eyebright, and bay are beneficial for you. Any antioxidant is helpful—particularly vitamins C, E, A or Lutein for your eyes, zinc, Co-Q10, Black Cohosh if you're a female in menopause, or Saw Palmetto if you're a man older than fifty. If you pull a muscle or throw your back out of whack, look for a good acupuncturist and avoid painkillers.

Taurus

Rules: neck, throat, cervical vertebrae

What You Look Like

In a Taurus, the neck is usually thick and sturdy and rises from broad, often muscular shoulders that seem to bear the weight of the world. They tend to be attractive individuals with broad foreheads and expressive faces. Yet their faces can be as inscrutable as fortune cookies when they are hiding something or feel threatened in some way. They usually look more youthful than other people their age, the result of good genes and a daily regimen of exercise.

Health and Fitness Tips

Thanks to the sensuality of your sign, you may be a gourmet cook and enjoy rich foods. But because your metabolism may be somewhat slow, you benefit from daily exercise and moderation in your diet. In fact, moderation in all things is probably a good rule to follow.

As a fixed earth sign, you benefit from any outdoor activity, and the more physical it is, the better it is for you. Hiking, skiing, windsurfing, biking are all excellent pursuits. You also benefit from any mind/body discipline like tai chi or yoga. The latter is especially good since it keeps you flexible, and that flexibility spills over into your attitudes and beliefs and the way you deal with situations and people. You probably enjoy puttering in a garden, but because you have such an artistic side, you don't just putter. You remake the garden into a work of art—fountains, bold colors, mysterious paths that twist through greenery and flowers. Once you add wind chimes and bird feeders, nature's music adds the finishing touches.

If your job entails long hours of sitting in front of a computer, your neck and shoulders may be more tense than usual. You would benefit through regular massage and hot tub soaks.

If you're the silent type of Taurus, then chances are you don't discuss your emotions. This tendency can cause health challenges if you keep anger or resentment bottled up inside you. Best to have an outlet—through exercise, for example, or through some sort of creative endeavor. Art, music, photography, writing: any of those would help. Better yet, learn to open up to at least one or two people!

Gemini

Rules: hands, arms, lungs, nervous system

What You Look Like

Geminis generally radiate a lot of nervous energy. It keeps them slender and wiry, and they're always on the move—if not physically, then mentally. They often have twinkling eyes, clear-cut features, a nose that turns up slightly at the end. Some of them have thick hair. They talk and move fast, many are ambidextrous and usually have excellent coordination.

Health and Fitness Tips

You benefit from periodic breaks in your established routine. Whether it's a trip to some exotic port or a trip to the grocery, it's a breath of fresh air, a way to hit the pause button on your busy mind. Regular physical exercise helps to bleed off some of your energy and keeps your already youthful body supple and in shape.

As a mutable air sign, you need intellectual stimulation and a constant array of experiences and information to keep your curiosity piqued. Otherwise it's too easy for all that nervous energy to turn inward and affect your health. The kind of work you do is important in the overall scheme of your health. You do best in non-routine kind of work with flexible hours or, preferably, in a profession where you make your own hours! Any job in communication, travel, public relations, would suit you. When you're passionate about what you do, you're happier. If you're happy, your immune system remains healthy.

With your natural dexterity and coordination, you

would do well at yoga. If you don't take classes yet, sign up for some. Not only will it keep you flexible, but you'll benefit mentally. Meditation would also be an excellent practice for you. Anything to calm your busy head!

Since your respiratory and nervous systems are your most vulnerable areas, your diet should include plenty of fish, fresh fruits, and vegetables. If you live in a place where you can garden, then plant some of these items for optimum freshness. Vitamin C, zinc, the B vitamins, and vitamins E and A are also beneficial for you. With your energy always in fast-forward, it's smart to get at least seven and preferably eight hours of sleep a night. If you're the type of Gemini with a high metabolism, then you benefit from eating several small meals throughout the day rather than just the usual three.

Cancer

Rules: breasts, stomach, digestive system

What You Look Like

Cancers are recognizable because of their round faces. Their bodies are sometimes round, too, though not necessarily overweight. Those who don't have roundness as part of their physical appearance may have some other distinguishing trait—liquid, soulful eyes, a lovely-shaped mouth, generally expressive features. They're moody individuals, and their moods are often reflected on their faces and in the way they walk and carry themselves.

Health and Fitness Tips

As a cardinal water sign, you benefit from proximity to water. If you can live or work close to a body of water, you'll notice a marked difference in your energy and intuition and how you feel and think. Even a vacation close to the water is healing. This seems to hold true not only for Cancer sun signs, but for moon and rising signs in Cancer too. The body of water can be anything—a lake, river, ocean, salt marsh, even a pond!

Not surprisingly, you benefit from any kind of water sport, even a day at the beach or a picnic by the river. The point is that water speaks to you. It feels like your natural element. You might want to read *The Secret of Water* or any of the other books by Masaru Emoto. You will never think of water in the same way again and will be more conscious of how human emotions affect water—and thus our bodies, since we consist of nearly 70 percent water.

Emotionally, you may cling to past injuries and hurts more than other signs or may still be dragging around issues from childhood or even from a past life. Unresolved emotional stuff can lodge in your body and create problems. So it's important that you rid yourself of past resentments and anger. Use hypnosis to dislodge these feelings. Forgive and forget. Have a past-life regression. Read Louise Hay's book *You Can Heal Your Life.*

If you have a moon, rising, or another planet in an earth sign, then consider regular workouts at a gym.

Leo

Rules: heart, back, spinal cord

What You Look Like

From Jacqueline Kennedy to Madonna to Presidents Obama and Clinton, the typical Leo looks regal. Hair that is thick or in some way distinguished, compelling eyes, a smile that can light up the dark side of the moon: these are the Leo hallmarks. Male or female, they project dignity and intelligence and move with a certain elegance. In a crowded room, the Leo is usually the one surrounded by people!

Health and Fitness Tips

Leo rules the heart. So you benefit from a low-fat diet, exercise, work that you love, and relationships in which you are recognized as the unique person that you are. Yes, those last two things count in the overall picture of your health!

Let's talk about your work. Acting, of course, is what you're known for. And performance. And politics. And, well, anything where you can show off your abundant talents. So if right now you're locked into a humdrum job, are the low person on the bureaucratic totem pole, and don't receive the attention you feel you deserve, then your pride and ambition are suffering. That, in turn, creates resentment that could be eating you alive. Turn the situation around by finding a career or an outlet where your talents shine and you're appreciated and recognized. You're a natural leader whose flamboyant style and magnetism attract the supporters who can help you.

You have a temper, but once you blow, that's it. Unlike Cancer, you don't hold on to grudges or harbor resentments or anger from childhood. You tend to be forward looking in your outlook, and your natural optimism is healthy for your heart and immune system. Anything you can do to maintain your cheerful disposition is a plus. When you feel yourself getting down, rent comedies, find books that make you laugh out loud, blog about your feelings.

Virgo

Rules: intestines, abdomen, female reproductive system

What You Look Like

Their physiques are usually slender and distinctive in some way—beautifully sculpted fingers and hands, for instance, nice legs, gorgeous teeth. They're physically attractive as a rule, which they enhance through their fastidious attention to detail. Their eyes may be unusual in some way, and their features tend to be sharp, clearly defined. They're fastidious about personal hygiene.

Health and Fitness Tips

If you're the type of Virgo who worries and frets a lot, then the first place it's likely to show up is in your digestive tract. You might have colic as an infant, stomach upsets as a teenager, ulcers as an adult. The best way to mitigate this tendency, of course, is to learn how NOT to worry and to simply go with the flow.

You do best on a diet that includes plenty of fresh fruits and vegetables, fish, and chicken. Try to stay away from fried or heavily spiced foods. Red meat might be difficult to digest. If you live in a place where fresh fruits and vegetables are difficult to find during the winter, then supplement your diet with the appropriate vitamins and minerals. If you're a fussy eater—and some Virgos are—then the vitamin and mineral supplements are even more important.

You benefit from hot baths, massages, anything that allows you to relax into the moment. Yoga, running, swimming, gym workouts, any of these exercise regimens benefit you. Some Virgos, particularly double Virgos— with a moon or rising in that sign—have an acute sense of smell. If you're one of those, then be sure to treat yourself to scented soaps and lotions, fragrant candles and incense, and any other scent that soothes your soul.

Virgo is typically associated with service, and you may find that whenever you do a good deed for someone, when you volunteer your time or expertise, you feel better about yourself and life in general. The more you can do to trigger these feelings, the healthier you'll be. You have a tendency toward self-criticism that's part and parcel of your need for perfection, and whenever you find yourself shifting into that critical frame of mind, stop it in its tracks. Reach for a more uplifting thought. This will help you to maintain your health.

Libra

Rules: lower back, kidney, diaphragm

What You Look Like

Even in a crowd of beautiful people, they stand out in some way. As a Venus-ruled sign, they have distinctive features—beautiful eyes, gorgeous skin, well-formed bodies, expressive mouths. They're often slender, good-looking. They enjoy beauty—in their partners, their surroundings, their aesthetic tastes. So it isn't surprising that they often dress beautifully and have homes that are boldly colored and uniquely decorated.

Health and Fitness Tips

If your love life is terrific, then your health probably is too. You're happiest when you're in a relationship, preferably a committed, lifetime relationship. When things between you and your partner are on an even keel, your energy is greater, your immune system works without a hitch, you sleep more soundly, and you're more apt to have a healthier lifestyle.

You prefer working in an environment that's aesthetically pleasing, where there's a minimum of drama with congenial people. If your work situation doesn't fit that description, then it could affect your health—and for the same reasons as a love life that is lacking. Emotions. Your lower back, kidneys, and diaphragm are vulnerable areas for you, and unvented emotions could manifest in those areas first. If it isn't possible to change jobs or careers right now, then find an artistic outlet for your creative expression. Music, photography, art, writing, dance, any area that allows you to flex your creativity.

123

You benefit from yoga, walking, swimming, and any kind of exercise that strengthens your lower back muscles. Meditation is also beneficial, particularly when it's combined with an awareness of breathing.

The healthiest diet for you should consist of foods with varied tastes, plenty of fresh fruits and vegetables, organic if possible, and a minimum of meats. Anything that benefits your kidneys is good. Drink at least eight glasses of water a day, so that your kidneys are continually flushed out.

Scorpio

Rules: sexual organs, elimination

What You Look Like

The body types vary, but the eyes ... well, the eyes are nearly always compelling, intense, piercing. They rarely reveal what they're feeling and are masters at disguising their expressions. Their masks are carefully honed through years of hiding their emotions. Many Scorpios have thick eyebrows, sharp noses, seductive mouths. Their voices are often husky and low.

Health and Fitness Tips

As a fixed water sign, you probably benefit by a proximity to water every bit as much as Cancer does. Lake, ocean, river, pond, salt marsh: take your pick. If none of these is available, then put a fountain in your backyard or somewhere in your house and create a meditation area. It's important that you have a quiet center where you can decompress at the end of the day, particularly if you have a busy family life and a lot of demands on your time.

You tend to keep a lot of emotion locked inside, and if the emotions are negative—resentment, anger—they fester and affect your health. So try to find someone you can talk to freely about your emotions—a partner, friend, family member. Or pour these feelings into a creative outlet. One way or another, get them out.

Scorpio rules the sexual and elimination organs, so these areas could be where ill health hits first. Be sure that you eat plenty of roughage in your diet and enjoy what you eat while you're eating it. Stay away from the usual culprits—fried or heavily processed foods. You do best with plenty of fresh food, but may want to consider eliminating red meats. Consider colonics treatments for cleaning out the bowels.

For your overall health, it's important to enjoy sex with a partner whom you trust. Avoid using sex as a leverage for power in a relationship.

Sagittarius

Rules: hips, thighs, liver

What You Look Like

They tend to come in two types—tall and broad through the shoulders or shorter and heavier. The second description comes in part from Jupiter, which rules the sign and causes them to indulge their appetites. They look athletic and have high foreheads that get higher in men as they age and their hair recedes. They move quickly, but not necessarily gracefully.

Health and Fitness Tips

As a mutable fire sign, you can't tolerate any kind of restriction or limitation on your freedom. You must be able to get up and go whenever you want. If you work in a job that demands you punch a time clock, where your hours are strictly regulated, or are in a relationship where you feel constricted, then you probably aren't happy. For a naturally buoyant and happy person like you, that could spell health challenges. Sadge rules the hips, the sacral region of the spine, the coccygeal vertebrae, the femur, the ileum, the iliac arteries, and the sciatic nerves, so any of these areas could be impacted health-wise.

You benefit from any kind of athletic activity. From competitive sports to an exercise regimen you create, your body craves regular activity. You also benefit from yoga, which keeps your spine and hips flexible.

If you're prone to putting on weight—and even if you're not!—strive to minimize sweets and carbs in your diet. The usual recommendations—abundant fresh vegetables and fruits—also apply. If you're the type who eats on the run, then you may be eating fast or heavily processed foods and should try to keep that at a minimum or eliminate it altogether. Even though your digestive system is hardy enough to tolerate just about anything, the fast foods and processed foods add carbs and calories.

Antioxidants are beneficial, of course, and these include vitamins C, A, and E. Minerals like zinc should be included in your diet and also a glucosamine supplement for joints.

Capricorn

Rules: knees, skin, bones

What You Look Like

As a cardinal earth sign, these individuals understand the benefits of exercise, and their bodies show it. While they generally aren't muscular—some are, but not as a rule—they look to be in shape. Their bodies are often angular and slender, and their faces, regardless of their age, have a maturity about them.

Health and Fitness Tips

Since you seem to have been born with an innate sense of where you're going—or want to go—it's likely that

Booksellers store or Barnes & Noble.com with the below exceptions:

A store credit for the purchase price will be issued (i) for purchases made by check less than 7 days prior to the date of return, (ii) when a gift receipt is presented within 60 days of purchase, (iii) for textbooks, or (iv) for products purchased at Barnes & Noble College bookstores that are listed for sale in the Barnes & Noble Booksellers inventory management system.

Opened music CDs/DVDs/audio books may not be returned, and can be exchanged only for the same title and only if defective. NOOKs purchased from other retailers or sellers are returnable only to the retailer or seller from which they are purchased, pursuant to such retailer's or seller's return policy. Magazines, newspapers, eBooks, digital downloads, and used books are not returnable or exchangeable. Defective NOOKs may be exchanged at the store in accordance with the applicable warranty.

Returns or exchanges will not be permitted (i) after 14 days or without receipt or (ii) for product not carried by Barnes & Noble or Barnes & Noble.com.

Policy on receipt may appear in two sections.

you take care of yourself. You know the routine as well as anyone—eat right, stay fit, exercise, get enough rest. But there are other components to living long and prospering (to paraphrase Spock!), and that's your emotions.

You, like Scorpio, are secretive, although your motives are different. For you, it's a privacy factor more than anything else. You keep your emotions to yourself and may not express what you feel when you feel it. This can create blockages in your body, notably in your joints or knees. It's vital that you learn to vent your emotions, to rid yourself of anger before it has a chance to move inward.

You're focused, ambitious, and patient in the attainment of your goals. But your work—and your satisfaction with it—is a primary component in your health. If you feel you've reached a dead end in your career, if you're frustrated more often than you're happy with what you do, then it's time to revamp and get out of Dodge. By taking clear, definite steps toward something else, you feel you're more in control of your destiny and mitigate the possibility of health challenges.

Since your knees are vulnerable, running is probably not the best form of exercise for you, unless you do it only once or twice a week and engage in some other form of exercise the rest of the time. For a cardio workout that isn't as tough on your knees, try a rowing machine. For general flexibility, there's nothing like yoga!

Aquarius

Rules: ankles, shins, circulatory system

What You Look Like

Tall and slender or short and round, their body types are as different and varied as they are. But many have deeply set eyes and classic profiles. Many of them move as quickly as Geminis; others move like molasses. Most aren't particularly coordinated, but some are. So, bottom line, it's tough to spot these individuals in a crowd. But as soon as you listen to them for five minutes, they're easier to peg. They talk eloquently about their ideas and ideals, and you'll recognize them by their discussions of alternative foods, alternative fuels, alternative lifestyles, alternative everything.

Health and Fitness Tips

Let's start with the effect of Uranus ruling your sign. It sometimes can set your nerves on edge—too many sounds, too much chaos around you, loud noises deep into the night, the backfiring of cars, the incessant drone of traffic, even a crowd at the local mall. You're sensitive to all of that. It's part of what makes it important for you to have a private space to which you can withdraw—a quiet back yard filled with plants, a room inside your house with an altar for your Wiccan practice filled with scents from candles or incense that soothe your frazzled nerves. Or perhaps a book on tape can shut it all out. But shut it out you must to protect your health.

Because you live so much inside your own head, exercise is definitely beneficial for you. It doesn't have to be anything complicated—yoga done in the privacy of your own home, long walks, regular bike rides. But do *something* to ground your body, to get your blood moving, to silence the buzz inside your head. It will all benefit your health.

Nutrition? Well, for an Aquarian, this can go any number of different ways. You enjoy different types of food, so that's a place to start—with what you *enjoy*. The foods are likely to be unusual—organically grown, for instance, prepared in unusual ways, or purchased from a local co-op. If you live in the city, then perhaps you purchase food from a grocery store you've been frequenting for years. The idea here is that *you* know what's best for your body, what you can tolerate, what you need. Even though Aquarians aren't generally as in touch with their bodies as earth signs, they have an intuitive sense about what works for them. In the end, that's all that matters.

Pisces

Rules: the feet, is associated with the lymphatic system

What You Look Like

Common wisdom in astrology says there are two types of Pisces—the whale and the dolphin. And this goes for the sun, moon, or rising in Pisces. The whale is, well, large, but also tuned into everything and everyone on the planet. The dolphin type is slender, sleek, quick, joyful, graceful. But both body types usually have extraordinary eyes that are not only soulful, but seem to be able to peer through time.

Health and Fitness Tips

Let's start with emotions. Let's start with the fact that you're a psychic sponge, able to absorb other people's moods and thoughts with the ease of magnet attracting every other piece of metal around it. Yes, let's start there. It's why you should associate only with optimistic, upbeat people. The negative types steal your energy, wreck your immune system, and leave you in a tearful mess at the end of the rainbow with nothing to show for your journey.

Like your fellow water signs Cancer and Scorpio, you probably benefit from proximity to water. Whether you live near water, work near it, vacation near it, water refreshes your soul, spirit, intuition, and your immune system. Read Masaru Emoto's books on how water responds to emotions and intent. You'll never think about water in the same way again. You'll never think about your sun sign in the same way again, either.

You benefit from any kind of exercise, but try something that speaks to your soul. Swimming. Rowing, but in an actual boat, on an actual river instead of in a gym. Even a hot tub where you kick your legs is beneficial. Pay attention to the water you drink. Is your tap water filled with fluorides? Then avoid it and look for distilled water. Drink at least eight glasses a day. Indulge yourself in massages, foot reflexology, periodic dips in the ocean. Any ocean.

Meditate. Find the calm center of your storm.

CHAPTER 9

Aspects

Throughout this material, we've talked about beneficial or challenging angles that a transiting planet makes to your sun sign or that transiting planets make to each other. These angles are called *aspects*. Think of them as a symbolic network of arteries and veins that transport the blood of astrology. In a natal chart, these angles connect our inner and outer worlds, accentuate certain traits and play down others. Each aspect represents a certain type of energy, so there really aren't any good or bad aspects because energy is neutral. It's what we do with the energy that counts. It comes back to free will. When transiting planets make angles to each other, energy is also exchanged.

For instance, every year there is at least one very lucky day when the transiting sun and transiting Jupiter form a beneficial angle to each other—a conjunction (same sign and degree), a sextile (60 degrees apart), or a trine (120 degrees apart). The lucky day in 2012 falls on May 13, when the sun and Jupiter are exactly conjunct. This means that the sun's life energy and Jupiter's expansive energy combine and create, well, some magic for all of us! It's especially good for Taurus and other earth signs, but since we all have Taurus somewhere in our charts, everyone benefits.

If you look back to the presidential election in November 2008, Saturn in Virgo and Uranus in Pisces formed an exact opposition to each other. They were 180 degrees apart, an aspect that is like a tug-of-war. In this case, the tug-of-war was between the candidate that represented the old paradigm, the established order—Saturn—and the candidate who symbolized sweeping change—Uranus.

Aspects are most powerful as they are approaching exactness. So even though a conjunction, for example, is 00 degrees of separation or a square is technically 90 degrees of separation, many astrologers use *orbs* that can be as wide as five or ten degrees. Some astrologers use small orbs, but others assign larger orbs for the sun and moon and smaller orbs for other planets. The closer the orb, the more powerful the combination. If you're sensitive to transits, then, you may be feeling lucky for several days before May 13!

In terms of a natal chart, any transiting planet that is approaching an aspect with one of your natal planets is also most powerful on its approach. The traditional aspects have been used since the second century A.D. They are the conjunction, sextile, square, trine, and opposition. These aspects are considered to be the major or hard angles and are also the most powerful. There are other minor aspects that astrologers use, but for the purpose of this chapter, we'll only talk about the traditional aspects.

At the end of this chapter is a natal chart. We'll be referring to it as we go through the aspects.

Conjunction, major hard aspect, 0 degrees

This aspect is easy to identify—clusters of planets within a few degrees of each other, usually but not always in the same sign and house. But it's a complex aspect because energies combine, fuse, merge. Think of it as power, intensity. So if you have conjunctions in your natal chart, the astrologer who reads for you should address what it means and how you can use it to maximize your potential.

Let's look at the young woman's chart. With her Saturn—♄—and Neptune—♆—conjunct in her tenth house of career, there's already a tension and power in her chart. Saturn builds structures and boundaries and seeks to hold back, restrict. It's about rules and responsibilities. Neptune urges us to allow boundaries to dissolve, to release the ego, to reach for higher ideals. So this woman will confront these dualities in her career—her tenth house.

With Uranus—♅—thrown into the mix, these experiences and dualities will come at her out of the blue, suddenly and without warning. Her career will be unusual, strange, filled with idiosyncratic people and defined by strange experiences—the Uranus influence. Uranus shakes up the status quo and when it's conjunct Saturn—even widely, by 7 degrees in this case—she will feel conflicted at times about which path to follow, which choices to make.

In this same chart, notice the close conjunction between the moon—☽—and Mars—♂—in the sixth house. One degree of separation. One possible repercussion is that her emotions are especially intense, even volatile at times, when it comes to her daily work routine and the maintenance of her health. Her health stuff may occur in fits and starts—one week she'll run two miles a day, the next week she's a couch potato, and the next week she meditates and practices yoga. It's the same way with her work. Erratic, moved by the spirit and passion of the moment. But because Mars is in Virgo, she's diligent, a hard worker at whatever she takes on.

Since Mars is within a degree of the seventh-house cusp, this passion she has spills over into her personal and business partnerships.

Sextile, major soft aspect, 60 degrees

Again, look at the young woman's chart. An example of a sextile occurs between her sun—☉—at 8 degrees Virgo in her sixth house and her Jupiter—♃—at 5 degrees Cancer in her fourth house . The orb, according to the aspect grid, is 2 degrees and 41 minutes. Close enough to have significant impact.

A sextile is a point of ease. It represents a free-flowing energy between the planets involved. No tension. The sextile is a kind of buffer, a shield against turmoil, indecision, instability. But if there are too many sextiles, then the person may be too passive!

In the young woman's chart, her Pluto in Scorpio in the eighth house—12♀♏49—is closely sextile her Neptune in the tenth, within 5 degrees of her Saturn in the tenth, within a 6-degree orb of her Virgo Mars in the sixth, and within 5 degrees of her Virgo moon in the sixth. That's a whole lot of energy stacked in her favor and suggests that whatever she does on a daily basis with her work somehow feeds into the larger picture of her career. During her college years, she was able to manifest jobs out of thin air while in school and during the summers.

When she was in high school, for instance, she and her parents vacationed in windsurfing spots in the Caribbean and South America because her dad is a windsurfer. So she learned to windsurf and became so proficient at it that she was able to teach windsurfing at her college, through the sailing club, to any students who were interested. The college paid her ten bucks an hour. Gas money! Food money!

From the time she was old enough to walk, she enjoyed horseback riding and loved working with horses, being around them. She lived near an equestrian community, so becoming a barn rat was not a tough thing to do. During the summer of her freshman year, with her parents breathing down her back about getting a job, she manifested a job teaching riding at an equestrian summer camp.

These examples are precisely the kinds of experiences that accompany the sextiles in her chart. That Pluto in Scorpio, a sign that planet rules, gives her enormous power and ability to hone in on what she needs and wants and make it happen.

Square, major hard aspect, 90 degrees

Friction, angst, *oh my God, the sky is falling*: that's how squares feel in a natal chart. The sky, of course, is never falling, but the friction and angst are quite real and act as triggers for action, forward thrust. They force us to develop, evolve, and reach aggressively for our desires.

How's this play out in real life? Look at the young woman's chart. She has three squares to her natal Mercury in Libra, in her seventh house of partnerships, all of them from that cluster of planets in her tenth house of career. Her natal Mercury—05☿♎33—is square to those tenth house planets from between 2 to 4 degrees. Ouch. The need to achieve something professionally is very strong. But it's not just about achieving. She wants to make her mark on the world, to leave something behind, some sort of legacy, something unique that bears *her stamp*. Because Mercury rules communication and this young woman enjoys writing and is good at it, that could be one of her signatures.

Mercury is also square her Jupiter in Cancer in the fourth house, suggesting that she may try to take on too much—in her writing, her life, her partnerships. Hit the pause button, breathe, ask for guidance through imagination, visualization, your family (fourth house), and dreams.

Squares spur us to action.

Trines, major soft aspect, 120 degrees

This aspect works like a sextile, linking energies in a harmonious way. It's associated with general ease and good fortune. Again, though, if there are too many in the chart, passivity may result.

Look at the chart again. The young woman's 8-degree Virgo sun in her sixth house is closely trine to both Neptune and Saturn in Capricorn. The Saturn/Sun trine enables the young woman to set realistic goals and to attain them. The Neptune/Sun trine gives her deep compassion, psychic and artistic ability. She's able to attract the right opportunities for her career. The trine to Uranus is a bit wider—7 degrees—but is still significant. It suggests that her profession is or will be unusual and that her freedom is important to her. It's doubtful this young woman will be found in an office, confined to a 9 to 5 job. Whatever she does is likely to be unique.

Opposition, major hard aspect, 180 degrees

This aspect feels like a persistent itch that you can't reach and usually involves polarities—Taurus/Scorpio, for example, or Aries/Libra. It brings about change through conflict and sometimes represents traits we project onto others because we haven't fully integrated them into ourselves.

In the woman's chart, her natal Jupiter in Cancer is opposed to all three planets in her tenth house. Jupiter expands everything it touches, so with Saturn, the woman's professional success comes about through persistence and dedication and by working with her beliefs in a constructive, positive way. With her Jupiter opposed to Uranus, the freedom to call her own shots, make her own schedule, to do her own thing, is paramount. In a chart that lacks direction and focus, this aspect can lead to involvement with revolutionary groups or religious cults. In a strong chart like this one, however, the Uranus/Jupiter opposition can indicate involvement in humanitarian efforts. The Neptune/Jupiter opposition can indicate utopian ideals, getting suckered by a sob story or trusting smooth talkers with a devious agenda. But it can also lead to great spiritual awareness and enhanced psychic ability.

Some other minor aspects that astrologers use are:

- the semi-square, 45 degrees. It creates irritation and friction between the planets involved.
- the septile, 51 degrees. Indicative of harmony and union in a nontraditional way. Can suggest spiritual power.
- the quincunx or inconjunct, 150 degrees separation. Indicates a need for adjustment in attitude and beliefs.

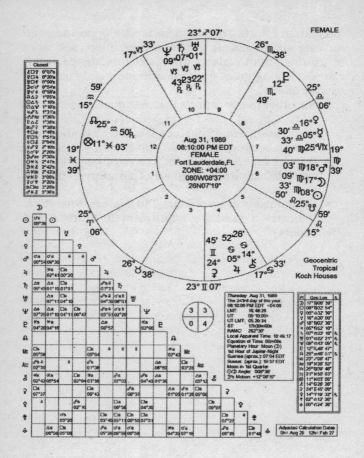

FEMALE

Aug 31, 1989
08:10:00 PM EDT
FEMALE
Fort Lauderdale,FL
ZONE: +04:00
080W08'37"
26N07'19"

Geocentric
Tropical
Koch Houses

Thursday Aug 31, 1989
The 243rd day of the year.
08:10:00 PM EDT +04:00
LMT: 18:49:26
UT   00:10:00
UT-LMT: 05:20:34
ST: 17h30m00s
RAMC: 262°30'
Local Apparent Time: 18:49.17
Equation of Time: 00m06s
Planetary Hour: Moon (☽)
1st Hour of Jupiter-Night
Sunrise (aprox.) 07:04 EDT
Sunset (aprox.) 19:37 EDT
Moon in 1st Quarter
⊙/☽ Angle: 008°36'
☽% Motion: +12°08'19"

Adjusted Calculation Dates
0h= Aug 29 12h= Feb 27

Pl	Geo Lon	
♇	17°♏08' 38"	
♀	08°♏32' 54"	
♀	16°♎00' 00"	
♂	25°♍00' 00"	
⊙	18°♍02' 36"	
☿	05°♎52' 10"	
☽	17°♍23' 16"	
♄	01°♍22' 21"	
♃	05°♊43' 09"	
♇	12°♏48' 47"	
☊	25°♒40' 51"	
⊕	23°♐02' 46"	
⚷	19°♓38' 53"	
⚸	21°♓50' 03"	
⚵	11°♓03' 08"	
⚶	14°♋26' 28"	
⚴	24°♊45' 09"	
⚳	14°♓19' 32"	
♆	02°♉12' 36"	
⚕	00°♈24' 30"	

CHAPTER 10

The Astrological Neighborhood

Whether you're just learning astrology or are a seasoned pro or somewhere in between, the Internet is a wonderful tool for studying astrology. You can Google anything—a planet, an aspect, some obscure detail about astrology—and some Web site or blog undoubtedly has the information you're looking for.

Astrology sites offer a vast spectrum of services, from free natal charts, daily transits, and monthly horoscopes to political and world predictions—it's all at your fingertips. Here are some of the best sites:

www.astro.com: Enter your birth data and obtain a free natal chart. This site is also chocked full of information about astrology. Great for the beginner, the intermediary, and the advanced astrologer. Something for everyone here. There are also some terrific articles by well-known astrologers.

www.astrologyzone.com: Susan Miller's site is a favorite for neophytes and pros alike. Every month she writes around three thousand words per sign about what you can expect in the upcoming month. Her predictions are eerily accurate!

www.moonvalleyastrologer.com: Celeste Teal is *the* expert on eclipses, a specialized area of astrology that few have researched the way she has. Her two books on eclipses are seminal works.

www.astrocollege.com: Lois Rodden's site is extraordinary. This woman spent most of her life collecting birth data and then created a piece of software that is invaluable in research. This site also rates and sells astrology software. Lois has passed on, but her work survives.

http://astrofuturetrends.com: Author and astrologer Anthony Louis does just what the site says. He predicts future trends, covers political stuff, and provides an overall view of astrology.

www.starlightnews.com: Click on Nancy's blog. Here you'll find the latest predictions and insights about world affairs. Nancy's predictions about politics have been right on. Before the 2004 election, she made some predictions about tight senatorial races that were totally accurate. She also called the presidential race in 2008. We've been following her closely ever since.

www.astro-yoga.com: This site combines astrology and yoga. We created it and this system of yoga.

www.tjmacgregor.com: Here you'll find monthly astrological predictions for writers.

www.ofscarabs.blogspot.com: About synchronicities—what they are, how they show up in our lives, what they might mean, and hundreds of stories.

Software

Computers have transformed everything about astrology. In the days before, you had to figure all this stuff by hand, through complicated mathematical formulas that left you gasping.

Our first piece of software was a really simple program we found at some computer store for ten bucks. It erected a chart in about sixty seconds. There it was—rising, moon, sun, planets, the houses—everything set up on the computer screen as if by magic. In the late 1990s, we bought our first really terrific astrology software from Matrix for about $300. In the years since, http://www.astrologysoftware.com has supplied us with endless data and information and revolutionized the study of astrology.

But it's not just enough to have a great piece of software. When your computer crashes, when you receive updates that screw up, when windows updates to a new system, you call the Matrix help line and their people walk you through it until everything works. The employees on their help lines aren't outsourced. You won't reach India. You'll talk to someone in Michigan who is not only an astrologer, but a computer geek who knows how to fix your problem. If by some fluke they can't fix your problem, they'll credit you for one of their other terrific programs.

The only complaint we have about Matrix is that to activate the software, you have to call or contact them through the Internet to receive a special code. If your computer crashes, if you buy a new PC or laptop . . . well, it's annoying. When you pay this much for software, you shouldn't have to obtain a special access code.

Another great piece of software is SolarFire. Astrologers are as dedicated to this program as they are to Matrix's software. Check out http://www.alabe.com for current prices. While the two programs offer similar features and capabilities, preferences seem to be individual. Both Matrix's Winstar and astrolabe's SolarFire offer many alternative features—like reports for natal, transit, and progressed interpretations.

Kepler's astrology program—http://www.astrosoftware.com—is beautiful in its rendition of charts, interpretations, and just about anything any astrologer could use or need. We like it for its ease, its beauty. But it's not a Winstar or SolarFire.

If your exploration of astrology takes you deeper, there are other software programs that take you there. Bernadette Brady is the undisputed mistress of fixed stars. Her software program, Starlight, is remarkable not only for its accuracy, but for its presentation. You will never think of fixed stars in the same way once you play with this program. What won't make sense in a natal-chart interpretation suddenly snaps into clarity when you use Brady's software. Be sure to download a print to file version for the software—through a PDF file—so that you can maximize usage. Their Web site: http://www.zyntara.com.

Lois Rodden's AstroDatabank is the software that Lois Rodden developed. It contains over thirty thousand birth records, "carefully documented and coded for accuracy with the popular Rodden Rating system. AstroDatabank includes intriguing biographies, revealing personality traits, important life events, and significant relationships." For the curious, the researcher, the neophyte and pro alike.

Both Winstar and SolarFire produce computerized report software. These reports are handy for when a friend of a friend is in a fix and you don't have the time to interpret transits and progressions for the person's birth chart. Winstar also produces software on the tarot and numerology.

Day Watch, another Winstar program, is forecasting software that is invaluable for astrologers. From their site: "Certainly it creates personalized astrological calendars, a great tool for professional astrologers and those who have an understanding of astrological terms, symbols, and technique. But Day Watch also contains a full range of onscreen and printable interpretations of events that even someone with absolutely no astrological training can read, understand, and immediately put to use in their daily lives."

At the beginning of every month, we bring up our personalized calendars that tell us what is happening daily in our natal charts and also lists which planets are changing signs in that month, on what date, and which planets are turning retrograde or direct. Each month includes an ephemeris and lunar charts for the new and full moon. The program also offers various types of reports.

Getting a Reading

So now you're ready for an astrological reading. But where do you start? Which astrologer should you use?

The best way to find an astrologer is through soeone who has gotten a reading and recommends the individual. If you don't know anyone who has had an astrological reading, then the next best course is to head over to the nearest bookstore and look through the astrology books. Browse through titles that interest you. Note the author's style. If the author uses a lot of astro jargon or seems to write in a depressing or heavy-handed way, move on. Once you find an author whose book you like, check to see if he or she has a Web site and get in touch with the person.

Rates for a reading vary from one astrologer to another and usually depend on what you want. Would you like just an interpretation of your natal chart? Would you like a forecast for the next six months or a year? Do you want a compatibility chart for you and your partner? Some astrologers prefer to do phone readings and record the reading. Others prefer to work through e-mail. If the astrologer you've chosen lives close to you, all the better. Have the reading done in person.

What to Expect During a Reading

Every astrological reading begins with your natal chart, so an accurate birth time is essential. It should come from your birth certificate or a parent's memory. An approximate time means the entire reading won't be as accurate.

This reading differs from a daily horoscope you find in a newspaper or on a Web site because it's tailored to your specific chart rather than just to your sun sign. If you're getting a reading only on your birth chart, then the astrologer interprets the entire chart, not just pieces of it. The astrologer looks at the signs and house placements of the various planets and the angles the planets make to each other.

Think of a natal chart as a holographic depiction of who you are. It's an organic blueprint, where the parts fit together in certain ways. In a reading, the signs of your sun, moon, and rising are where most astrologers begin. The sun represents your total personality, the moon symbolizes your inner world, and your rising sign is the doorway to your chart—the portal through which all your experiences enter. So an astrologer would look at the mix of these planets and then look at how they meld or oppose, facilitate or challenge other planets in your chart.

In addition to planets and aspects, astrologers also look at some other things in natal charts: the Nodes of the moon, part of fortune, various asteroids, Chiron, Vertex, and Sabian symbols. The Nodes are discussed in the next chapter, so let's go through the other parts of the list.

Part of fortune ⊗ : This is the most commonly used Arabic part, of which there are dozens. Its placement by sign and house designates where your "pot of gold" lies. It's your luck factor.

Asteroids: There are probably hundreds of asteroids, but astrologers use only a handful of them. Thanks to the work of astrologer Demeter George, four asteroids are the most commonly used: Vesta, Ceres, Athena, and Juno. Here are their general meanings:

Vesta ⚶: This asteroid's position in a natal chart describes where we are dedicated and how we can use our energies to bring about the greatest change in the larger world.

Ceres ⚳: How were we nurtured and how do we nurture others? That's what Ceres shows us, according to the sign and house position.

Pallas Athena ♀: How do you fight for what you want? How do you pursue what you desire? Pallas, the warrior queen, describes the battles we choose to fight.

Juno ⚵: The asteroid of marriage. It generally describes the romantic/marriage partner we need and get.

Chiron ⚷: Known as the wounded healer, this planetoid describes where we are wounded and how healing this wound, which often stems from early childhood, can lead to greater wisdom and the healing of others.

Vertex: It's a point that describes agreements we made prior to being born into this life, a point of destiny. Since we have free will, we can choose not to keep these appointments, but it's probably a good idea if we do. Often the sign of our Vertex is the sign of someone to whom we're close—parent, partner, child, friend, mentor.

Sabian Symbols: Back in the early part of the twentieth century, astrologer Marc Edmund Jones spent hours with a clairvoyant, Elsie Wheeler, who gave him psychic impressions of each of the 360 degrees of the zodiac. The impressions are usually couched in metaphors, but over the years have proven to be eerily accurate. To test it, go to one of the sites listed in this chapter and get a free birth chart. Then go to www.cafeastrology.com, search for Sabian symbols, and look up the degree of your sun sign.

There are other points and asteroids that astrologers use, but when you're just starting out in your interpretation of your own chart—or of someone else's—keep the chart as clean as possible. Stick to the planets. Once you've got those meanings down, start adding other elements to the chart.

CHAPTER 11

Your Soul's Agenda

The Soul

There are various ways to look for spiritual aspects in a chart. Some astrologers use Neptune and the angles it makes to other planets. Others use the moon and its aspects. We use the North and South Nodes of the moon.

The Nodes aren't planets. They're points formed by the moon's orbit around Earth that intersect with the Earth's path around the sun. They're always separated by 180 degrees, so they form an axis of energy. If your North Node falls in Gemini, then your South Node falls in Sagittarius, the sign that is six away from Gemini. If you haven't done so already, turn to the appendix, locate the time span that includes your birth date, and find out the sign of your North Node. Then look at the table below to find your South Node.

The South Node represents our comfort zone, the accumulation of characteristics, attitudes, and talents that we bring into this life from other lives or—if you don't believe in reincarnation—that are laid down early in childhood. We retreat to our South Node when we're hurt, feel sick or threatened, or perhaps when we're in a new relationship and aren't sure yet where things are going. We also retreat here when we feel unsure of ourselves. The South Node is the psychological equivalent of comfort food.

The North Node symbolizes the direction we should move in this life to fulfill our talents and potential and to evolve spiritually. It represents the soul's agenda this time around, the qualities, traits, and experiences our higher selves felt that we need to evolve spiritually and to reach our potential.

LUNAR NODES

If your north node is in	*your south node is in*
Aries	Libra
Taurus	Scorpio
Gemini	Sagittarius
Cancer	Capricorn
Leo	Aquarius
Virgo	Pisces

The sign of your North Node describes the types of experiences you should strive for in this life. It can also describe the psychological bent, potential, and talents that you should try to develop, to reach for, in order to attain your soul's agenda and to achieve your creative and spiritual potential. The sign of the South Node describes all of the above, but from previous lives. It's "been there, done that, and still feel comfortable here."

The house placement of your South Node describes the area that is your comfort zone. The house placement of your North Node describes the area where your greatest potential and talent can be achieved and the way in which you can evolve spiritually.

Take a look at the natal chart at the end of chapter 9. The woman's South Node in Leo—☋12♌32—falls in her fourth house of the home, her domestic environment. Her North Node in Aquarius—☊12♒32—falls in her tenth house of career. These signs suggest that to evolve spiritually, to achieve her full potential, she should strive to create a career that helps others. Aquarius is the sign of the humanitarian, who often works with groups to achieve a common goal.

She feels most comfortable when she's in the spotlight, or when she's involved in some drama involving her family and personal environment. She's such a warm, caring person that she's a people magnet (South Node in Leo). The house placement of her South Node suggests that she feels most comfortable in her personal environment. But the path to her spiritual evolution and to her achievement lies in the public arena.

Nodes Through the Signs

Aries North Node

Your soul craves independence. But your comfort zone lies in the embrace of others. You're at ease in most relationships, within groups, and seek balance in everything you do. Sometimes your need for balance is so great that you bend over backward to accommodate others and end up compromising your own values. That's your comfort zone—Libra South Node—speaking.

It's your South Node, too, that constantly sends you off in search of the perfect partner, the elusive soul mate. But you probably won't find the ideal partner until you know who *you* are and what you believe separate from your parents, family, authority figures, and anyone else who seeks to define you. That's where your Aries North Node comes in, where you must reach for your independence and freedom.

This node is about *you*—your independence rather than your codependence, about following your impulses, passions, and hunches rather than pressing the pause button on all that and doing something to please someone else. You're here this time to develop independence in thought, action, words, deeds. You're here to define your values according to who *you* are rather than through group consensus. Don't hesitate to take risks. Live like the *Star Trek* motto, boldly going where no man (or woman!) has gone before. Spiritually, you must sprout your wings and fly.

Easier said than done because it begins with solitude, a state of being that is foreign to you. As you begin to carve time for yourself, your Libra South Node may throw a major tantrum and urge you to get out and about, to hurry to that party, that get-together, that crowd of friends and strangers so that you can work the room. Resist those temptations, regardless of the comfort they promise. Ignore the criticisms of others—a difficult challenge because Libra South Node can't abide disapproval. The moment it detects disapproval, it causes you to run around apologizing to everyone, making excuses, laughing, oh, you were just kidding, really, and how about if we all get together tomorrow night for another party?

While your Libra South Node seeks to smooth things over with family, friends, coworkers, and everyone else who disapproves, your Aries North Node coaxes you to continue following impulses and forging your own path. It urges you to be spontaneous, to take off at a moment's notice with just a backpack and your ATM card and head for parts unknown. It demands that you become an individual separate from the collective called family, relationships, the community. It pushes you beyond consensus reality to test the limits of your soul. Once you're able to do that, you can successfully draw on your Libra South Node for harmony and balance.

Examples: Ram Dass, Jay Leno, Neil Armstrong.

Taurus North Node

Your soul seeks stability. With this fixed earth-sign node, your mission this time around is to define your values and realize your potential through everything the physical universe has to offer. It's a magnificent banquet of sensual delights, glittering beauty, unimagined riches. Your playground is physical reality, and you're supposed to build something meaningful and lasting while you're here. You're supposed to do it patiently, with resilience to any obstacles in your way, and whatever you tackle isn't done until it's done!

But your Scorpio South Node resists. It demands that you merge with whatever you're doing, that you become the project, the relationship, the ideal, and that you control it. It urges you to work privately, in secrecy, never letting on what your real agenda is. Your South Node investigates, researches, digs for answers and truth, and does it with a kind of terrible impatience and intensity. Your North Node asks that you take some things on faith and trust, that you let your soul speak, and allow events to unfold naturally, organically.

The Scorpio South Node suggests that in past lives, you've dealt with crisis, calamity, excessive sexuality, suspicion, deceit, profound transformation. This time around, one of your callings is to find the calm center of the storm. While everything is collapsing around you, while people you care for are losing their minds and swept up in high drama, you are as still and centered as Buddha.

To achieve this requires enormous practice and patience. Start meditating. Have a physical exercise routine that grounds you completely in physical reality. Yoga, running, swimming, tai chi, biking, the gym: do anything that heightens your awareness of your physical body. And be selfish. Yes, that last part sounds strange because we're taught from a young age to practice the opposite. But for the Taurus North Node, selfishness is self-empowerment. It means you put your own needs and desires first. You're a survivor. Once you do that, you won't feel the need to manipulate and control others.

The sensuality part of the Taurus North Node can be

troublesome because all too often you're working from the raw sexuality of your Scorpio South Node. Try to balance your sensuality. Instead of leaping into sexual relationships, ease yourself into sensual relationships. Experiment, follow your passions in areas other than sex. Otherwise, the seductiveness of the Scorpio North Node takes you into the really dark places—excessive sex, drugs, eating, spending, booze. Kurt Cobain, heroin addict and suicide, is the dark example of this nodal axis. Jacques Cousteau, underwater explorer, and J. R. R. Tolkien, author and creator of the Hobbit world, are more evolved examples. They built legacies and worlds and touched the lives of millions.

Other examples: Greg Allman, Lucille Ball, Pearl Buck, Harry Houdini

Gemini North Node

Your soul seeks diversity and wants to tell everyone about the journey. It is as if you're searching for a unified theory of the universe. Why, why, why? Your insatiable curiosity urges you to gather information to answer these burning questions and then to disseminate what you learn in any way you can, through many venues simultaneously. That's why you're here this time around. As one of the two signs symbolized by two of something, you multitask with ease.

Your Sagittarius South Node practically guarantees that you have a worldview or belief system that serves as a solid foundation in your life. It enables you to take in other people's belief systems and to compare and contrast them with your own. But when you're deep inside this comfort zone, you may think *your* belief system is the only truth. You may become intolerant of other people's spiritual and political beliefs and become a self-righteous stick in the mud.

It's likely that someone in your immediate circle of family and friends holds a belief system radically opposed to yours—parent, friend, partner, sibling, other relative, neighbor, coworker. This opposition probably leads to heated discussions and arguments. You're intent on convincing the other person that you're right, but this only creates further dissension. Instead, look at this person as your teacher. What can you learn from him or her? Listen with an open mind—and *really* listen. Also listen to what your soul whispers in the silence of your own mind and body. All too often, you're so intent on what you're going to say next that you're deaf to what the other person is saying and dismiss the whispers of your soul as nonsense.

Once you're aware of this pattern within yourself, you can catch yourself before it happens. Here are some guidelines to help you along:

Maintain your curiosity. It's one of your most valuable resources. When someone says something that pushes your buttons, ask yourself why you feel the way you do. Resistance is usually a clue to something within yourself that you should explore and strive to understand.

Always believe in yourself. Yes, this can be challenging for a Gemini North Node person. The twins that symbolize Gemini indicate a duality in your personality. One twin urges you to reach for the seemingly impossible and the other twin is laughing into her hands, snickering, *Yeah, right.* The best way to reconcile this duality is to develop a firm certainty about your talents that gets you through both good times and bad.

Examples: Susan Sarandon, Deepak Chopra, Bill Clinton

Cancer North Node

Your soul searches endlessly for someone or something to nurture—a person, a cause, a mission. You're here to navigate the world of your emotions and intuition, to learn to nurture others as you have nurtured yourself in past lives. You need to discover what makes you feel emotionally secure and to establish that security in your life in order to achieve your potential.

Your Capricorn South Node brings clear goals and ambitions. But because work, goals, and ambition are your comfort zone, you may feel you have to control everything and everyone within your environment. You have a heightened sense of responsibility too, believing that you must assume all the responsibility—at work, at home, with your family. Your desire to achieve and be recognized for those achievements suggests that you work extremely hard. But since these traits come from your South Node, you may not make significant progress until you're living from a centered, emotionally secure place.

If you can stay in tune with your emotions, they will act as an infallible guide. When a negative emotion surfaces, don't just shove it aside, but don't obsess about it, either. Take note of it—then release it and let it flow out of you. In the same way, you should release your need for control too. Control of others is an illusion fostered by your South Node. The only person you can control is yourself—your own thoughts, actions, choices, your home and personal environments. You can't control what others think, and do, and believe.

The Cancer/Capricorn axis is about how we live our private and public lives. Home and family versus career and profession, right brain versus left brain, the inner world versus the outer world. The Cancer North Node urges you to open your heart, to listen to the whispers of your intuition, to lower your defenses. As a cardinal water sign, this node also urges you to explore the unknown.

Examples: Elisabeth Kübler Ross, Erma Bombeck, Daphne du Maurier

Leo North Node

Your soul craves recognition, so baby, let the good times roll! You're here this time around to explore all forms of creative expression. You're supposed to learn what you love, what you truly desire, to have fun and be happy and how to manifest all of it. Along the way, you're also supposed to learn how to give and receive unconditional love. Sounds like a Disney movie, right?

Thanks to your Aquarius South Node, you're tolerant of people who are different from you, understand group dynamics, believe that we're all created equal. Your comfort zone is the world of ideas, the mind, the intellect. In fact, you may be more comfortable with ideas than you are with people or more comfortable putting the group before the individual, friends before partner and family. But your Leo North Node urges you to reach beyond ideas, beyond the group, to plunder the depths of your creativity and express yourself as an individual.

To navigate your Leo North Node successfully, here are some essentials:

- Nurture your creativity on a daily basis—not just whenever the spirit moves you. Once you learn to do this out of sheer enjoyment, your heart opens wide, and you start to realize that it's okay to be recognized for your achievements. It's okay to stand out from the group, to step out into the limelight and announce who you are.
- Ignore peer pressure. Whether this is difficult or easy depends on your age, of course, and the type of work you do.
- Create your life consciously. This requires awareness of your internal patterns. If you dislike some of the patterns you find, then reshape them or break them altogether.
- Don't depend on others to make you happy. Whenever you find yourself doing this, break the habit by

making a conscious decision to create your own joy. Then go do exactly that.

The beauty of the Leo North Node is about *you*—as an individual separate from any collective, any tribe. Love yourself first so that you're whole enough to love others.

Virgo North Node

Details, perfection: that's what your soul hopes to find this time around. You're the Swiss watchmaker, immersed in the details of creating the best watch in the world. All those intricate levers, the beveled glass face, the tiny little hands. Somehow you bring all these parts together and do it with utter perfection. Now apply the watchmaker analogy to your life. Somehow you're supposed to bring all these disparate bits and pieces together, analyze your experiences, and then manifest your beliefs and ideals in a practical way. The heart of your journey is self-perfection.

Your Pisces South Node offers some of the tools you need—a deep compassion, magnificent imagination, excellent intuition and healing ability. But when your inner critic is screaming, and you retreat into your Pisces South Node out of fear, then it's easy to become trapped in a victim consciousness. You know the routine—you're not good enough, not quite up to the task, there are others more qualified . . . and so on. First, silence the inner critic and resolve not to quit. Once you do that, the rest becomes easier.

When you feel that coiled serpent of fear in the pit of your stomach, tackle it. When you feel unable to make a decision, take a few deep breaths and try to explore your resistance. Don't obsess about the fear or tear it apart, scrutinizing every bit of it. Just acknowledge it and try to move through it.

Share your knowledge and skills with others, without

thought of compensation, but do so only because you want to, not because you feel obligated. By performing a service out of compassion rather than obligation, you mitigate the risk of victim consciousness.

Remain in the moment. Or, as Ram Dass said, *Be here now.* By being fully rooted in the moment, fear can't choke you. Read Eckhart Tolle's *The Power of Now.* By doing this, you also mitigate self-criticism. Any time you find yourself falling into this frame of mind, tell yourself that you're perfect as you are. *Love and approve of yourself.*

Your Virgo North Node urges you to navigate your daily life with reason, logic, and attention to detail. Once you're able to do this, you can draw on the South Node's power of imagination and intuition and can manifest virtually anything you desire.

Examples: Harrison Ford, Michael J. Fox, Kurt Vonnegut Jr.

Libra North Node

Your soul seeks balance: that's what this lifetime is about. Specifically, you're here to learn how to balance your needs with those of your partner, kids, friends, parents, and just about everyone else. You do it by walking in the other person's shoes.

Your comfort zone, of course, is the exact opposite of everything in the first paragraph. When you're afraid or uncertain, hurt or not feeling well, you retreat into an independent, *I can do it myself* frame of mind. You become selfish, intolerant of people who are different from you, and aren't open to any kind of compromise.

This *me first* attitude can be tough to overcome. But a good first step is to put others first. Yes, balk all you want, but it's the perfect place to start. Try it in small increments at first. Perhaps your partner needs the car at the same time that you're scheduled to have lunch with someone. Instead of insisting that you should get the car, make other arrangements. Or once a week or once a month, put someone else before yourself—let someone else go before you in the grocery store line, at the theater, the gas station. When you start doing this on a regular basis, then you're moving along the path of your North Node.

The Aries South Node prompts you to act decisively, impulsively, rashly because you assume you know what's going on, that you've got the right information and the right answers, and it inadvertently hurts someone. Better to pace yourself, ask questions, interact with people around you, and gather the information you need. Use tact and diplomacy rather than the blunt force of words and actions.

Once you're able to embrace the art of relating to others, then you can successfully draw on the independence and fearlessness of your Aries South Node.

Examples: Madonna, Frédéric Chopin, Anaïs Nin

Scorpio North Node

Your soul cries out for personal power. You're here to learn about using that personal power and magnetism in a positive, constructive way. Through intense experiences, you learn to purge your life of the nonessential or of whatever is stagnant in any area—relationships, jobs, careers, belief systems, habits. Then you can draw on your Taurus South Node to build what is durable, lasting.

You've got plenty of help on this journey. Your South Node gives you ample physical energy, practicality, and a stubborn determination that can see you through anything. Your Taurus South Node urges you to collect things—old books, stamps, art, jewelry—and it whispers, *I want to be surrounded by comfort and beauty.* But when you become obsessively attached to these possessions, to comfort and beauty for their own sake, you may attract a situation that teaches you possessions are just stuff we own.

Your work ethic is stellar, nose to the ground, immersed in whatever you're doing, for as long as it takes. But you make some things harder than they need to be. That's when you know you're being resistant to change. Yet change is part of what you're here to learn.

When change knocks at your door, invite it in for coffee and a chat. If you can't learn to do that, then circumstances will force change and it will be something profoundly transformative and probably not pleasant. Again, take small steps. Once a week, do something you've never done before. If you're terrified of heights, then the step could be something as dramatic as skydiving or as small as walking to the end of a high diving board.

Empower others by supporting their creative endeavors, spiritual values, raises and promotions, or anything else that is important to them. Use your exceptional intuition to gain insight into others—who are they in the privacy of their own hearts? What are their dreams, motives, and hopes? Use your intuition as often as you can. It's like a muscle. The more you use it, the stronger it becomes.

When you feel fear that threatens to send you scampering back to your comfort zone—to the nearest mall to shop for anything, to the comfort of rich foods, booze, drugs, the entire physical spectrum of sensual delights—stop. Breathe. Then investigate. What are you afraid of? Has it happened yet? Or are you afraid of something that *may* happen? Once you become aware of the pattern, you can break it, and when you break it, you're truly advancing along the path of your Scorpio North Node.

Examples: Tiger Woods, Edgar Allan Poe, Francis Ford Coppola

Sagittarius North Node

Your soul is seeking truth—specifically, your personal truth. It may sound like a major undertaking, but you can achieve it by using your intuitive ability to grasp the big picture rather than collecting endless, disconnected facts. The emphasis for you in this lifetime is on right brain, intuition, and imagination rather than logic and reason.

Your comfort zone—the Gemini South Node—is about information, facts, and figures. You can talk to anyone about anything, have terrific communication skills, and are one of the most social creatures in the zodiac. But when you feel threatened and afraid, you retreat into the darker aspects of your South Node—you talk when you should be listening, second-guess what people are thinking and feeling, make up facts, change rules in the middle of the game.

To use your North Node energy successfully, learn to trust yourself. To trust that inner voice of your intuition rather than the voices of everyone you consult before you make a decision. Strive to be more spontaneous. By allowing yourself freedom to take off at a moment's notice for an exotic port, to call in sick to work so you can attend your kid's play at school, to run off and get married in Vegas—well, it's part and parcel of the Sadge North Node. Honor it! Spontaneity is the manifestation of your intuition.

Strive to be more patient. Yeah, your Gemini South Node won't want to hear about it, but patience leads you to realize there are no quick fixes, and what's the big rush about, anyway?

Your North Node urges you to explore the unknown, to delve into spiritual, political, and metaphysical issues that people around you may not want to discuss. Just resist the temptation for self-righteousness and go about your business. This journey doesn't belong to anyone else. It's *yours*.

Examples: Drew Barrymore, Colin Powell, Zelda Fitzgerald, Angelina Jolie

Capricorn North Node

This time around, your soul seeks to control its own destiny. That's it in a nutshell, that's why you're here this time around. Already, your Cancer South Node is sobbing in a corner for that orphan on the news tonight, for the starving animals roaming the ruins of the latest disaster, for the most recent genocide somewhere. She doesn't want to hear about your ambitions, about you taking charge, about you controlling your destiny. So she pouts, she plunges you into a depression, and here *you* now sit, worrying yourself into a frenzy about stuff that hasn't even happened yet.

Let's back up. Your Cancer South Node offers plenty of tools for your journey—intuition and compassion, a sense of personal history, deep emotions that are your gauge to what's really going on in your life. Your South Node knows how to comfort anyone and anything in need that's hurting, that needs a shelter for the night—or for a year. This includes strays—cats, dogs, birds, whatever finds its way to your doorstep. The problem arises when you nurture and heal at the expense of your own needs or when you nurture others without first nurturing yourself. That's when your South Node becomes an impediment to achieving your potential. That's when you become like Rapunzel, trapped in her tower.

Your Capricorn North Node urges you to reach for everything you want and to achieve your potential through careful planning, strategizing, and hard work. But your Cancer South Node keeps hurling up images of your past mistakes, the issues you dealt with in childhood, how your mom or dad or family might object to what you're doing. You stop in your tracks, suddenly paralyzed and filled with doubt.

So your first order of business is to release the past.

The present is your point of power. The present is the place from which you write the script of your life. Honor the past, certainly, but recognize that your childhood, your parents, the bully in the sixth grade have no say over your life now.

Your second order of business—and imagine this as a Power Point presentation—is to stay tuned in to your feelings. But don't use your emotions to manipulate or control others. When you feel negative, don't dwell on it. Let the negativity wash through you, put one foot in front of the other, and move forward again.

Third point? Always express what you feel, when you feel it. Don't keep it all bottled up inside, as your South Node would like. Let it all out. Not only will you feel better, you'll be advancing on the path of your North Node.

By the way, you are in illustrious company! Examples: Indira Gandhi, Robert Redford, Oprah Winfrey

Aquarius North Node

Your soul searches for the collective experience, so this time around, you're here to learn about the importance of groups. Whether it's your family group, your community, a social circle, a political or spiritual movement, or some massive humanitarian effort that impacts the family of man, you're supposed to learn you can't always be the center of attention.

Your Leo South Node won't be happy about this development. It basks in applause and recognition. Yet your South Node also confers a terrific personality, great warmth and magnetism, and such radiant joy for life that if you can direct those qualities toward something larger than yourself, you will succeed at everything you do.

Your ego is well developed, thanks in large part to your Leo South Node. But ego alone won't do the job this time around. You're called upon to reach beyond the self, to extend yourself into the larger world, into the family of man, where you can make a tremendous difference, an integral component in a paradigm shift. You may do this through any number of creative venues, through your career, through volunteering, through your family life or the way you earn your living. But there are some definite steps you can take toward embracing your North Node, and foremost among them is to minimize drama.

Your South Node, see, is all about drama—in temperament, relationships, activities. In every single phase and area of your life there may be drama that your South Node stirs up, stokes. So strip away the drama, and what do you have? Someone with great talents and potential who can achieve that potential through shifting focus from self to the group, the tribe, the community, whatever it is.

Use your Leo South Node to cultivate and nurture your creative passions. If you can pour your emotions into a creative outlet, especially one that brings insights and pleasures to a larger group, you're well on your journey into your North Node.

Examples: Leonard Cohen, F. Scott Fitzgerald

Pisces North Node

Your soul wants to sink into the depths of imagination and intuition to discover the larger spiritual and creative picture that governs your life. This lifetime is about unearthing everything that is hidden in your life—power you have disowned, secrets that are kept in family vaults, in genealogy books, in the deepest reservoirs of your DNA. Your life is about bringing all this stuff into the light of day.

Your Virgo South Node brings a lot to the table for this journey—a discriminating intellect, a penchant for details, a remarkable ability to connect the dots in any situation, event, crisis, relationship. You name it, the Virgo South Node grasps how all the connections are made. Your South Node is terrific in any situation where rapid solutions are needed, where connections must be made at the speed of light, and where everything—all the information and details—are *correct*.

But, *correct* aside, this is the life where you go with the flow, avoid self-criticism, trust the universe to deliver what you need and desire, and develop your spiritual beliefs. All of this can be done through your daily work, but in terms of the big picture, the larger canvas of possibilities, the forest as opposed to the trees. Maybe you blog about your experiences. Maybe you set up a Web site that sells a particular product or service that helps others to reach their highest potential. The bottom line about the Pisces North Node is, ultimately, unknown and unknowable, too mystical to penetrate unless it's your conscious path, and too complex to decipher unless your intuitive skills are remarkably developed.

But remember this. When your Virgo South Node slaps its ruler across your desk in ninth grade and demands that you memorize how to conjugate the verb "to be" in Latin, Spanish, French, and German, it's your Pisces North Node that hurls your arm upward, knocking that ruler away, and says, "Chill. I'm on my own path to enlightenment."

Examples: Matt Damon, Naomi Campbell, Isadora Duncan

CHAPTER 12

By the Numbers

Even though this is an astrology book, we use numbers in some of the daily predictions because we're attempting to remain true to what Sydney Omarr did. The legendary astrologer was also a numerologist and combined the two forms in his work. So let's take a closer look at how the numbers work.

If you're familiar with numerology, you probably know your life path number, which is derived from your birth date. That number represents who you were at birth and the traits that you'll carry throughout your life. There are numerous books and Web sites that provide details on what the numbers mean regarding your life path.

But in the daily predictions, what does it mean when it's a number 9 day, and how did it get to be that number? In the dailies, you'll usually find these numbers on the days when the moon is transiting from one sign to another. The system is simple: add the numbers related to the astrological sign (1 for Aries, 2 for Taurus, etc.), the year, the month, and the day.

For example, to find what number June 14, 2011, is for a Libra, you would start with 7, the number for Libra, add 4 (the number you get when you add 2011 together), plus 6 for June, plus 5 (1+4) for the day. That would be 7+4+6+5 (sign + year + month+ day) = 22= 4.

So June 14, 2011, is a number 4 day for a Libra. It would be a 5-day for a Scorpio, the sign following Libra. So on that number 4 day, Libra might be advised that her organizational skills are highlighted, that she should stay focused, get organized, be methodical and thorough. She's building a creative future. Tear down the old in order to rebuild. Keep your goals in mind, follow your ideas.

Briefly, here are the meanings of the numbers, which are included in more detail in the dailies themselves.

1. Taking the lead, getting a fresh start, a new beginning
2. Cooperation, partnership, a new relationship, sensitivity
3. Harmony, beauty, pleasures of life, warm, receptive
4. Getting organized, hard work, being methodical, rebuilding, fulfilling your obligations
5. Freedom of thought and action, change, variety, thinking outside the box
6. A service day, being diplomatic, generous, tolerant, sympathetic
7. Mystery, secrets, investigations, research, detecting deception, exploration of the unknown, of the spiritual realms
8. Your power day, financial success, unexpected money, a windfall
9. Finishing a project, looking beyond the immediate, setting your goals, reflection, expansion.

Simple, right?

CHAPTER 13

Love and Timing in 2012 for Virgo

You are one of the most discriminating signs in the zodiac, with precise ideas about love and romance—and just about everything else, too! But as a mutable sign, like Gemini and Sagittarius, you're adaptable and can change as needed. As an earth sign ruled by Mercury, any relationship begins in the mind first, with a mental and intellectual chemistry.

How do the stars stack up in the romance department in 2012? Let's take a closer look.

Whether you're flying solo or in a committed relationship, timing is often the crux on which success and happiness rest. The faster-moving planets—Mercury, Venus, and Mars—tend to have less of an impact on our lives because of the speed at which they move. Venus, for instance, stays in a sign for about three weeks, unless it's moving retrograde, then the transit can last several months. The transit of Venus through Virgo, for example, lasts from October 3 to 28. But Venus in Gemini, where it turns retrograde this year, extends from April 3 to June 27.

Mercury, unless retrograde, zips through a sign in just under three weeks. Mars, unless retrograde, takes about forty-five days to move through a sign. Compare this to the snail of the zodiac—Pluto, which entered Capricorn in 2009 and won't leave until 2024.

Venus rules love and romance, Mars governs sexuality, Mercury rules communication. Beneficial angles among these three planets or from these planets to your sun sign usually indicate a winning combination for relationships. We'll include new and full moons in the love and romance equation, too, since the moon rules our emotions and intuitive selves. New moons generally usher in new opportunities, and full moons bring insights, news, and a touch of moon madness!

For the Single Virgo

You can talk circles around most other signs, although a Gemini will give you a run for your money. For any relationship to even get off the ground, you must be attracted to the other person's mind. There must be strong communication. The best times for connecting with a potential partner at that level are when Mercury is in your own sign, in a fellow earth sign, or in a compatible water sign.

The first period to watch for is between January 8 and 27, when Mercury is in fellow earth sign Capricorn in your solar fifth house. During this transit, be sure to get out and about, so that you're meeting new people. Accept all social invitations. Do whatever you enjoy the most. The more enjoyment you experience, the likelier it is that you'll attract exactly the right person at the right time. Romance is on your mind!

Between May 9 and 24, Mercury is in fellow earth sign Taurus in your solar ninth house. This transit is great for discussing your worldview and spiritual beliefs. You might meet your potential romantic interest at a workshop or seminar, at some sort of spiritual gathering, on a college campus, at a publishing function, or even while traveling.

Mercury will be in your sign between August 31 and September 16, an ideal time for a mind link with someone who interests you. Your head and heart are in complete agreement.

When Mercury is in a compatible water sign, your conscious mind is more intuitive. Information about the other person flows into you—through a touch, a look. Those dates? February 13 to March 2, Mercury in Pisces. Even though Mercury is opposed to your sun during this period, your imagination and intuition are working overtime! Between June 7 and 25, Mercury in Cancer. October 5 to 29, Mercury in Scorpio.

The most romantic time occurs when Venus is in your sign or fellow earth signs. The best of the lot is when Venus is in Capricorn in your solar fifth house, that section of your chart that symbolizes love and romance, creativity, enjoyment, and children. Unfortunately, Venus doesn't transit Capricorn in 2012, so the next best time frame is between October 3 and 28, when Venus transits your sign. During this transit, others find you attractive, appealing, and seductive. Your self-confidence soars. Again, be sure to make yourself available during this time period. You never know where you may meet the love of your life!

Even if Venus doesn't transit Capricorn and your romantic sector this year, Mars does, between November 16 and December 25. This transit heats up your sex life and brings a lot of activity generally to romance and whatever you do for fun and pleasure.

From January 1 to June 11, Jupiter transits Taurus and your solar ninth house, where it has been since June 2011. By now, you have some idea of just how lucky and expansive this transit is, and that trend should continue. While Jupiter forms a beneficial angle to your sun, everything in your life runs a bit more smoothly. Others are attracted to your expansive, buoyant nature.

From June 11 to June 25, 2013, Jupiter transits Gemini and the career area of your chart. In terms of romance, this could lead to romance with a coworker or boss. Circle the period from June 27 to August 7, when Venus will be traveling with Jupiter. That time frame should be very pleasant.

Although we're going to talk more about Uranus in

Aries in the next chapter, let's look at this transit in terms of love and romance. Until March 2019, Uranus in Aries transits your solar eighth house. This transit may require you to adjust your attitude about your partner's income and about any resources you share with others. In terms of romance and love, it's possible that romance could find you at a workshop or seminar dealing with metaphysical topics or through any involvement you may have with banks, insurance companies, or inheritances. These two areas are leagues apart, but both are covered by the eighth house.

This year, Uranus and Venus connect between February 8 and March 5, so anyone you meet during this period is going to appeal to you on a wildly visceral level. You may not have a clue why you're attracted to this person, but attracted you will be.

A Venus retrograde isn't as eventful as Mercury retrogrades are. This year's, in Gemini, occurs between May 15 and June 27. It can heighten tensions with a partner—mostly through misunderstanding.

Mercury (communication) turns retrograde three times a year, so be sure to note those dates and ramifications in the Big Picture section for Virgo. A relationship that begins under any of those retrograde periods will be messed up in the communication department. Those dates:

March 12–April 4, in Aries
July 14–August 8, in Leo
November 6–26, in Sagittarius

For the Committed Virgo

The dates listed above for the single Virgo also apply to the committed Virgo, but for different reasons. Venus doesn't transit Capricorn and your solar fifth house this year, so let's look at some other propitious dates when your relationship with a partner is running smoothly and romantically. March 5 to April 3, when Venus is in fellow earth sign Taurus, is a perfect time to plan a trip with your partner. Pick some far-flung location where neither of you has been and make an adventure of it. Or plan a creative project together. Or refurbish your home, if that's something you both enjoy doing.

When Venus transits Pisces and your solar seventh house—January 14 to February 8—you and your partner may decide to deepen your commitment to each other in some way. Maybe you move in together, get engaged or married, or start a family. Perhaps you buy a home together.

If you're looking for a home, one of the best times falls between December 15 and January 9, 2013, when Venus transits Sagittarius and your solar fourth house. This transit helps you to grasp the larger context of "home"—neighborhood, neighbors, schools, the whole nine yards.

When Mercury transits compatible water sign Scorpio and your solar third house, your communication skills are heightened. You're able to express the deep stuff that matters. This, in turn, encourages your partner to do the same.

So let's look for some dates this year that favor marriage and which dates you might want to avoid:

- Avoid the Mercury retrograde dates mentioned above
- When Venus is in your sign between October 3 and 28
- On or after the new moon in your sign on September 15
- On or after the full moon in your sign on March 8
- On or after a new or full moon in your partner's sign
- Avoid eclipse dates
- Any time between August 31 and September 16, when Mercury is moving direct in your sign

For All Virgos

Virgos can be adept at visualizing to attain what they want. But first you need to know what you're looking for in a romantic partner. List every quality you can think of, regardless of how absurd it seems. Then during your daily meditations or as you're falling asleep at night, visualize this person in great detail. Then let the universe do its work!

CHAPTER 14

Career Timing in 2012 for Virgo

Virgos are consummate communicators, and this year you'll have plenty of opportunities to exhibit your talents professionally. We've talked about Jupiter's transit through fellow earth sign Taurus in terms of romance, but what sort of impact does it have this year on your career?

As mentioned before, Jupiter transits Taurus and your solar ninth house from January 1 to June 11. During this transit, you are actively working with your beliefs, which have been expanding since the transit began in June 2011. As your beliefs expand to accommodate new ideas and experiences, your options in every area of your life—including your career—multiply. In a sense, you're seeding your life during this transit for a professional payoff once Jupiter enters Gemini and your career area. Circle these dates: June 11, 2012, to June 25, 2013. Here are some possibilities for the Gemini transit:

- You land a significant promotion and raise
- You start your own business
- You change jobs/career for something more in alignment with your values
- You start traveling abroad frequently for business
- Your products and services expand to overseas markets
- You write a novel

- You start a blog promoting your services and products
- You build a Web site
- You do more public speaking

While Jupiter is transiting Gemini, it forms a beneficial angle to Uranus in Aries, which brings an element of surprise and unpredictability to your professional picture this year. You attract unusual individuals who are helpful to you professionally.

In 2012, when paradigms are shifting, take stock early on. Are you happy in your job? Is your career satisfying? What kind of work would you do if you had the opportunity? Would you like to go to graduate school to study something else? Is there a talent or interest you would like to develop more fully? Does your job just pay your bills, or is it a focal point in your life?

Once you answer these questions, you can start putting the energies of 2012 to work for you. So let's take a closer look at how you can create a professional life that you love. If you already have that, then let's see how you can improve what is nearly perfect.

Why 2012?

Most metaphysical teachers talk about the importance of being fully present, fully grounded in the moment. In *The Power of Now*, *The Law of Attraction,* and *Seth Speaks,* the message is the same: our point of power is the present. We may cling to the past and yearn for the future, but neither will bring us the power we have in this moment, in this breath, in this present action.

So before this year is already behind you, make a list of your professional goals and dreams. If you haven't attained all of them, what's holding you back? Chances are that the only thing holding you back is ... well, *you.* Perhaps you think you might fail at something new.

Maybe you think you lack the proper education or skills. In other words, your insecurity could be your obstacle to attaining your goals.

As a mutable earth sign, you generally aren't rigid in your beliefs. You're willing to change as needed. That will be an asset this year.

Dates to Watch For

In addition to the Jupiter transits, let's take a look at the new and full moons this year and how you can use their energies to your benefit.

New moons generally mean new opportunities. Full moons are usually equated with news, insights, and a tad of craziness tossed in just to keep things interesting!

The September 15 new moon in your sign is the most important one for you all year. It's worth preparing for—through visualizing, making lists of your wishes and desires, laying out a left-brain strategy for attaining what you want. Mercury forms a beneficial conjunction to this new moon, suggesting a lot of communication and activity generally. Your daily life could be very busy around the time of this new moon, and you are likely to feel pressed for time! In terms of your career, expect new opportunities to surface that will please you. But be vigilant, Virgo. Some of these opportunities could unfold quickly.

The new moon in fellow earth sign Taurus that occurs on April 21 should be beautiful for you. It coincides nicely, too, with Jupiter's transit through Taurus, so any new opportunities that occur on or around this date will be major. The career possibilities with this one depend, of course, on your situation, beliefs, and how actively you're working with those beliefs. But if you're in the right space mentally, spiritually, and emotionally, then you reap the benefits.

The new moon in compatible water sign Cancer on

July 19 is a good time to get out and about, to accept social invitations, hang out with friends. It's possible that new people enter your life around this time who are helpful professionally.

What the Planetary Transits Reveal

We've talked about some of the transits and the moons in 2012 that are favorable for career matters. Now let's take a look at some other things that are going on that will impact your professional life.

Mercury rules your sign, so its transits are important for you. When Mercury transits Gemini and your career sector, you've got a great opportunity to really speak your mind. It's a favorable time to pitch ideas, garner support among coworkers and bosses, and to generally finish up projects that require sharp communication skills. It's also a favorable time to create a Web site or blog for your company or services. The dates? May 24 to June 7.

Another favorable period, particularly for brainstorming with coworkers about cutting-edge ideas and technologies, falls between January 27 and February 13. Mercury transits Aquarius then and forms a beneficial angle to your career area.

From March 2 to 12 and April 16 to May 9, Mercury transits Aries and your solar eighth house. This could be the period where your client base expands to overseas markets, where you travel abroad for business, or when you have increased contact with people overseas.

During any of the Mercury retrograde periods mentioned in the previous chapter, avoid pushing forward on new projects. Review and revise is the best way to navigate these periods.

Saturn's Movements

Until October 5, Saturn is in Libra, your solar second house of finances. This transit, which has been going on since October 2009, prompts you to pay closer attention to your money. You may find the right structure for handling your money or may encounter restrictions and delays with money. Or both. But with Saturn forming a beneficial angle to your career area, chances are good that a raise could be in the offing, and this will urge you to pay closer attention to what you earn, how you spend it and save it, and what your deeper beliefs are about money.

Once Saturn enters Scorpio on October 5—for a run of two and a half years—your comfort level will be higher. Your mind will excel at research and investigation, which will become components of whatever you do on a daily basis. You'll be after the bottom line, Virgo, and won't act until you have it.

Parting Thoughts About Career Matters

Whenever you feel discouraged about your career or anything else this year, get out and do something you enjoy. Virgos enjoy anything connected to intellectual and mental pursuits—books, good conversation, ideas, movies, communication, travel. Do what you love. Do what makes your heart sing.

The more you do what you enjoy, the better you feel. The better you feel, the more likely it is that you'll attract experiences, people, and situations that increase that feeling. The law of attraction.

CHAPTER 15

Navigating Uranus in Aries in 2012

Even though we talked about Uranus in Aries in the last chapter as it relates to your career, let's take a look here at its impact on your life generally.

Uranus's transit through Aries until early March 2019 will be forming a challenging angle to your sun that will call for attitude adjustments. This transit stimulates that area of your chart related to your partner's income, to mortgages, loans, income tax. This area of your chart also governs large questions—life after death, communication between the dead and the living, and just about anything else that goes bump in the night.

With Uranus in this section, you may have sudden psychic experiences that prompt you to question the fundamentals of your belief system. Your partner's income may soar or plunge, and he or she will find innovative ways of making money. It may be more difficult to obtain a mortgage or other loan, or you may have sudden opportunities to get these loans and will have to act quickly.

With any Uranus transit, there's always a thrust for independence and freedom, so it's possible that you'll want to be free of a mortgage and will be able to purchase a home with cash or lay off your existing mortgage. You won't want to be burdened by any debt, especially credit-card debt, and will work hard to pay it off.

One repercussion of Uranus's transit is that psychic

ability increases. You may have prophetic dreams or experiences with telepathy and clairvoyance, or you may take seminars and workshops on honing your abilities. You may take up the study of astrology or start using divination systems like the I Ching and runes.

In any area where your life is stuck in a rut or routine, Uranus is going to shake things up and sweep things clean, and when the dust settles, you'll be amazed that you have arrived in a better place.

During these seven years, Uranus will be forming a beneficial angle to that area of your chart that governs your daily work routine and the maintenance of your health. This means there will be plenty of excitement and unpredictability in your daily work that will stimulate your creativity. During tumultuous times, meaningful coincidences—synchronicities—are frequent. Pay attention to these nudges from the universe, decipher their messages, and know that every time you experience one of these, you're on the right track or are being warned that a particular path isn't in your best interest.

What's particularly notable about the Uranus transit is that from June 11, 2012, to June 25, 2013, it fits in nicely with Jupiter's transit through Gemini and your solar tenth house—your career area. The two planets form harmonious angles to each other; the unpredictability that accompanies Uranus allows Jupiter to expand your professional opportunities. Until October 5, Saturn in Libra is moving in opposition to Uranus. If we look at Saturn as representing the established way of doing things and Uranus as the new way, there can be some significant tug-of-wars. Just let the new win!

Here are some possibilities that may unfold with this Uranus transit. The abrupt changes can be troubling, but the end result seven years from now will be beneficial to you.

Possibilities

1. You change jobs
2. Your career heads in a new direction
3. Your partner's income increases or plunges
4. Relationships end
5. New relationships begin
6. New, exciting experiences are the norm
7. You take more risks
8. The risks pay off
9. You start your own business
10. You sell a novel or screenplay
11. You're recognized in some way by your peers
12. The people around you are confused by your behavior
13. Loss of a loved one
14. You inherit money
15. You win or lose an insurance settlement
16. You find innovative ways to perform your job
17. Your marital status changes
18. You pay off your home
19. Your need for personal freedom and self-expression increases
20. You start meditating, take up yoga
21. You encounter people from past lives

These possibilities are just that—merely possibilities. To really grasp how the transit will affect you, get out your natal chart. Look at the house where Aries is found in your chart. Look for any planets you have in Aries. These areas—plus your sun—are the ones that will be impacted more strongly by Uranus's transit through Aries.

Turn to the natal chart at the end of chapter 9. This woman is a Capricorn with a tenth-house sun, has a Leo moon in the fifth house, and has Aries rising at 19 degrees and 54 minutes—19♈54. The rising is the cusp of her first house, which governs the self. So Uranus has been in her twelfth house since it was at 17 degrees and 16 minutes of Pisces—17 ♓ 16—the cusp of her twelfth house.

During this period, with Uranus stirring up all the hidden stuff in her unconscious, she got married and divorced, landed a great job in an assisted living facility as the wellness director (she's an RN), was nearly forced to resign by an abusive boss, fought it, held onto her job, and got a raise. All three of her sons left home during this transit—to jobs and college. She moved twice.

As of this writing, in 2010, she is now accustomed to this Uranian energy and is planning to branch out as a consultant in her field, helping other men and women to navigate the labyrinth of health care and options for their aging parents and grandparents. In other words, she sees a gap in the health-care market and is figuring out ways she might fill that gap. That's the innovation part of the equation.

Once Uranus enters Aries in March 2011, it will be on its approach to her rising—an important, major life transit. The rising, as the portal to our charts, is where our experiences enter into our lives. The closer Uranus gets to her ascendant, the more unpredictable, exciting, and high energy her life will become. The conjunction is exact in March 2016, but she may start feeling it as early as the summer of 2012, when Uranus reaches 8 degrees Aries (eleven degrees from her rising) before it turns retrograde. It turns direct again in early December 2012 and gets to within 7 degrees of her ascendant by July 2013, before it retrogrades again. By July 2014, Uranus gets to within 3 degrees of her rising before it retrogrades once more. In late May 2015, it hits her rising.

What all this means is that each year as Uranus inches closer to that exact hit on her rising sign, she feels a progressively stronger urge to break free of any restrictions that are holding her back. The closer it gets to her rising, the closer it also gets to forming beautiful angles—trines—to her South Node in Leo (fourth house)—☊ 12 ♌ 32, and her natal moon and Pluto in

Leo in the fifth house—☽21♌48 and ♇22♌54. So while she's feeling this tremendous urge for freedom, Uranus is making it easier for her to bring about major changes in her emotional, inner life (moon). A new relationship could enter the picture, and it will be one wild, wonderful ride, different from anything she has experienced before. She might move.

With Pluto thrown into the mix, she has a marvelous opportunity to understand her innermost being—the unconscious beliefs and attitudes that have resulted in negative situations or relationships in the past. The trine to Pluto from Uranus gives her enormous personal power. One of her sons (fifth house) may get married. She might do or create something so innovative that she is recognized for it by peers. The trine to her South Node and sextile to her North Node in Aquarius in the eleventh house—♌12♒32—suggests that people she has known in the past (this life or others) may surface. She will have an opportunity to attain her dreams.

These possibilities are due to the transit of just one planet, Aries. So when you look at your natal chart to see where Uranus's impact will be felt most strongly, look beyond your sun sign. Look at other planets and points too.

Notice, for instance, that in this same chart, the woman has Jupiter in Taurus in her first house—♃10♉59. This means that during the first six months of 2012—as well as the last six months of 2011—this woman enjoys a Jupiter return. This is when Jupiter returns to the place it was when you were born, which happens every twelve years. It marks the beginning of a new cycle. So even while Uranus is upsetting the apple cart, she's benefiting tremendously from her Jupiter return during the first six months of 2012. New opportunities will surface in her personal life; she may have opportunities to travel internationally, she might get married.

In addition, see her Capricorn sun up there in the tenth house—☉13♑ 03? Pluto in Capricorn is now transiting her tenth house—her career area—creating profound change in her professional path. In March 2014, Pluto will conjunct her sun, so as it approaches, the changes will become more intense. She'll feel a greater urge to alter her path and will gain insight into her own motives and psyche.

So when you look at your own chart, study how the other transiting planets are affecting your natal blueprint. You probably will find there's a balance. If one area of your life is chaotic, there will be other areas where life is truly exciting and prosperous.

Dates to Watch For

March 22: On or around this new moon in Aries, life is going to get chaotic. A mortgage may come through or be denied, or you'll have to scramble to get in certain papers. Uranus will be close to this moon, suggesting sudden, unexpected events that catch you by surprise.

May 20: Solar eclipse in Gemini, in your solar tenth house of career. This one attracts new professional opportunities that should be very positive. Take time to consider these opportunities and choose the path that feels right to you.

June 4: Lunar eclipse in fire sign Sagittarius, in your solar fourth house. News about a domestic situation, one of your parents, or some deeper issues triggers your emotions. The news looks positive.

One powerful period this year occurs between **November 16 and December 25,** when Mars joins Pluto in fellow earth sign Capricorn in your solar fifth house. The power generated by these two planets traveling together can be considerable, and you can now harness and use it on your creative ventures. One of your children may encounter a wonderful opportunity for growth. In terms of romance and enjoyment, you'll be focused, energetic.

Pluto will be in Capricorn and your fifth house until 2024 and will be forming a beneficial angle to your sun.

You should be able to make tremendous strides creatively during this transit.

Between **February 8 and March 5,** Venus and Uranus are traveling together in Aries, a surefire combination that revs up your love life. This individual may be psychic or as intuitively inclined as you are. This period also favors obtaining mortgages, loans, and breaks on insurance and taxes.

From **October 3 to 28,** Venus transits your sign, a wonderful period for meeting someone new and for creative work. Others find you appealing during this transit, and people generally are open to your ideas.

Venus is retrograde in Gemini between **May 15 and June 27,** a period when there may be some bumps in the road in your career. These aren't major hurdles, more petty annoyances. If you're involved in a romance with someone at work, things could be confusing during this retrograde.

CHAPTER 16

Virgo and Mars in 2012

In the old science fiction books and movies of the 1950s, the invading aliens were usually Martians. They had powers that we humans lacked and were obviously more technologically advanced, but could be brought down by simple science: Earth germs against which they had no immunity.

These days, of course, the bad aliens might be from anywhere. In ABC's remake of *V*, the aliens look like us, talk like us, are all enormously attractive and cultured, but they have an insidious agenda. We don't really know what the true physical appearance is of these "visitors." Mars is never mentioned.

Our cultural fascination with invading aliens and Mars probably began with the publication of H. G. Wells's *War of the Worlds* in 1898. The novel's story idea is simple: Mars is dying and the Martians flee their world and invade Earth, planning to take over the planet and all its resources. Their first attack on London with advanced weaponry seems to ensure their victory. But they're defeated by—you guessed it!—germs.

Edgar Rice Burroughs had a thing or two to say about Mars too. In 1911, he wrote *A Princess of Mars,* the first of eleven novels about the red planet. The protagonist was John Carter, a confederate Civil War veteran who ends up being transported to Mars. Over the course of the eleven books, he settles into life on his adopted planet—gets married, involved in Martian politics, fights the good fight.

In 1951, Ray Bradbury's *Martian Chronicles* twisted the idea of a Martian in a new way. Human settlers arrive on Mars, and the Martians are killed by the bacteria that the humans bring with them. But these Martians capture our hearts because they are beautiful people of an ancient civilization.

Robert Heinlein, with his 1961 publication of *Stranger in a Strange Land*, brought another curve into the Martian theme. His story centers on a human born on Mars, the only survivor of the first manned space mission to the planet. The protagonist, Valentine Michael Smith, is raised and educated by Martians, then is returned to Earth when he's a young man with the sensibilities of a human, the perspective of an alien, and incredible psychic powers.

In addition to *V*, television has mined the alien and Mars theme too. There was *My Favorite Martian, Alien Nation, Battlestar Galactica,* and of course, *X-Files*.

In film, there were a host of many forgettable movies, but an exception was *Total Recall,* based on a Philip K. Dick short story. Arnold Schwarzenegger plays a man haunted by suppressed memories—specifically, journeys to Mars. The story has all the complex hallmarks of Philip K. Dick—paranoia, duplicity, deep and powerful secrets, and plenty of corrupt bad guys. The ending takes place on Mars, when atmospheric gases and water are freed from deep within the planet's rocks.

But what do we actually know about the red planet? We know that it bears some similarities to Earth and may have been habitable at one time in the past—and may be in the future. Its surface has been dramatically altered by volcanism, impacts by asteroids and meteors and other celestial bodies, violent movements in its crust, and great cyclonic dust storms that frequently swallow the entire planet. Its polar ice caps grow and recede, like ours, with the change of seasons. Near the poles, the layered soil indicates that the planet's climate has changed more than once. Its ancient volcanoes, once powered from the heat of the Martian core, rise against the starkness with a kind of fierce purity. The largest volcano, Olympus Mons, is seventeen miles high and may be the largest in the solar system. There's also a titanic canyon about the size of the distance between New York and L.A.

Due to several unmanned missions to Mars, our knowledge about the planet is growing. Thanks to the Mars Odyssey spacecraft, launched in 2001, it's now believed that billions of years ago Mars was inundated by the largest floods in the solar system. No one knows where all that water went, but the Mars Odyssey detected substantial quantities of water mixed into the soil about three feet down, near the Martian south pole.

On August 12, 2005, the Mars Reconnaissance Orbiter was launched, and it entered the orbit of Mars on March 10, 2006. After five months of a technique called aerobraking (a three-step procedure that cuts in half the fuel needed to achieve a lower, more circular orbit), the orbiter started its scientific tests. These lasted until November 2008. Since then, NASA has released thousands of high-resolution photos of the Mars surface that have broadened our knowledge about the fourth planet from the sun. The photos may answer the basic questions about whether Mars had water, if it was once inhabited and if so, was it destroyed by a catastrophe? Can it sustain human life in the future?

Images of recent impact craters on Mars have revealed subsurface ice midway between the planet's north pole and equator. A geologist with the U.S. Geological Survey claims he has found evidence of an extensive cave system among ancient volcanoes at Mars's equator. He believes the depressions visible in the high-resolution photos are consistent with lava flows on Earth that produce caves. Some of these depressions are more than 60 miles long and 150 feet across. If the geologist is right, then caves may provide early colonists with protection from the harsh environment and lethal cosmic rays.

On a clear night at certain times of the year, you can walk outside after dark and glimpse Mars in the sky, a speck of rose-tinted light between 56,000,000 and 399,000,000 kilometers from Earth. Its diameter is a little more than half that of Earth, the length of a Martian day is 24.6 Earth hours, a Martian year is 1.88 Earth years, and gravity on the surface is about a third of Earth's. Ninety-five percent of the atmosphere consists of carbon dioxide, it's toxic. It has two moons, but both are so small they may not be moons but just rock formations that have gotten trapped in the planet's gravitational pull. They are named after the two squires who served Ares, the Greek god of war: Phobos, which means "fear," and Deimos—"panic."

Mars in Astrology

To the ancient Greeks, he was Ares, a savage god who was little more than a bloodthirsty SOB. In the *Iliad,* Zeus says it like he sees it, that he finds Ares, his son, completely odious because he enjoyed nothing but "strife, war, and battles." On Olympus, he was intensely disliked for his blind violence and brutality.

This theme is beautifully illustrated in the movie *Gladiator.* Times are brutal, and brute strength is held in such high esteem that the populace turns out to watch men kill each other in the stadium. Not surprisingly, Aries Russell Crowe won an Oscar for his performance. Now skip ahead a couple thousand years. In *The Running Man,* one of the novellas that Stephen King wrote as Richard Bachman, this same theme is repeated, but now the protagonist (played by Arnold Schwarzenegger in the film) is running for his life on national TV and surviving by his wits and brute strength. Same theme, different century.

But aggression, survival, and war are only one side of Mars. The Greek side. On the Roman side, he was called by the name we know him—Mars. He was first and foremost the god of agriculture—the protector of cattle, the preserver of corn—and was associated with the woodpecker, the horse, and the wolf. As the husband of Rhea Silvia, a vestal virgin, he fathered Romulus and Remus, who were suckled by a wolf.

The connection between Mars and sex probably came about as a result of Ares's affair with the goddess Aphrodite. She was married to a cripple, Hephaestus, and compared to him Ares was handsome, dashing, courageous, all the things the Olympians looked for in a mate. Ares, of course, took advantage of the situation, and their lustful encounters on the "marriage couch" became well known to the other gods when Hephaestus ensnared the adulterous couple in an invisible net.

In 2012, Mars makes it through six signs and spends less than a week in a seventh. Let's take a look at what these transits mean for you, Virgo.

Important Dates

January 1 to July 3: Mars in Virgo. This transit stimulates every area of your life. It provides the physical energy to get things done, heats up your sex life, hurls open doors to new opportunities. During this transit, tackle any obstacles that may be preventing you from achieving a goal. Others see you as a powerhouse with answers, drive, ambition. During this period, Mars forms a beneficial angle to Pluto, which is in fellow earth sign Capricorn and puts you in a powerful position.

July 3 to August 23: Mars in Libra, transiting your solar second house. Finances are highlighted. You may be working harder to make ends meet or simply because you love what you're doing. Mars in Libra suggests you may be socializing more than usual, with people who share your values. The people you meet during this time may be helpful financially. You may have to strike a more balanced approach to spending, i.e., sticking to your budget!

August 23 to October 6: Mars in Scorpio in your solar third house. Whenever Mars transits Scorpio, things can get emotionally intense. But with Mars forming a beneficial angle to your sun during this transit, intensity doesn't intimidate you. In fact, you use it to your advantage in all your communications. You may be checking out new neighborhoods in anticipation of a move. This transit also brings more frequent contact with siblings, other relatives, neighbors. A romance is possible with someone who may live as close to you as your own neighborhood!

October 6 to November 16: Mars in Sagittarius, your solar fourth house of home and family. Unless you have natal planets in fire signs, this probably won't be your favorite transit of the year. It may create friction at home as you feel pulled between responsibilities there and obligations at work. That said, consider using this energy for refurbishing your home in some way—fresh paint on the walls, new floors, or just general cleaning out of the garage, attic, closets.

November 16 to December 25: Mars in Capricorn, your solar fifth house. Mars now forms a beneficial angle to your sun sign and enables you to accomplish quite a bit. Your creative projects take on new life and energy, you make more time for enjoyable activities, and your love life (and sex life!) also improve.

Capricorn's energy is familiar to you, and it also enables you to focus more clearly on your goals. So know where you're going and what your end point is. Have a plan B.

December 25 to February 2, 2013: Mars in Aquarius in your solar sixth house. This transit brings your focus to your daily work routine and the maintenance of your health. Its energy is mental, visionary, concerned not only with teamwork, but with what each individual brings to the table. Use this time frame to brainstorm with coworkers for new ideas, new methods, new ways.

Even though Aquarius is an air sign that isn't especially compatible with your sun sign, it's a sign that thinks, and you, Mercury ruled, appreciate the intellectual process and the communication that accompanies it.

CHAPTER 17

The Big Picture for Virgo in 2012

Welcome to 2012, Virgo. This year is marked by partnership, cooperation, patience, kindness and understanding. It's a year for an important relationship to develop—in business, in your personal life, or even both! Let's take a closer look.

Pluto, the snail of the zodiac, starts off the year in Capricorn, in your solar fifth house, where it has consistently been since November 2008. You're accustomed to its energy now. Its transit, which lasts until 2024, is bringing profound and permanent change globally, evident in the economic challenges that now face the U.S. Most institutions are in the throes of great change—the healthcare industry, the petroleum and insurance industries, mortgages/lending, housing, aviation, even the Internet. You name it, and Pluto's fingerprint can be found.

On a personal level, this planet's transit through that area of your chart that represents romance and love, enjoyment, children, and creativity will continue to transform these things at profound levels. On the creative front, you will become more aware of your needs and motives. Your muse will be whispering in your ear 24/7. If you've wanted to start a family, consider doing it during this transit. Everything you do for fun and pleasure will have a deeper aspect to it. In other words, instead of just taking a trip somewhere, there will be a purpose behind the trip—to learn something, to expose yourself to new venues, or perhaps you'll travel as part of a spiritual quest. Romantically, you may be attracting unusual, idiosyncratic individuals who give you plenty of personal freedom and encourage your self-expression.

Neptune entered Pisces, your opposite sign, on April 4, 2011. But by early August 2011, it had slipped back into Aquarius. On February 3, 2012, it enters Pisces again and won't move on until January 2026. This transit forms a challenging angle to your sun, so its initial impact can create confusion. For hints about what this may mean for you, look back to that period in 2011 when Neptune was in Pisces.

Neptune symbolizes our higher ideals, escapism, fiction, spirituality, and our blind spots. It seeks to dissolve boundaries between us and others. One possible repercussion of this transit is prolonged religious wars, which proliferated during Uranus's transit in Pisces in early 2003. On a personal level, though, Neptune's transit through your solar seventh house suggests that you may try to integrate your spiritual beliefs more readily into your partnerships—both business and personal. Your partnerships may also become more spiritual, idealistic, even more psychic. In fact, if you can focus on these three elements in your relationships, there's less likely to be confusion during this transit. Given the spiritual aspect of this transit, it's quite possible that a relationship develops with someone you knew in a past life.

Uranus entered Aries and your solar eighth house in March 2011. This transit is discussed at some length in chapter 15, on Uranus's transit through Aries, so take a look there for in-depth information. But know that one repercussion of this transit is that unusual and exciting people are going to be entering your life and shaking things up. The biggest changes are likely to be to your partner's income.

Saturn begins the year in Libra in your solar second house. It has been there since the summer of 2010 and will be there until October 2012. This transit brings greater structure to your finances and values. It may also restrict your earnings in some way, or perhaps for a time you have to take on a part-time job. But try to use this energy in terms of structure. Start a budget—out of every check you receive, pay yourself a percentage first, pay cash for purchases, avoid credit-card debt. You know the drill here, Virgo. Make it happen.

Once Saturn enters compatible water sign Scorpio on October 5, the transit will have a greater level of comfort. It will be forming a beneficial angle to your sun in your solar third house. You will find a strong structure for your intuition, perhaps through writing—a blog, Web site, novel, self-help book—and your relationships with siblings, other relatives, and neighbors will benefit.

One of your best periods this year falls between January 1 and June 11, when Jupiter transits fellow earth sign Taurus and your solar ninth house. This transit expands your worldview, spirituality, personal philosophy. It highlights higher education, publishing, overseas travel, foreign cultures. It's possible that your company's products or your services/products expand to overseas markets. You may be traveling overseas more frequently, which opens your consciousness to new experiences, thoughts, ideas.

From June 11, 2012, to June 25, 2013, Jupiter transits Gemini and your career area. This is a big wow, Virgo, and it's smart to plan for it. Seeds planted during Jupiter's transit through Taurus can sprout fast during its transit through Gemini. You may change jobs, land a promotion and raise, change careers, start your own business, write a novel . . . well, there are many possibilities. The more focused you are, the clearer your intentions, the greater the possibilities with this transit.

They say that timing is everything, so with that in mind, let's look at some specific areas in your life in 2012.

Romance/Creativity

The most romantic and creative time for you all year falls between March 5 and April 3, when Venus transits fellow earth sign Taurus. You feel more sensual and appealing, and your self-confidence soars. Other people pick up what you radiate and respond accordingly. If you're in a committed relationship, then you and your partner rediscover each other. Plan a trip out of town to some secluded, romantic spot. Spend time together doing whatever you both enjoy.

Another good period: October 3 to 28, when Venus is moving direct in your sign. Things really seem to flow your way then in many areas, but particularly with romance and creative ventures. The best time for serious involvement and deepening commitment in an existing relationship occurs when Venus transits Pisces and your solar seventh house of partnerships, which occurs between January 14 and February 8. You and your partner may decide to move in together, get engaged, or get married. Just be sure that you don't do any of this under a Mercury retrograde period. Take a look under the appropriate section below to find out when Mercury will be retrograde this year.

Other good backup dates: August 23 to October 6, when Mars transits compatible water sign Scorpio, and between November 16 and December 25, when it transits Capricorn and the romance/love area of your chart.

Career

Career timing is covered in chapter 14, but here's some additional information about professional matters. Usually, Venus and Jupiter transits to your career area are the times to look for. This year, lucky you, Jupiter in Gemini transits your career area for more than a year, from June 11, 2012, to June 25, 2013. Venus transits this area from April 3 to August 7. However, it's retrograde between May 15 and June 27, so try not to start anything new during this period.

Another nice period is when Mercury transits your career area between May 24 and June 7. This is the time to pitch ideas, push your agenda forward, travel related to work, and socialize with peers. It also favors all professional communication.

Between November 16 and December 25, Mars in Capricorn links up with Pluto, and both planets form a beneficial angle to your sun. This period is when you should seek creative solutions. Brainstorm. Don't be afraid to try the untried.

Best Times For

Buying or selling a home: December 15 to January 9, 2013, when Venus is in Sagittarius and your solar fourth house; December 10 to 31, Mercury transits the same sign and house.

Family reunions: Any of the dates above or when Venus is in your sign between October 3 and 28.

Financial matters: The period from October 28 to November 21, when Venus transits Libra and your solar second house.

Signing contracts: When Mercury is moving direct!

Mercury Retrogrades

Every year, Mercury—the planet of communication and travel—turns retrograde three times. During this period, it's wise not to sign contracts (unless you don't mind renegotiating when Mercury is moving direct), to check and recheck travel plans (or, better yet, don't travel), and to communicate as succinctly as possible. Refrain from buying any large-ticket items or electronics during this time too. Often, computers and appliances go on the fritz, cars act up, data is lost . . . you get the idea. Be sure to back up all files before the dates below:

March 12–April 4: Mercury retrograde in Aries, your eighth house—shared resources, mortgages, loans, insurance, partner's income.

July 14–August 8: Mercury retrograde in Leo, your solar twelfth house—personal unconscious, what's hidden.

November 6–26: Mercury retrograde in Sagittarius, your solar fourth house of the home.

Eclipses

Solar eclipses tend to trigger external events that bring about change according to the sign and house in which they fall. Lunar eclipses trigger inner, emotional events according to the sign and house in which they fall. Any eclipse marks both beginnings and endings. The solar and lunar eclipse in a pair falls in opposite signs. If you're interested in detailed information on eclipses, take a look at Celeste Teal's excellent and definitive book, *Eclipses: Predicting World Events & Personal Transformation.*

If you were born under or around the time of an eclipse, it's to your advantage to take a look at your birth chart to find out exactly where the eclipses will impact you.

Most years feature four eclipses—two solar and two lunar, with the set separated by about two weeks. In November and December 2011, there were solar and lunar eclipses, so this year the first eclipses fall during May and June.

May 20: Solar eclipse at 0 degrees Gemini. This one should bring in new professional opportunities.

June 4: Lunar eclipse in Sagittarius, your solar fourth house. Positive eclipse for your family life.

November 13: Solar eclipse in Scorpio in your solar third house. New opportunities surface for communication.

November 28: Lunar eclipse, Gemini. Jupiter forms a five-degree conjunction to the eclipse degree, suggesting that professional news you receive around this time will be cause for celebration!

Luckiest Day of the Year

Every year there's one day when Jupiter and the sun meet up, and luck, serendipity, and expansion are the hallmarks. This year that day falls on May 13, with a conjunction in Taurus.

CHAPTER 18

Eighteen Months of Day-by-Day Predictions: July 2011 to December 2012

Moon sign times are calculated for Eastern Standard Time and Eastern Daylight Time. Please adjust for your local time zone.

JULY 2011

Friday, July 1 (Moon in Cancer)   New opportunities come your way related to a group activity, especially one that involves friends. You have a chance to expand whatever you're doing. But it's also a good time to begin a new project. Focus on your wishes and dreams.

Saturday, July 2 (Moon into Leo, 5:44 p.m.)   With Mercury moving into your twelfth house, your thinking is influenced by your subconscious. You tend to act on your feelings rather than on logic. You're also secretive about your plans. However, you could confide at great length to a friend. ˙

Sunday, July 3 (Moon in Leo)   Yesterday's energy rolls into your Sunday. Think carefully before you act. There's a tendency to undo all the positive actions you've taken. Avoid any self-destructive behavior. Be-

198

ware of hidden enemies. As yesterday, it's a good idea to keep your thoughts to yourself and remain behind the scenes.

Monday, July 4 (Moon into Virgo, 9:16 p.m.)   Venus moves into your eleventh house. You can achieve your goals through your social contacts. Friends play an important role in your day, especially those with artistic talent. Spread your good news, and take time to listen to others.

Tuesday, July 5 (Moon in Virgo)   The moon is on your ascendant. The way you see yourself is the way others see you. You're recharged for the month ahead, and this makes you more appealing to the public. It's a great day for starting something new. Your appearance and personality shine. Your feelings and thoughts are aligned.

Wednesday, July 6 (Moon into Libra, 11:54 p.m.) Promote new ideas; follow your curiosity. Freedom of thought and action is key. However, avoid excess in whatever you're doing. It's a good time for travel, adventure, and meeting new people. You're seeking new horizons. You're motivated and inspired.

Thursday, July 7 (Moon in Libra)   You identify emotionally with your possessions or whatever you value. Watch your spending. You feel best when surrounded by familiar objects. It's not the objects themselves that are important, but the feelings and memories you associate with them. Put off making any major purchases.

Friday, July 8 (Moon in Libra)   Romance is highlighted. Relationship issues figure prominently in your day. You're seeking harmony and peace. Go to an art gallery opening or a museum or to the theater or a concert. Your creativity, personal grace, and magnetism are highlighted.

Saturday, July 9 (Moon into Scorpio, 2:32 a.m.)
Uranus goes retrograde in your eighth house. In the coming weeks, you could experience erratic ups and downs, especially related to joint finances. It's a time for looking inward. Slow down and contemplate some of the larger mysteries of life.

Sunday, July 10 (Moon in Scorpio)   The moon is in your third house. You write from a deep place. It's a good day for journaling or working on any writing project. Matters from the past influence your thinking. A female relative plays a role.

Monday, July 11 (Moon into Sagittarius, 3:47 a.m.)
It's a number 1 day, and you're at the top of your cycle again. Be independent and creative. Take the lead, and don't be afraid to turn in a new direction. You're inventive; you make connections that others overlook. Refuse to deal with people with negative attitudes. Stress originality.

Tuesday, July 12 (Moon in Sagittarius)   The moon is in your fourth house. Work at home, if possible. Spend time with your family and loved ones. You're dealing with the foundations of who you are and who you are becoming. Retreat to a private place for meditation. Remember your dreams. A parent plays a role in your day.

Wednesday, July 13 (Moon into Capricorn, 10:14 a.m.)
You're creative, and you express yourself well. Your artistic talents are highlighted. Your attitude determines everything. Spread your good news. Your charm and wit are appreciated.

Thursday, July 14 (Moon in Capricorn)   You're emotionally in touch with your creative side. Take a chance; experiment. Be yourself. Be emotionally honest. In love, there's greater emotional depth to a relationship. Try to avoid being possessive of loved ones.

Friday, July 15 (Moon into Aquarius, 4:30 p.m.)
You gain insight and illumination related to a romantic relationship or a creative project. Your emotions tend to overpower your intellect. You reap what you've sown. Children play a role in your day.

Saturday, July 16 (Moon in Aquarius) It's a service-oriented day. Help others, but don't deny your own needs. Take care of any health issues. Watch your diet, and take time to exercise. You could be somewhat emotionally repressed.

Sunday, July 17 (Moon in Aquarius) Groups and social events are highlighted. Your individuality is stressed. Your visionary abilities are heightened. You have a greater sense of freedom. You're dealing with new ideas, new options, and originality. You get a new perspective.

Monday, July 18 (Moon into Pisces, 1:13 a.m.) It's a number 8 day, your power day again. Open your mind to a new approach that could bring in big bucks. Business discussions go well. You could pull off a financial coup. You're playing with power, so be careful not to hurt others. You're being watched by people in power.

Tuesday, July 19 (Moon in Pisces) You get along well with others. You can fit in just about anywhere. Loved ones and partners are more important than usual. You could be dealing with a legal matter, possibly related to a partnership or a marriage. You comprehend the nuances of a situation, but it's difficult to go with the flow.

Wednesday, July 20 (Moon into Aries, 12:26 a.m.)
Get out and meet new people and have new experiences. Express your opinions dynamically. Explore, discover, and create. You're determined and courageous today. In romance, something new is developing.

Thursday, July 21 (Moon in Aries)   The moon is in your eighth house. Your sense of security or duty plays a major role in your day. You help others, especially a partner. You could be managing another person's money or an inheritance. You're dealing with mortgages, taxes, or insurance. Alternately, you're attracted to the goals of a large social movement.

Friday, July 22 (Moon into Taurus, 12:59 p.m.) You're innovative and creative; you communicate well. Your attitude determines everything. You're warm and receptive to what others say. Your charm and wit are appreciated. Take time to relax, enjoy yourself, and recharge your batteries.

Saturday, July 23 (Moon in Taurus)   The moon is in your ninth house. You're a dreamer and a thinker. You may feel a need to get away. Plan a long trip. Sign up for a workshop or seminar. Publicize and advertise whatever you're doing. If you're involved with a publishing project, expect some positive answers.

Sunday, July 24 (Moon in Taurus)   Use common sense, and take a down-to-earth perspective on whatever you're doing. Health and physical activity are highlighted. Garden, cultivate ideas, and do practical things. Go hiking, have a picnic, and get out into nature.

Monday, July 25 (Moon into Gemini, 12:35 a.m.) Service to others is the theme of the day, and diplomacy wins the way. Be sympathetic and kind, generous and tolerant. Do a good deed. Focus on making people happy. Be understanding, and avoid confrontations. At the same time, dance to your own tune.

Tuesday, July 26 (Moon in Gemini)   With the moon in your tenth house, professional concerns are highlighted. You gain a boost in prestige, possibly an advancement and a raise. You're warm and friendly toward coworkers. It's a good day for sales and dealing with the public.

Wednesday, July 27 (Moon into Cancer, 9:12 p.m.) It's another power day. You can go far with your plans and achieve financial success, especially if you open your mind to a new approach. Keep in mind that you're playing with power, so be careful not to hurt others. Business discussions go well.

Thursday, July 28 (Moon in Cancer) With Mercury moving into your first house, you're talkative and express yourself well. You're mentally restless, looking for information and new ideas. Meanwhile, Venus moves into your twelfth house, indicating a love of secrecy and a desire for solitude over the next three weeks. Your introspective side reveals itself, balancing the need to get out and communicate at other times. You also feel a sense of compassion toward those who are less fortunate than you.

Friday, July 29 (Moon in Cancer) The moon is in your eleventh house. You get along better with friends and associates. You find meaning through your involvement in a group, especially one that works for the common good. Take time to focus on your wishes and dreams, and examine your overall goals.

Saturday, July 30 (Moon into Leo, 2:16 a.m.) There's a new moon in your twelfth house. New opportunities arise that could make you the power behind the scenes. You also could find new opportunities working in a large institution, such as a hospital or government agency. Alternately, you could gain new opportunities to delve into the unconscious. It's a good time for therapy, meditation, and taking up yoga.

Sunday, July 31 (Moon in Leo) Drama is highlighted today, perhaps involving children. You're creative and passionate now, impulsive and honest. Animals and pets figure prominently. Romance and love play a role.

AUGUST 2011

Monday, August 1 (Moon into Virgo, 4:42 a.m.) You start the month at the top of your cycle. You can take the lead now. You get a new beginning. Stress originality. Trust your hunches. Intuition is highlighted. You're inventive; you make connections that others overlook. You're determined and courageous.

Tuesday, August 2 (Moon in Virgo) Mercury goes retrograde in your first house today and stays there until August 26. That means you could experience some confusion and delays related to your personal life. Try to be clear and concise in all your communication with individuals, a group, or the public at large. There's a tendency to procrastinate or change plans.

Wednesday, August 3 (Moon into Libra, 6:05 a.m.) Mars moves into your eleventh house. You're energetic; you take the lead to organize others, especially for a good cause. You work hard, but you can also be a disrupting force now among others.

Thursday, August 4 (Moon in Libra) The moon is in your second house. Your money-earning potential increases. You're taking an emotional look at your priorities related to money. Collect what's owed you, and pay what you owe. You feel best surrounding yourself with familiar objects that you associate with fond memories.

Friday, August 5 (Moon into Scorpio, 7:57 a.m.) Variety is the spice of life. Change, variety, and travel are highlighted. Think freedom, no restrictions. Think outside the box. Take risks; experiment. You're also more comfortable than usual in front of an audience.

Saturday, August 6 (Moon in Scorpio)   The moon is in your third house. Your mind is sharp, and you communicate well. You're busy interacting with neighbors or relatives in a social gathering. You get your ideas across, but try not to get too emotional. A female relative plays an important role.

Sunday, August 7 (Moon into Sagittarius, 11:21 a.m.) It's a number 7 day. You look behind the scenes, investigating a secret matter. You're a searcher, a seeker of truth. Make sure that you see things as they are, not as you wish them to be. You're a spy for your own cause.

Monday, August 8 (Moon in Sagittarius)   The moon is in your fourth house. You feel a close tie to your roots. You're dealing with the foundations of who you are and who you are becoming. A parent plays a role. Work on or plan a home-renovation or -repair project, especially if it provides a way of expanding your space.

Tuesday, August 9 (Moon into Capricorn, 4:38 p.m.) Look beyond the immediate. Finish what you started. Visualize the future; set your goals, and then make them so. Complete a project, and make room for something new.

Wednesday, August 10 (Moon in Capricorn)   With the moon in your fifth house today, take a chance and experiment. Be aware that your emotions tend to overpower your intellect. You're emotionally in touch with your creative side. Alternately, you are more protective and nurturing toward children.

Thursday, August 11 (Moon into Aquarius, 11:48 p.m.) It's a number 2 day. Use your intuition to get a sense of your day. Be kind and understanding. Cooperation, especially with partners, is highlighted. Don't make waves.

Don't rush or show resentment; let things develop. Marriage plays a key role.

Friday, August 12 (Moon in Aquarius)　　The moon is in your sixth house. It's a good day to clarify any health or work issues. It's best if you follow a regular schedule now. Stay positive. Help others where you can, but dance to your own tune, Virgo. You're the one others go to for help. You improve, edit, and refine their work.

Saturday, August 13 (Moon in Aquarius)　　There's a full moon in your sixth house today. You gain insight and illumination related to your everyday work or possibly to a health matter. You reap what you've sown. Efforts you've made to help others won't be overlooked.

Sunday, August 14 (Moon into Pisces, 8:55 a.m.) Approach the day with an unconventional mind-set. Release old structures; get a new point of view. Variety is the spice of life. Think freedom, no restrictions. Change and variety are highlighted.

Monday, August 15 (Moon in Pisces)　　It's all about partnerships, business and personal. You get along well with others. You can fit in just about anywhere. However, be careful that others don't manipulate your feelings. There could be a contract coming your way. It's Mercury retrograde until August 26, so read the fine print.

Tuesday, August 16 (Moon into Aries, 8:03 p.m.) Secrets, intrigue, and confidential information play a role today. You might feel best working on your own. You investigate, analyze, or simply observe what's going on. You quickly come to a conclusion and wonder why others don't see what you see. It's best to hold off on making any final decisions for a couple days.

Wednesday, August 17 (Moon in Aries)　　The moon is in your eighth house. You have a strong sense of duty;

you feel obligated to fulfill your promises. Security is an important issue with you right now. You could be dealing with your feelings about possessions, as well as things that you share with others, such as a spouse.

Thursday, August 18 (Moon in Aries)   It's a good day for completing a project, clearing up odds and ends, and brainstorming new ideas. Take an inventory of where things are going in your life. But don't start anything new until tomorrow. Get out into nature; have an adventure. Take time to reflect and get ready for something new.

Friday, August 19 (Moon into Taurus, 8:37 a.m.) It's a number 1 day, and you're at the top of your cycle. Now it's time to take the lead. Independence is the theme. You're inventive; you make connections that others overlook. Trust your hunches. You get a fresh start.

Saturday, August 20 (Moon in Taurus)   You're a dreamer and a thinker. You're captivated by new ideas and philosophies. You may feel a need to get away. You feel restless and yearn for a new experience. A foreign-born person or a foreign country could play a role in your day.

Sunday, August 21 (Moon into Gemini, 8:53 p.m.) Venus moves into your first house. You're feeling good about yourself. Your thoughts and feelings are well aligned. Your personal grace and charm are appreciated. You're also very socially oriented; you can develop new friendships and social contacts.

Monday, August 22 (Moon in Gemini)   The moon is in your tenth house, Virgo. Professional concerns are the focus of the day. You attend to details and seek perfection in whatever you're working on, but at the same time you're more in tune with fellow workers and more emotional in your interactions. However, don't blur the boundary between your personal and professional lives.

Tuesday, August 23 (Moon in Gemini)   You're feeling moody and sensitive to the moods of others. It's best to keep things to yourself. You're intuitive, nurturing, and protective of your personal environment and of those close to you. Work on a home-repair project. Take time to snuggle with your loved one.

Wednesday, August 24 (Moon into Cancer, 6:31 a.m.) Service to others is the theme of the day. Focus on making people happy. Be kind and understanding, and do a good deed. Help others, but avoid scattering your energies. Dance to your own tune. A domestic adjustment works out for the best.

Thursday, August 25 (Moon in Cancer)   With the moon in your eleventh house, you feel obligated and responsible to help others. You flow with the social currents. You could get involved with a group that seeks to improve living conditions of those in need.

Friday, August 26 (Moon into Leo, 12:09 p.m.)   Mercury goes direct in your twelfth house. Confusion, delays, and miscommunication are over, especially related to matters from the past. Any hidden enemies reveal themselves. You handle mental work very well, especially dealing with computers and electronic devices. The glitches you've experienced are in the past. Any matter related to your unconscious attitudes becomes clear. You see movement and growth related to any spiritual or mystical endeavor.

Saturday, August 27 (Moon in Leo)   The moon is in your twelfth house. It's best to work behind the scenes, and avoid any conflicts and confrontations, especially with women. Keep your feelings secret. Unconscious attitudes can be difficult.

Sunday, August 28 (Moon into Virgo, 2:13 p.m.)
There's a new moon in your first house with Venus
closely conjunct. That means new personal opportunities come your way. It could also mean that a new relationship is developing. You can earn money through the
arts. Overall, your life is unfolding very nicely. Go with
the flow.

Monday, August 29 (Moon in Virgo)   The moon is
on your ascendant. You're feeling physically vital and
recharged for the month ahead. You're assertive and
outgoing. Your appearance and personality shine. You
get along well with the opposite sex.

Tuesday, August 30 (Moon into Libra, 2:26 p.m.)   Jupiter goes retrograde in your ninth house and stays
there until Christmas Day. You look inward to expand
your worldview and spiritual beliefs. However, you will
probably slow down your spiritual work until the end of
the year. Your expansion is internal.

Wednesday, August 31 (Moon in Libra)   The moon
is in your second house. Money issues and your emotions
are on your agenda. Look for an investment, pay your
bills, and collect what's owed to you. You equate your financial assets with emotional security. Look at your priorities in handling your income. Put off making any major
purchases.

SEPTEMBER 2011

*Thursday, September 1 (Moon into Scorpio, 2:48
p.m.)*   It's a number 2 day. Partnerships are highlighted. Use your intuition to get a sense of your day,
and focus on relationships. Be kind and understanding.
Don't make waves. Don't rush or show resentment; let
things develop.

Friday, September 2 (Moon in Scorpio) The moon is in your third house. You're dealing with your everyday world, but you're thinking about power issues. You write from a deep place. It's a good day for journaling or working on any writing project. Be aware that your thinking could be unduly influenced by the past. A female relative plays a role in your day.

Saturday, September 3 (Moon into Sagittarius, 3:04 p.m.) It's a number 4 day. Your organizational skills are highlighted, but try not to wander off task. Emphasize quality; you're building a creative foundation for your future. Tear down the old in order to rebuild. Be methodical and thorough.

Sunday, September 4 (Moon in Sagittarius) The moon is in your fourth house. Spend quality time at home with loved ones. Beautify your surroundings with a home-repair or -redecoration project. Retreat to a private place for meditation.

Monday, September 5 (Moon into Capricorn, 10:04 p.m.) It's a number 6 day. Focus on making people happy. Be sympathetic, kind, and compassionate. Do a good deed for someone. But avoid scattering your energy. Dance to your own tune.

Tuesday, September 6 (Moon in Capricorn) The moon is in your fifth house. Follow your heart on a creative project. You can tap deeply into the collective unconscious for inspiration. In love, there's greater emotional depth than usual. However, make an effort to avoid being overly possessive with a loved one, even though that's your tendency.

Wednesday, September 7 (Moon in Capricorn) Your ambition and drive to succeed are highlighted. Your responsibilities increase. But you may feel stressed, overworked. Authority figures and elderly people play a role.

So do banks or financial institutions. Maintain emotional balance. Your domestic scene needs attention.

Thursday, September 8 (Moon into Aquarius, 5:43 a.m.)   It's a number 9 day. Finish what you started. Visualize the future; set your goals, and then make them so. Take an inventory of where things are going in your life. Make room for something new, and accept what comes your way. But don't start anything new.

Friday, September 9 (Moon in Aquarius)   It's another service day. Attend to daily details, Virgo, and be of service. Help your coworkers, but don't overlook your own needs. Make appointments that you've been putting off.

Saturday, September 10 (Moon into Pisces, 3:27 p.m.)   The spotlight is on cooperation. Emotions and sensitivity are highlighted. Don't make waves. Don't rush or show resentment; let things develop. There could be some soul-searching related to relationships.

Sunday, September 11 (Moon in Pisces)   The moon is in your seventh house. Partnerships play a key role in your day. You have a strong desire to be accepted. You can fit in just about anywhere. You get along with just about everyone.

Monday, September 12 (Moon in Pisces)   With the full moon showing up in your seventh house, yesterday's energy flows into your Monday. You gain insight and illumination related to a relationship. It all becomes clear. You reap what you've sown.

Tuesday, September 13 (Moon into Aries, 2:50 a.m.)   The emphasis is on freedom of thought and movement. Get ready for a change of scenery or a possible relocation. Experiment and find a new outlook. Variety is the spice of life.

Wednesday, September 14 (Moon in Aries) You can make money through an artistic endeavor. Security and material success are emphasized. You love the feeling of buying and accumulating. However, watch your spending, and avoid the tendency toward extravagance.

Thursday, September 15 (Moon into Taurus, 3:25 p.m.) You investigate, analyze, or simply observe what's going on. You quickly come to a conclusion and wonder why others don't see what you see. Gather information, but don't make any absolute decisions until tomorrow. You work best on your own. Knowledge is essential to success.

Friday, September 16 (Moon in Taurus) With Pluto going direct in your fifth house, you have a tendency once again to splurge. Your pleasures can be expensive. Gambling plays a role. Take a chance, but don't get yourself in so deep that you can't work your way out. Alternately, you could be dealing with children who are strong-willed and difficult to control.

Saturday, September 17 (Moon in Taurus) The moon is in your ninth house. You're feeling as if you need to get away. Plan a trip or sign up for a seminar or workshop. A foreign country or a person of foreign birth could play a role. Philosophy, religion, and mythology play a role in your day.

Sunday, September 18 (Moon into Gemini, 4:06 a.m.) With Mars moving into your twelfth house, you could feel like you're on a mission now. Whatever it is, you tend to keep it to yourself to avoid competition or naysayers. You work behind the scenes with a lot of energy. Any unconscious anger needs to be brought to the surface and released.

Monday, September 19 (Moon in Gemini) The moon is in your tenth house. Business dealings are highlighted on this Monday. It's a good day for sales and dealing with the public. You get along well with fellow workers. Avoid any emotional displays in public.

Tuesday, September 20 (Moon into Cancer, 2:54 p.m.)
It's a number 3 day. Enjoy the harmony, beauty, and pleasures of life. Remain flexible. Your popularity is on the rise. Your attitude determines everything. Spread your good news. Your charm and wit are appreciated.

Wednesday, September 21 (Moon in Cancer) The moon is in your eleventh house. Friends play an important role, especially Taurus and Capricorn. You find strength in numbers. You find meaning through friends and groups, especially a group of like-minded people working for the common good.

Thursday, September 22 (Moon into Leo, 9:56 p.m.)
Promote new ideas; follow your curiosity. Freedom of thought and action is key. It's a good day for a change of scenery. You could be planning a move to a new location. You can overcome obstacles with ease.

Friday, September 23 (Moon in Leo) The moon is in your twelfth house. Think carefully before you act or speak. If you're not careful, there's a tendency to undo all the positive actions you've taken. You might feel a need to withdraw. Take time to reflect and meditate.

Saturday, September 24 (Moon into Virgo, 10:50 p.m.)
It's a number 7 day. You work best on your own. You investigate, analyze, or simply observe what's going on now. Knowledge is essential to success. Gather information, but don't make any absolute decisions until tomorrow.

Sunday, September 25 (Moon in Virgo) Mercury moves into your second house today. It's a good time to come up with moneymaking ideas. You stick with your values, which tend to be oriented toward material goods. You communicate your values and moneymaking ideas to others.

Monday, September 26 (Moon into Libra, 12:51 a.m.)
Clear up odds and ends. Take an inventory of where things are going in your life. Visualize the future; set your goals, and then make them so. Look beyond the immediate. Get ready for something new. Strive for universal appeal.

Tuesday, September 27 (Moon in Libra)   There's a new moon in your second house. You get new opportunities related to finances. Money issues and your emotions are on your agenda. Collect what's owed you, and pay what you owe.

Wednesday, September 28 (Moon into Scorpio, 12:06 a.m.)   It's a number 2 day. The spotlight is on cooperation. Show your appreciation to others. Don't make waves. Your intuition focuses on relationships. Partnerships are highlighted. Use your intuition to get a sense of the day.

Thursday, September 29 (Moon in Scorpio)   The moon is in your third house. It's a good day for expressing yourself through writing. Take what you know and share it with others. As you go about your everyday life, look to the big picture. Expect an invitation to a social event.

Friday, September 30 (Moon into Sagittarius, 12:42 a.m.)   Your organizational skills are highlighted. Control your impulses. Take care of obligations. Tear down the old in order to rebuild. It's a good day to clean out a closet, the attic, or your garage.

Saturday, October 1 (Moon in Sagittarius)   The moon is in your fourth house. Spend time with your family and loved ones. Stick close to home. You're dealing with the foundations of who you are and who you are becoming. Take time to meditate. It's also a good day for dream recall or to change a bad habit.

Sunday, October 2 (Moon in Sagittarius)   You see the big picture, not just the details. There's passion in relationships. Spiritual values arise. Worldviews are emphasized. You're restless, impulsive, and inquisitive. It's a good day for traveling.

Monday, October 3 (Moon into Capricorn, 4:16 a.m.) Think freedom, no restrictions. Change and variety are highlighted now. Take risks; experiment. Approach the day with an unconventional mind-set. Freedom of thought and action is key. But so is moderation; avoid excess in whatever you're doing.

Tuesday, October 4 (Moon in Capricorn)   The moon is in your fifth house. You can move ahead on any creative project. You're emotionally in touch with your creative side. Meanwhile, you have an opportunity to achieve greater depth in a relationship, but it could take hard work. Be yourself; be emotionally honest. Children and pets play a role in your day.

Wednesday, October 5 (Moon into Aquarius, 11:19 a.m.)   You become aware of confidential information, secret meetings, and things happening behind closed doors. You investigate like a detective solving a mystery. Dig deep, gather information, but don't act on what you learn until tomorrow.

Thursday, October 6 (Moon in Aquarius)   With the moon in your sixth house, the emphasis turns to your daily work and service to others. Attend to details, and be careful not to overlook any seemingly minor matters that could take on importance. Keep up with your exercise plan, and watch your diet.

Friday, October 7 (Moon into Pisces, 9:14 p.m.) It's a number 9 day. Make room for something new. Clear your desk for tomorrow's new cycle. Visualize the future; set your goals, and then make them so. Look beyond the immediate. Strive for universal appeal.

Saturday, October 8 (Moon in Pisces) The focus turns to relationships, business and personal ones. You get along well with others and know how to approach people. You do whatever it takes to get accepted, and you're sensitive to the needs of others.

Sunday, October 9 (Moon in Pisces) Venus moves into your third house. You have a love of things from the past. You're artistic and creative. You get along well with family members and neighbors. You're also very persuasive in pursuing your ideas, but you're willing to compromise.

Monday, October 10 (Moon into Aries, 8:57 a.m.) The feeling of security is an important issue with you. Your experiences are more intense than usual. You have a strong sense of duty and feel obligated to fulfill your promises. It's a good time to get involved in a cause aimed at improving life for large numbers of people.

Tuesday, October 11 (Moon in Aries) There's a full moon in your eighth house. You gain illumination and insight related to whatever you share with another person. If you are planning on making a major purchase, make sure that you and your partner are in agreement. Otherwise, you could encounter intense emotional resistance. Issues of the day could include matters of sex, death, rebirth, rituals, and relationships. You reap what you've sown.

Wednesday, October 12 (Moon into Taurus, 9:35 p.m.)
Approach the day with an unconventional mind-set. Think freedom, no restrictions. You're versatile, changeable. Your creativity, personal grace, and magnetism are highlighted.

Thursday, October 13 (Moon in Taurus)   With Mercury moving into your third house, your mind is stimulated with new ideas. You express yourself well, and you're versatile, showing an interest and knowledge in several different fields. History and archaeology are two areas that might attract your attention.

Friday, October 14 (Moon in Taurus)   The moon is in your ninth house. It's a good time to plan a long journey to a foreign country. Alternately, you take a new interest in worldviews, ideas, philosophy, and mythology. Sign up for a workshop or seminar. Follow whatever opportunity opens for you.

Saturday, October 15 (Moon into Gemini, 10:15 a.m.)
Make room for something new. Clear up odds and ends; complete a project. Visualize the future; set your goals, and then make them so. Look beyond the immediate. Strive for universal appeal.

Sunday, October 16 (Moon in Gemini)   The moon is in your tenth house. Your tenacity is recognized. You gain an elevation in prestige related to your profession and career. Material success and financial security play a role in your day. You make a strong emotional commitment to your profession or to a role in public life.

Monday, October 17 (Moon into Cancer, 9:39 p.m.)
It's a number 1 day, and you're at the top of your cycle.

You get a fresh start. Be independent and creative. Stress originality. Trust your hunches; intuition is highlighted.

Tuesday, October 18 (Moon in Cancer)   The moon is in your eleventh house. Friends play an important role, especially Taurus and Capricorn. You find strength in numbers. You find meaning through a group of like-minded people working for a common good.

Wednesday, October 19 (Moon in Cancer)   Your home and personal life play a central role in your day. Spend time with family and loved ones. Tenderness is highlighted! Beautify your domestic scene. Take care of a home-repair project.

Thursday, October 20 (Moon into Leo, 6:07 a.m.)   It's a number 4 day. Your organizational skills are highlighted. Control your impulses. Take care of obligations. Emphasize quality. Tear down the old in order to rebuild. Be methodical and thorough. You're at the right place at the right time.

Friday, October 21 (Moon in Leo)   You might feel a need to withdraw and work behind the scenes. Things affecting the past play a role. Take time to reflect and meditate. Avoid any self-destructive tendencies. Communicate your deepest feelings to another person.

Saturday, October 22 (Moon into Virgo, 10:42 a.m.)   Focus on making people happy. Be sympathetic, kind, and compassionate. Avoid scattering your energies as you go about your day. Be aware that you could face emotional outbursts or someone making unfair demands. An adjustment in your domestic life may be necessary.

Sunday, October 23 (Moon in Virgo)   The moon is on your ascendant. The way you see yourself is the way others see you. You're recharged for the month ahead, and this makes you more appealing to the public. You're physically vital, and relations with the opposite sex go well. You're sensitive to other people's feelings.

Monday, October 24 (Moon into Libra, 11:50 a.m.) It's a number 8 day. You can go far with your plans and achieve financial success. Business discussions go well. You're playing with power, so be careful not to hurt others.

Tuesday, October 25 (Moon in Libra) The moon is in your second house. Expect emotional experiences related to money. You may be dealing with payments and collecting what's owed to you. You equate your financial assets with emotional security. Look at your priorities in handling your income.

Wednesday, October 26 (Moon into Scorpio, 11:09 a.m.) There's a new moon in your third house, and that indicates new opportunities related to your writing or speaking skills. Your mental abilities are strong now, and you have an emotional need to reinvigorate your studies, especially regarding matters of the past. It's a good time to begin a new project or get rid of an old habit. You accept an invitation to a social event that could involve relatives and neighbors.

Thursday, October 27 (Moon in Scorpio) Look for intense, emotional experiences today. You're passionate; your sexuality is heightened. Investigate, research, and dig deep. Be aware of things happening in secret and of possible deception. Forgive and forget; try to avoid going to extremes.

Friday, October 28 (Moon into Sagittarius, 10:46 a.m.) You're innovative and creative; you communicate well. Your artistic talents are highlighted. You see the big picture. Your attitude determines everything. Spread your good news. In romance, you're an ardent and loyal lover.

Saturday, October 29 (Moon in Sagittarius) The moon is in your fourth house. Spend time with your family and loved ones. Stick close to home. You're dealing with the foundations of who you are and who you are becoming. You could be dealing with parents or working on a home-improvement project.

Sunday, October 30 (Moon into Capricorn, 12:39 p.m.) Release old structures; get a new point of view. You're versatile, changeable. Be careful not to spread out and diversify too much. Promote new ideas; follow your curiosity. Look for adventure. Freedom of thought and action is key. But so is moderation; avoid excess in whatever you're doing.

Monday, October 31 (Moon in Capricorn) The moon is in your fifth house. You're emotionally in touch with your creative side, and that makes it a good day to pursue a creative or artistic project. Be yourself; be emotionally honest. In love, there's great emotional depth to a relationship. Take a chance; experiment. You're more protective and nurturing toward children.

NOVEMBER 2011

Tuesday, November 1 (Moon into Aquarius, 6:08 p.m.) Keep your goals in mind; follow your ideas. Be tenacious. It's best to stay with the tried and true. It's not a day for experimentation or new approaches. Be methodical and thorough. Tear down the old in order to rebuild. It's not a good day for pursuing romance, especially a new one.

Wednesday, November 2 (Moon in Aquarius) Mercury and Venus move into your fourth house. Mercury brings a substantial amount of mental activity into the home that could involve studying and research or debates on contested subjects. Venus, meanwhile, suggests a happy home life. You feel attached to the home and the domestic scene. You take great pride in your endeavors in your home.

Thursday, November 3 (Moon in Aquarius) The moon is in your sixth house. It's a service day. Others rely on you. You're the one they go to for help. You improve, edit, and refine their work. Clarify any health or work issues. It's best if you follow a regular schedule.

Friday, November 4 (Moon into Pisces, 3:18 a.m.) You work best on your own today. You're a spy for your own cause. Make sure that you see things as they are, not as you wish them to be. Knowledge is essential to success. Gather information, but don't make any absolute decisions until tomorrow. Go with the flow.

Saturday, November 5 (Moon in Pisces) Loved ones and partners are more important than usual. A legal matter comes to your attention. You get along well with others and feel a need to be accepted. You can fit in just about anywhere. You're looking for security, but you have a hard time going with the flow.

Sunday, November 6—Daylight Saving Time Ends (Moon into Aries, 2:02 p.m.) Finish what you started. Visualize the future; set your goals, and then make them so. Look beyond the immediate. Spiritual values arise. Take an inventory of where things are going in your life. Make a donation to a worthy cause.

Monday, November 7 (Moon in Aries) Your experiences are more intense than usual. Security is an important issue with you. It can affect your feelings about your possessions, as well as things that you share with others, such as a spouse. Get involved in a cause aimed at improving living conditions for large numbers of people.

Tuesday, November 8 (Moon in Aries) It's a great time for initiating projects, launching new ideas, and brainstorming. Emotions could be volatile, especially if you're dealing with shared resources. You're passionate but impatient. You're extremely persuasive, especially if you're committed to what you're doing, selling, or trying to convey.

Wednesday, November 9 (Moon into Taurus, 2:46 a.m.) Neptune goes direct in your sixth house. You feel as if it's your duty to help others. You might even see your task as heroic or in spiritual terms. However, everyday duties tend to be tedious and unappealing.

Thursday, November 10 (Moon in Taurus) There's a full moon in your ninth house. You gain insight and illumination related to higher education or plans for a foreign trip. Your mind is active, and you yearn for a new experience. You can create positive change through your ideas. You reap what you've sown.

Friday, November 11 (Moon into Gemini, 3:11 p.m.) With Mars moving into your ascendant, you're more assertive and self-confident than usual this month. You feel vital and outgoing. You also move right ahead into whatever you're doing rather than skirting around the edges and testing the waters.

Saturday, November 12 (Moon in Gemini) The moon is in your tenth house. You find meaning through friends and groups. There's strength in numbers. You work for the common good, and at the same time you keep your focus on your own wishes and dreams.

Sunday, November 13 (Moon in Gemini) You feel restless and need to communicate with others. Socialize and take a short trip for a gathering. You see two sides of an issue. You feel creative and need to express yourself.

Monday, November 14 (Moon into Cancer, 2:20 a.m.)
It's a number 8 day, a good day to buy a lottery ticket.
It's your power day and your day to play it your way. You
can go far with your plans and achieve financial success.
Unexpected money comes your way. Look for a windfall.

Tuesday, November 15 (Moon in Cancer) The
moon is in your eleventh house. Friends and associates,
especially members of a group, play a more important
role in your life. You work well with others, especially
Taurus and Capricorn. Focus on your wishes and dreams.
Examine your overall goals, and make sure that they're
still an expression of who you are.

Wednesday, November 16 (Moon into Leo, 11:18 a.m.)
It's a number 1 day, and you're at the top of your cycle.
Be independent and creative. Don't let others tell you
what to do. Get out and meet new people, and have new
experiences. Express your opinions dynamically.

Thursday, November 17 (Moon in Leo) The moon
is in your twelfth house. Take time to withdraw and work
behind the scenes. It's best to hide your emotions and
moodiness. Avoid stubbornness and any self-destructive
behavior. Things affecting the past play a role.

Friday, November 18 (Moon into Virgo, 5:20 p.m.)
Your attitude determines everything. Ease up on routines. Take time to relax, enjoy yourself, and recharge
your batteries. Have fun in preparation for discipline
and focus. In business dealings, diversify. Insist on all the
information, not just bits and pieces.

Saturday, November 19 (Moon in Virgo) The moon
is in your first house. You're dealing with your emotional self, the person you are becoming. You're sensitive to other people's feelings. The way you see yourself
is the way others see you. Your feelings and thoughts
are aligned.

Sunday, November 20 (Moon into Libra, 8:17 p.m.)
It's a number 5 day. Approach the day with an unconventional mind-set. Release old structures; get a new point of view. Variety is the spice of life. Think freedom, no restrictions. Change and variety are highlighted.

Monday, November 21 (Moon in Libra)   The moon is in your second house. Your values and what you value are highlighted today. You might react emotionally to a matter related to your personal finances. Whatever you value takes on greater importance. You feel best surrounded by your things.

Tuesday, November 22 (Moon into Scorpio, 8:59 p.m.)
You launch a journey into the unknown. Secrets, intrigue, and confidential information play a role. Be aware of decisions made behind closed doors. Make sure that you see things as they are, not as you wish them to be. Knowledge is essential to success.

Wednesday, November 23 (Moon in Scorpio)   The moon is in your third house. You can be quite opinionated, especially if you're talking with family members or neighbors. Try to stay in control of your emotions. You tend to be affected by the past.

Thursday, November 24 (Moon into Sagittarius, 8:58 p.m.)   Mercury goes retrograde in your second house and stays that way until December 13. That means you can expect some delays, misunderstandings, and miscommunication over the next three weeks, especially related to your home life or any work being done on your home. Relax and control your emotional reaction to situations.

Friday, November 25 (Moon in Sagittarius)   There's a solar eclipse in your fourth house. Expect new opportunities to arise related to your home and family. There

224

could be a new addition to your home, such as the birth of a child or construction of a new room.

Saturday, November 26 (Moon into Capricorn, 10:05 p.m.) Venus moves into your fifth house. Romance is definitely in the air. You appeal to the opposite sex. You're well liked, and you show your affection for children. Your artistic talents are highlighted.

Sunday, November 27 (Moon in Capricorn) The moon is in your fifth house as yesterday's energy flows into your Sunday. Your emotions tend to overpower your intellect. Be yourself. Be emotionally honest. In love, there's great emotional depth to a relationship. You're emotionally in touch with your creative side.

Monday, November 28 (Moon in Capricorn) Your ambition and drive to succeed are highlighted. Your responsibilities increase. You may feel stressed, overworked. Don't ignore your exercise routine. It's a good day to take a yoga class. Don't speculate or take any unnecessary risks. Maintain emotional balance. Other Virgos and Taurus play a role in your day.

Tuesday, November 29 (Moon into Aquarius, 2:02 a.m.) Promote new ideas; follow your curiosity. Approach the day with an unconventional mind-set. Think outside the box; get a new point of view. Change and variety are highlighted now. Think freedom, no restrictions.

Wednesday, November 30 (Moon in Aquarius) The moon is in your sixth house. Your personal health occupies your attention. Attend to details related to your health; make a doctor or dentist appointment. Keep your resolutions about exercise, and watch your diet. Be of service to others, but don't deny your own needs.

Thursday, December 1 (Moon into Pisces, 9:46 a.m.)
It's a number 5 day. Travel and variety are highlighted today. Variety is the spice of life. Think outside the box. Take risks; experiment. Think freedom, no restrictions. You're more comfortable than usual in front of an audience.

Friday, December 2 (Moon in Pisces)   The moon is in your seventh house. Partnerships are in the spotlight, private or business-related. Loved ones are more important than usual. Women play a prominent role. Be careful that others don't manipulate your feelings.

Saturday, December 3 (Moon into Aries, 8:52 p.m.)
Secrets, intrigue, and confidential information play a role in your day. You investigate, analyze, or simply observe what's going on. You quickly come to a conclusion and wonder why others don't see what you see. You detect deception and recognize insincerity with ease. Gather information, but don't make any absolute decisions until tomorrow. Go with the flow.

Sunday, December 4 (Moon in Aries)   The moon is in your eighth house. Your experiences are more intense than usual. Security is an important issue with you right now. It can affect your feelings about your possessions, as well as things that you share with others.

Monday, December 5 (Moon in Aries)   Emotions can get volatile. You're passionate but impatient. You're extremely persuasive, especially if you're passionate about what you're doing or selling or trying to convey. It's a great time for initiating projects, launching new ideas, and brainstorming.

Tuesday, December 6 (Moon into Taurus, 9:36 a.m.)
It's a number 1 day. You're at the top of your cycle again.

Get out and meet new people and have new experiences. Express your opinions dynamically. Stress originality.

Wednesday, December 7 (Moon in Taurus)   The moon is in your ninth house. Sign up for a workshop or seminar on a subject of interest. You could also follow your wanderlust and plan a long journey. Study and investigate possible destinations and sites along the way. You're a dreamer and a thinker, and you yearn for new experiences.

Thursday, December 8 (Moon into Gemini, 9:54 p.m.) Take time to relax, enjoy yourself, and recharge your batteries. You can influence people with your upbeat attitude. Your charm and wit are appreciated. Foster generosity. In romance, you're an ardent and loyal lover.

Friday, December 9 (Moon in Gemini)   Your life is more public. Business is highlighted. It's a good day for sales and dealing with the public. You're more emotional than usual regarding your work and business relationships. Be careful not to cross the line between your personal and professional lives.

Saturday, December 10 (Moon in Gemini)   There's a lunar eclipse in your tenth house. You could find emotional experiences surfacing related to your career, bosses, workplace, and coworkers. Stay in control of your emotions, especially in public. With Uranus going direct in your eighth house, you have a clearer belief about life after death or communication with the dead. You attract unusual people who may be geniuses in their field.

Sunday, December 11 (Moon into Cancer, 8:27 a.m.) It's a service day, and diplomacy wins the way. You offer advice and support. Be sympathetic and kind, generous and tolerant. Focus on making people happy. Avoid arguments.

Monday, December 12 (Moon in Cancer)   You have a deeper relationship with friends, especially Taurus and Capricorn. You feel highly emotional about a group effort. You work for the common good, and your heart is in the right place. Follow your wishes and dreams.

Tuesday, December 13 (Moon into Leo, 4:49 p.m.) Mercury goes direct in your fourth house. That means any confusion and miscommunication that you've experienced recently, especially related to your home life, recede into the past. Things move smoothly. You can take care of a home-repair project, especially one that has been put off. You get along better with family members.

Wednesday, December 14 (Moon in Leo)   With the moon in your twelfth house, withdraw and spend time in private. Relax and meditate. Keep your feelings to yourself, unless you confide in a close friend. Follow your intuition. It's a great day for a mystical or spiritual discipline.

Thursday, December 15 (Moon into Virgo, 10:59 p.m.) You're at the top of your cycle again. Trust your hunches. You're inventive; you make connections that others overlook. You're determined and courageous. A flirtation turns more serious.

Friday, December 16 (Moon in Virgo)   The moon is on your ascendant. The way you see yourself is the way others see you. Your face is in front of the public. You're recharged for the rest of the month, and this makes you more appealing to the public. Your appearance and personality shine. Your feelings and thoughts are aligned.

Saturday, December 17 (Moon in Virgo)   Yesterday's energy flows into your Saturday, but you're more sensitive to other people's feelings. You may feel moody one moment, happy the next, then withdrawn and sad. It's all about your emotional self and the person you are becoming. It's difficult to remain detached and objective.

Sunday, December 18 (Moon into Libra, 3:07 a.m.)
It's a number 4 day. Control your impulses. Fulfill your obligations. You're building foundations for an outlet for your creativity. Revise; rewrite. Emphasize quality. You're at the right place at the right time. Missing papers or objects are found.

Monday, December 19 (Moon in Libra) The moon is in your second house. Money and material goods are important to you and give you a sense of security. You have a tendency to collect things, and those objects make you feel at home and at peace. It's not the objects themselves that are important, but the feelings and memories you associate with them. Put off making any major purchases.

Tuesday, December 20 (Moon into Scorpio, 5:33 a.m.)
With Venus moving into your sixth house, an office romance is possible. Your routines will go smoothly for the next three weeks. Your relationships with coworkers and employees are warmer. A love affair in the office could develop, if you're interested.

Wednesday, December 21 (Moon in Scorpio) The moon is in your third house. Your mental abilities are strong, and you have an emotional need to express your ideas. Take what you know and share it with others, but keep conscious control of your emotions when communicating. Your thinking is unduly influenced by the past. You accept an invitation to a holiday gathering.

Thursday, December 22 (Moon into Sagittarius, 7:03 a.m.) It's a number 8 day, your power day. You get an opportunity to expand and grow. Be courageous. You're playing with power, so be careful not to hurt others. Be aware that others in power may be watching your moves.

Friday, December 23 (Moon in Sagittarius) With the moon in your fourth house, there's plenty of energy in your home life. Work at home if possible, or take the day off and work on a project to repair or beautify your house. Spend some time in quiet meditation. Recall your dreams.

Saturday, December 24 (Moon into Capricorn, 8:48 a.m.) There's a new moon in your fifth house. That indicates new opportunities related to a creative project coming your way. You also gain insight into a love relationship.

Sunday, December 25 (Moon in Capricorn) With Jupiter going direct in your ninth house, you expand your knowledge. You're looking at the big picture related to religion, philosophy, mythology, or higher education. Initiate plans for a long journey. You will benefit by foreign travel over the next year. Merry Christmas!

Monday, December 26 (Moon into Aquarius, 12:15 p.m.) Ease up on your routines, and spread your good news. You communicate well. You're warm and receptive to what others say. Your imagination is keen. You're curious and inventive. Enjoy the harmony, beauty, and pleasures of life. Beautify your home.

Tuesday, December 27 (Moon in Aquarius) With the moon in your sixth house, the emphasis turns to your daily work and service to others. Attend to all the details, Virgo. Be careful not to overlook any seemingly minor matters that could take on importance. Keep up with your exercise plan, and watch your diet. Don't let your fears hold you back. Help others, but don't deny your own needs.

Wednesday, December 28 (Moon into Pisces, 6:46 p.m.)
You're restless and looking for change, a new perspective. You're versatile and changeable, but don't make too many commitments now. Stay focused as best you can. Take risks; experiment. Pursue a new idea. Freedom of thought and action is key.

Thursday, December 29 (Moon in Pisces) The moon is in your seventh house. The focus turns to relationships, business and personal ones. You get along well with others and can fit in just about anywhere. You comprehend the nuances of a situation, but it's difficult to go with the flow. Be careful that others don't manipulate your feelings.

Friday, December 30 (Moon in Pisces) It's a day for deep healing. Imagination is highlighted. Watch for psychic events, synchronicities. Keep track of your dreams, including your daydreams. Ideas are ripe. Compassion, sensitivity, and inspiration are highlighted.

Saturday, December 31 (Moon into Aries, 4:49 a.m.)
It's your power day and your day to play it your way. You're in the power seat. Buy a lottery ticket. Take a risk. You attract financial success. Unexpected money arrives.

HAPPY NEW YEAR!

JANUARY 2012

Sunday, January 1 (Moon in Aries) You're quite the entrepreneur today, filled with ideas for the new year. Your main challenge is to garner support among family, friends, and coworkers and enlist their aid in implementing a big idea. Your penchant for details will be a major plus in this endeavor.

Monday, January 2 (Moon into Taurus, 5:17 p.m.)
Your emotions are grounded today, and your focus is bringing ideas to a practical, useful level. You may be more stubborn than you usually are, but that's fine if you're sure you're right. Just don't be stubborn out of spite.

Tuesday, January 3 (Moon in Taurus)   The moon joins expansive Jupiter in your ninth house. Thinking about foreign travel, Virgo? Make it more real by selecting a location and dates and then checking with online travel sites for the best deal. Visualize the trip happening. The more vivid the visualization, the greater the possibility that the trip will happen.

Wednesday, January 4 (Moon in Taurus)   Stick to your position, Virgo. You've got facts and figures on your side and can talk circles around the competition. Your worldview and/or spiritual beliefs are highlighted today. Perhaps a trip you want to take is actually part of a spiritual quest.

Thursday, January 5 (Moon into Gemini, 5:45 a.m.)
Your emotional focus is on career matters. Once Jupiter enters Gemini and your career area in June, you're in for a treat! Plant the right seeds now so that once Jupiter enters your professional picture, you can take advantage of all the opportunities that come your way.

Friday, January 6 (Moon in Gemini)   The moon and Mercury are compatible today, giving your communication skills a major boost. Don't hesitate to speak your mind. Ignore the naysayers who insist something can't be done the way you envision it. You've connected the dots and are on your way to implementing what you envision.

Saturday, January 7 (Moon into Cancer, 4:06 p.m.)
The Cancer moon is compatible with your earth-sign

sun. It brings a strong intuitive and emotional flavor to all the day's activities and interactions. Keep your social calendar open, so that you can enjoy the company of close friends today.

Sunday, January 8 (Moon in Cancer)   Mercury enters fellow earth sign Capricorn, where it will be until January 27. This transit brings real drive to your communication skills and career ambitions. It also forms a beneficial angle with Jupiter in Taurus—and to your sun—so you are in rare shape for much of the month. Proceed fearlessly.

Monday, January 9 (Moon into Leo, 11:35 p.m.)   The full moon in Cancer (before it enters Leo) highlights friends, groups, and your wishes and dreams for yourself. Expect news about one of these areas. There could also be news about your mother or her equivalent—a nurturing figure.

Tuesday, January 10 (Moon in Leo)   With the moon in Leo and your solar twelfth house, you may want to lie back and chill today, preferably by yourself or with a couple of close friends. Do your work from home, through the Internet and e-mail. You'll have a chance to strut yourself when the moon transits your sign between January 12 and 14.

Wednesday, January 11 (Moon in Leo)   Your own psyche is wide open to you today, so dive in and figure out your motives, true dreams, and aspirations. Try to resolve old issues that may surface. You have a lot of insight into your unconscious and may get even more information with some sort of divination system.

Thursday, January 12 (Moon into Virgo, 4:44 a.m.) It's your day. The moon is in your sign, so the inner and outer you are in total agreement. You may be a tad too picky today—toward others or yourself—so it's to your advantage to back off on criticisms. It may sound hokey, but the old Dale Carnegie adage still holds true—don't criticize, condemn, or complain!

Friday, January 13 (Moon in Virgo)   Life goes your way today. Not only are Mars and the moon in your sign, but Mercury, Jupiter, and Pluto are in fellow earth signs. In other words, the astrological deck is so stacked in your favor, Virgo, that you should be able to make tremendous headway in any area you choose.

Saturday, January 14 (Moon into Libra, 8:29 a.m.) Venus enters Pisces, your opposite sign, where it will be until February 8. This transit bodes well for all the partnerships in your life, but if you're in a committed relationship, things should be stellar. Plan something special this evening with the one you love.

Sunday, January 15 (Moon in Libra)   Emotionally, you're focused on your finances—how you earn and spend money, what you believe and think about money. You may be worried that you don't earn enough or that you spend too much. Instead, focus on appreciating what you do have, so that the universe will bring you more of it!

Monday, January 16 (Moon into Scorpio, 11:34 a.m.) The Scorpio moon is compatible with your earth-sign sun and brings a deep intensity and intuition to everything you do. This intensity is especially true in your communication today. You're after the bottom line, Virgo, and won't stop until you find it.

Tuesday, January 17 (Moon in Scorpio)   Passions run deep today. You may be spending time with siblings or neighbors and find that you have to bite your tongue to keep from saying something the other person won't want to hear. This moon forms a beautiful angle to Venus in Pisces, so it would be a great time to delve into a creative project that requires imagination.

Wednesday, January 18 (Moon into Sagittarius, 2:30 p.m.)   Once the moon enters Sagittarius, a situation at home or someone in your personal life requires additional attention from you. You seem to grasp the larger picture and are able to do exactly what's needed. Restlessness may shadow you throughout the day, so be sure you have an exercise routine that takes your mind off things.

Thursday, January 19 (Moon in Sagittarius)   Yesterday's situation could turn into today's nightmare if you don't intervene and resolve the issue, whatever it is. Sometimes confrontation is the only way to move on. It doesn't mean the confrontation has to be loud or nasty, just decisive.

Friday, January 20 (Moon into Capricorn, 5:42 p.m.) Ah. Late this afternoon the moon enters Capricorn, and the tension eases up. You're ready for a long, lazy evening with your current romantic interest. Or you get moving on a creative project and are delighted to find that your muse is ready and willing to help.

Saturday, January 21 (Moon in Capricorn)   Your physical energy is remarkable. You're like the Energizer battery—you just never quit. So tackle everything you've put off and then some. You'll be burning the midnight oil tonight. If travel is one of your greatest pleasures, then take a virtual trip sometime today and figure out your next destination!

Sunday, January 22 (Moon into Aquarius, 9:54 p.m.) You may spend the day figuring out your agenda for the upcoming week. You're looking for cutting-edge ideas, future trends, new ways of doing things to make your job easier or more meaningful. You'll find them, Virgo. You're the zodiac's expert at connecting the dots!

Monday, January 23 (Moon in Aquarius) With today's new moon in Aquarius, new opportunities surface in your daily work and the maintenance of your daily health. Perhaps someone gives you a gym membership. Or maybe you land a nice promotion that also increases your pay. Whatever the opportunities are, you seem quite pleased!

Tuesday, January 24 (Moon in Aquarius) Go for it. Change is in the air, and you're primed, ready. Embrace whatever comes your way today—unless you feel resistance. In that case, reach for better and more positive thoughts, and explore your emotional resistance; then let it go.

Wednesday, January 25 (Moon into Pisces, 4:12 a.m.) The moon joins Venus in Pisces, in your opposite sign. This combination brings your attention to your spouse or partner—or to a business partner. Venus here suggests the arts and creativity and/or money. So perhaps you and your partner embark on a creative journey together, or you find the right partner for your business. Either way, money and the arts are part of the picture.

Thursday, January 26 (Moon in Pisces) Imagination can sometimes work to your disadvantage if you let it run wild. Try to pour it into a project or visualization for something you really desire. Or experiment with your psychic ability, and attempt to see tomorrow's headlines. Jot down your impressions.

Friday, January 27 (Moon into Aries, 1:29 p.m.) Mercury enters Aquarius, where it will be until February 13. This transit ramps up your daily work life. You may have more contact than usual with coworkers or employees or may be doing more writing—perhaps a newsletter, blog, even a Web site. You're very on top of things, and the people around you know it.

236

Saturday, January 28 (Moon in Aries) This probably isn't your favorite lunar transit. The Aries moon may make you impatient and frustrated, or you may feel rushed, constantly pressed for time. It's to your advantage to pause when you feel that way and take a few deep breaths. Think before you speak. And take up yoga! If you have a yoga practice already, carve out extra time for additional yoga today.

Sunday, January 29 (Moon in Aries) You share your time, money, and energy today without expecting compensation. Or someone else does such for you, maybe your partner or spouse. Maybe the help is extended to or comes from a stranger. Be alert; be compassionate.

Monday, January 30 (Moon into Taurus, 1:29 a.m.) The last two days of January fit you like the proverbial glove. You're more practical today, more grounded, and there's a certain sensuality about you that attracts attention from a possible romantic interest. If you're involved already, then your partner is paying close attention to you. Nice, isn't it, Virgo?

Tuesday, January 31 (Moon in Taurus) If you've thought about going to grad school or to college, now is the time to get the ball rolling for the next fall enrollment. Set goals. Figure out how you're going to reach those goals. Then set things in motion. Sometimes all it takes is a firm decision to move ahead.

FEBRUARY 2012

Wednesday, February 1 (Moon into Gemini, 2:15 p.m.) Emotionally, you may feel torn in two directions. Discuss it with a boss, peer, friend, or family member. Your communication abilities are strong today, and it helps to talk and write about whatever is bothering you. Professional matters are front and center.

Thursday, February 2 (Moon in Gemini) Move forward with your projects and activities at work. It's a good day to get your desk cleared, to tie up loose ends, and basically consolidate before the weekend. You'll want to have your time free and unfettered this weekend so you can enjoy yourself!

Friday, February 3 (Moon in Gemini) Neptune enters Pisces, your opposite sign, where it will be for the next fourteen years. Read more about this transit in the Big Picture for your sign. One possible repercussion is that your ideals will become vastly more important in all your partnerships. Your intuitive ability should deepen too, particularly in regard to a spouse or partner.

Saturday, February 4 (Moon into Cancer, 1:04 a.m.) This water-sign moon is more to your liking and compatible with your earth-sign sun. It highlights friends and social functions, so get out there and enjoy yourself. You might consider having an impromptu party at your place—nothing fancy, just a few friends and great conversation and music.

Sunday, February 5 (Moon in Cancer) This moon forms a strong angle to your sun and to Mars in your sign. Your intuitive energy is strong, and you're able to figure out people and situations without much effort. You may be nurturing a friend. One of your parents is highlighted today, too.

Monday, February 6 (Moon into Leo, 8:24 a.m.) You may be tackling tricky people today—through e-mail or by phone, but probably not in person. Avoid confrontation, keep your plans to yourself, but try to clear the air. You can be tactful when you need to be, Virgo. Use diplomacy today.

Tuesday, February 7 (Moon in Leo) Today's full moon in Leo brings an old issue into stark relief. Deal with it. There could also be news about someone from the past. Saturn turns retrograde in Libra, in your solar second house, and remains that way until June 25. During this period, be sure you have your financial ducks in a row. Stay on top of bank accounts, credit card payments, and the like.

Wednesday, February 8 (Moon into Virgo, 12:33 p.m.) Venus enters Aries and your solar eighth house, where it will be until March 5. This transit should make it easier for you to obtain loans and mortgages, but also brings a kind of restless passion to your love life. You're filled with entrepreneurial ideas and can use that legendary Virgo penchant for details to nail down the specifics. With the moon in your sign today, you're in tiptop shape to take on just about anything.

Thursday, February 9 (Moon in Virgo) With the moon and Mars both in your sign, you're able to move through your day with utter confidence. In a sense, you can do no wrong because you believe in yourself so strongly. Take on detail work today, stuff you ordinarily shove aside. Tomorrow, you'll be glad you did.

Friday, February 10 (Moon into Libra, 2:55 p.m.) Artistic sensibilities soar today. You may be trying to figure out how to make your art, writing, or some other creative endeavor pay off. Do some research on the Internet. Join online groups that share your creative interests. Do your homework; find the facts.

Saturday, February 11 (Moon in Libra) Balance and harmony are high on your list today. You may end up mediating an argument or heated discussion. It's easy for you to walk in someone else's shoes, to see the world as this person does. It brings greater understanding of the person's situation—and your own.

Sunday, February 12 (Moon into Scorpio, 5:02 p.m.) Secrets, what's hidden, the bottom line: that's the tone for the day. Your intuition is strong, and you're able to use it during your normal activities throughout the day. Synchronicities—meaningful coincidences—abound! Figure out the message.

Monday, February 13 (Moon in Scorpio)   Mercury enters Pisces, your opposite sign, so it's time for a heart-to-heart with your business or romantic partner. What you learn should delight you. Your imagination is gearing up for something big, so be sure to jot notes on ideas that occur to you. You'll be able to use them later.

Tuesday, February 14 (Moon into Sagittarius, 7:57 p.m.)   Happy Valentine's Day! With both Mercury and Neptune in your opposite sign, be sure to make time for the one you love. Buy a gift that expresses your true feelings. It doesn't have to be expensive, merely personal and meaningful.

Wednesday, February 15 (Moon in Sagittarius)   With the moon in a fire sign, in your solar fourth house, you grasp the larger picture about your family and personal environment. Now you simply have to act on what you know to bring about changes. If you're considering an overseas trip, now is the time to plan.

Thursday, February 16 (Moon in Sagittarius)   Feeling a bit restless, Virgo? Then start the day with some yoga postures and a few minutes of meditation. These two practices will help to ground you and start you off on the right path today. Your plate is full, and you have to use your time wisely.

Friday, February 17 (Moon into Capricorn, 12:04 a.m.)   This earth-sign moon is friendlier for you and forms a beneficial angle to Mercury in Pisces, to your sun sign, and to Mars in your sign. The combination serves to bolster your career ambitions, brings your feeling toward romance and love, and generally grounds you. Could it be, Virgo, that the one you love is also someone with whom you work?

Saturday, February 18 (Moon in Capricorn) If you live in the northern hemisphere, then chances are that by February you're ready to blow the cold and head for warmer climates. Perhaps you and your partner or a friend should get away for a long weekend. Pick a spot where the sun shines and the beaches beckon!

Sunday, February 19 (Moon into Aquarius, 5:29 a.m.) As you work up to the new moon in Pisces on the twenty-first, you feel a shift in the air. Your ability to think way outside the box is enhanced under the Aquarian moon, however, so make good use of the energy. Plan today for what you would like the new moon on the twenty-first to bring into your life. New relationships? A new job with better pay? Something else?

Monday, February 20 (Moon in Aquarius) You're able to breeze through your work day with a minimum of hassles. The Aquarius moon enables you to detach emotionally and simply move on through whatever challenges you encounter. It's a good feeling, isn't it?

Tuesday, February 21 (Moon into Pisces, 12:32 p.m.) Today's new moon in Pisces should bring new partnership opportunities—personally and professionally. If you're involved already, then you and your partner may be taking the relationship to the next level. Maybe you move in together or get engaged or married. Maybe you decide to start a family.

Wednesday, February 22 (Moon in Pisces) Your imagination is as expansive as the great outdoors. Every scrap of information, every thought, feeling, and intuition is caught in the net of your imagination and converted into something magical. You might as well take the day off from work, Virgo, and lose yourself in a creative project. Your imagination will thank you!

Thursday, February 23 (Moon into Aries, 9:48 p.m.)
You and your partner usually see eye to eye on the important issues. But with Neptune also in Pisces, there could be some confusion between you. Neptune blurs the boundaries between self and others and leaves no room for ego. So speak from the heart.

Friday, February 24 (Moon in Aries)   Every bit the entrepreneur today, you figure you can go it alone and accomplish everything on your list before noon. Think again. Enlist the help of others, if you need to. Delegate responsibility to coworkers. The job will get done much more quickly, and you won't feel stressed.

Saturday, February 25 (Moon in Aries)   Life could be a bit frantic today, chaotic. You may feel pressed for time. But perhaps it's because you've left all your personal chores for the weekend instead of spreading them out through the week. So next week do it differently. Create a new MO for yourself!

Sunday, February 26 (Moon into Taurus, 9:30 a.m.)
The Taurus moon feels like an old friend with whom you enjoy spending time. You might be attending a workshop or seminar concerning a topic that intrigues you. Or perhaps you're cooking up a storm, trying new recipes. Or—another Taurean pursuit—maybe you're creating a garden of some sort. If you live where it's cold now, it could be an indoor garden or simply adding plants that bring beauty to your surroundings.

Monday, February 27 (Moon in Taurus)   Your life feels solid and grounded, and the feeling radiates from you and affects the people around you. Your worldview and/or spiritual beliefs come into play today, perhaps through a conversation with a foreigner. You're updating your Facebook page, your Web site, your blog.

Tuesday, February 28 (Moon into Gemini, 10:28 p.m.)
Your career takes center stage today. You may be pitching ideas and pushing your projects forward and have to communicate your ideas to bosses and peers to gain their support. Don't worry about it. You're adept at thinking on your feet and can easily play to the mood of the crowd.

Wednesday, February 29 (Moon in Gemini) It's leap year, remember? With the moon still in Gemini, you're in rare form, rushing ahead faster than the competition. Your ideas are strong and vivid in your mind. If you need to put something in writing, though, give it thought, and organize the ideas so others really understand what you're saying.

MARCH 2012

Thursday, March 1 (Moon in Gemini) It's a prime day to pitch ideas to bosses and coworkers and to communicate your ideas to whoever will listen! You may be working longer hours to meet a deadline—self-imposed or otherwise—or simply to clear your desk before the weekend. With Mars still in your sign—until July 3 your physical energy is plentiful, and you're able to get things done.

Friday, March 2 (Moon into Cancer, 10:09 a.m.)
Mercury enters Aries today, where it will be until May 9 because it will be retrograde part of the time. Read about the retrograde in the Big Picture section for your sign. While Mercury is moving direct, your mind is sharp, edgy, fearless. You try new things, test out new ideas, and seek a niche in the market that your skills or product might fill.

Saturday, March 3 (Moon in Cancer)   With the moon in nurturing Cancer, you may be spending time with a friend or friends who are in need of emotional support. Or perhaps a friend extends her compassion toward you. You also may feel drawn toward group activities with people whose passions are like yours. It's a good day to intuitively explore your wishes and dreams and to visualize what you desire.

Sunday, March 4 (Moon into Leo, 6:19 p.m.)   With the moon entering your solar twelfth house this evening, you may be ready to kick back and tackle your own psyche. Wrestle it to the floor, Virgo! Find out what your true motives are, and heed the guidance you receive in dreams and meditations. You're preparing the way for the moon entering your sign on the sixth.

Monday, March 5 (Moon in Leo)   Venus enters fellow earth sign Taurus today and remains there until April 3. During this transit, your love life and creativity should hum along pleasantly. This transit certainly favors foreign travel, business dealings with foreign countries, and even love and romance while you're traveling.

Tuesday, March 6 (Moon into Virgo, 10:28 p.m.)   The moon enters your sign late tonight, so it's a good time to prepare for whatever you're taking on tomorrow. Line up your priorities, lay down your strategy, connect the dots. On a personal level too this transit suits you. Your head and heart are in complete agreement.

Wednesday, March 7 (Moon in Virgo)   Get ready for tomorrow's full moon in your sign. If fact, you may be feeling its effects today, with a lot of general craziness around you. Stick to what you know today and don't implement anything new just yet. Be fearless, but keep your secrets to yourself!

Thursday, March 8 (Moon into Libra, 11:51 p.m.)
Today's full moon in Virgo occurs at 4:40 a.m., and
thanks to a close conjunction from Mars, you've got
plenty of drive, energy, and ambition. Don't be reckless,
however. Move through your day at the same measured
pace that you bring to all facets of your life.

Friday, March 9 (Moon in Libra)   The Libra moon
strives to bring you into emotional balance. Consider
the areas of your life where you feel an imbalance, and
figure out how to rectify the situation. Perhaps you need
more free time or feel you should be spending more
time with your family. Or maybe you feel you must de-
vote more time to launching your own business. Whatever your concern, time may be at the heart of it all.

Saturday, March 10 (Moon in Libra)   If you haven't
read *The Law of Attraction* by Esther and Jerry Hicks,
buy the book today and get started. It will help you to
realize how you create your reality from the inside out,
through your focus and beliefs. With the moon in your
financial sector, the book could help you realize how to
attract more money!

***Sunday, March 11—Daylight Saving Time Begins
(Moon into Scorpio, 1:25 a.m.)***   With the moon
in compatible water sign Scorpio, you're set up nicely
today for research, investigation, and psychic development. In fact, your intuition should be quite strong today and tomorrow, and it would be beneficial to heed
that inner voice. With Mercury turning retrograde tomorrow in Aries, be sure to back up computer files, finalize travel plans, and make your submissions.

Monday, March 12 (Moon in Scorpio)   Mercury
turns retrograde and will remain that way until April
4. Reread the section on Mercury retrogrades in your
sign's Big Picture section. One possible repercussion of
the retrograde is that old issues and old friends, lovers,

and ex-partners surface. The best advice for this period is to revise, rethink, review.

Tuesday, March 13 (Moon into Sagittarius, 2:54 a.m.)
You're on the go today, and the pace you keep is wild, frantic. By the time you pause to breathe and gather your thoughts, you pinpoint the source of your need to move at such a pace. Be sure to carve out time for your family and loved ones.

Wednesday, March 14 (Moon in Sagittarius) Unless you have planets in fire signs, this moon probably isn't your favorite. However, it enables you to adapt emotionally to a fluid situation and roll with the punches. Just remember to offer no resistance to events. Accept what is, and move on.

Thursday, March 15 (Moon into Capricorn, 6:24 a.m.)
The day shapes up perfectly. With the moon, Venus, Mars, and Pluto all in earth signs, you are firmly grounded and are seeking practical methods and solutions. In the romance department, Venus in Taurus brings a certain sensuality that manifests itself in a craving for good foods, an excellent wine, and quality time spent with the one you love.

Friday, March 16 (Moon in Capricorn) If you don't have a regular exercise routine yet, today is an ideal day to start one. Design something that you know you'll do daily or five times a week minimum. You may also want to experiment with new nutritional programs, vitamins, herbs, and even alternative therapies.

Saturday, March 17 (Moon into Aquarius, 12:12 p.m.)
Think of the Aquarius moon as the visionary's moon. You can use the visionary ability in any way you want. If you have today off, imagine how your house would look if you had the money, time, and energy to overhaul it. What would you change? Colors? Furniture? Wallpa-

per? Figure out how much the overhaul would cost, and then decide how to implement these changes.

Sunday, March 18 (Moon in Aquarius)   How far can you take an idea today? You may want to get together with friends or coworkers and brainstorm. Or do the same with your family. Are all of you on the same page? Do you have the same goals? What can you change in your ideas to make them practical and appealing to a wider audience?

Monday, March 19 (Moon into Pisces, 8:05 p.m.) Your partner or spouse is your focus today as the moon joins Neptune in Pisces, your opposite sign. The two of you could become involved in some sort of charity or volunteer function. If you're animal lovers, then perhaps you and your partner volunteer at your local shelter and decide to foster animals until they're adopted.

Tuesday, March 20 (Moon in Pisces)   Your imagination is expansive, all encompassing. You may feel you live with a foot in two worlds—daily reality and the world of imagination and dreams. Your ideals are front and center in your life for today and tomorrow. What do you value most and why?

Wednesday, March 21 (Moon in Pisces)   Once you realize that change begins with just one person, you know you're on the right track. The only question is how to bring about the change you envision. With your skill for details, you solve the challenge and move full steam ahead.

Thursday, March 22 (Moon into Aries, 5:58 a.m.) Today's new moon in Aries ushers in new opportunities to be an entrepreneur, a trailblazer, a pioneer. You're like the *Star Trek* motto, boldly going where no one has gone before. With both Mercury and Uranus conjunct this moon, the opportunities could involve writing or some other form of communication, and they surface quickly and unexpectedly. Be on your toes, Virgo, prepared to move at a moment's notice.

Friday, March 23 (Moon in Aries) One such opportunity that could accompany yesterday's new moon is breaks on insurance, taxes, and mortgages. Or, equally possible, you have an opportunity to hone your intuitive ability, have a past-life regression, or investigate some facet of psychic phenomena.

Saturday, March 24 (Moon into Taurus, 5:44 p.m.) The moon joins Jupiter in Taurus, in your solar ninth house, and you may be thinking of some foreign port that calls to you in dreams. You may also be considering college or grad school. If so, set things in motion now for fall of 2013. Get your ducks lined up, Virgo. The better prepared you are, the greater your success.

Sunday, March 25 (Moon in Taurus) You may be quite stubborn today about an issue, situation, or relationship. It's probably a good thing too, as someone may be pushing you to do something you don't want to do. Just stick to what you know, Virgo, and don't worry about everyone else.

Monday, March 26 (Moon in Taurus) Your worldview and spiritual beliefs may be front and center in your day. Perhaps someone is challenging what you believe, and you feel you must defend those beliefs. But the bottom line, Virgo, is that you're not here to defend yourself. You're here to explore, learn, and enjoy.

Tuesday, March 27 (Moon into Gemini, 6:44 a.m.) With the gift of gab today, you're able to sell anything to anyone. Whether it's a product or an idea, you show your complete grasp of what you're doing, and that's what convinces the other guy that your product or idea is worth its weight in gold. Just try not to talk circles around your boss. He or she may resent it!

Wednesday, March 28 (Moon in Gemini) Remember that unfinished manuscript in a bottom desk drawer? Get it out, dust it off, and get to work. You've got plenty to say and wisdom and stories to share, and there's no time like the present. Believe in what you're doing. After all, if you don't believe, no one else will either.

Thursday, March 29 (Moon into Cancer, 7:08 p.m.) With the moon in Cancer most of the weekend, set up your social schedule this evening. If there's nothing special on your calendar yet, then consider having a party or some sort of get-together at your place. Mercury is still retrograde, so hold off on new projects until after April 4.

Friday, March 30 (Moon in Cancer) Despite the retrograde, you feel superb when you wake up, and that feeling probably follows you throughout the day. There could be some moments of nostalgia for the good ole days—whenever they were. It might be triggered by a certain scent. Remind yourself that your point of power lies in the present.

Saturday, March 31 (Moon in Cancer) If you live in the northern latitudes, can you now smell the approach of spring? If so, this boosts your sense of optimism and general mood. Throughout the day, practice what Esther and Jerry Hicks call rampaging appreciation—find something in your environment to appreciate and then something else and something else . . . You get the idea, right?

APRIL 2012

Sunday, April 1 (Moon into Leo, 4:37 a.m.) This moon works for you if you have natal planets in fire signs, or if you think of it as spring cleaning. Instead of closets, you're cleaning out the basement of your psyche—old issues, power you have disowned over the years, the worn wishes and dreams you buried. Psychic housecleaning.

Monday, April 2 (Moon in Leo)   In some area of your life today you shine, and your peers recognize you for a job well done. Accept the recognition with thanks and appreciation, and then get on with whatever you're doing. In two days, Mercury turns direct again, and you'll be able to move forward with plans and projects.

Tuesday, April 3 (Moon into Virgo, 9:54 a.m.)   Venus enters Gemini and your tenth house of career today. This transit, which ends August 7, should spell a nice period of professional success and ease. The tides move with you. Others accept your ideas and admire your drive and ambition. Venus will be retrograde, though, between May 15 and June 27, so consider that period one of dormancy, when your love life may suffer some bumps and bruises.

Wednesday, April 4 (Moon in Virgo)   Finally. Mercury turns direct in Pisces, your opposite sign. Wait a few days before you bring things full speed ahead. With the moon and Mars still in your sign, you're at the top of your game. Make it count! Do important stuff today. Prioritize.

Thursday, April 5 (Moon into Libra, 11:33 a.m.)
Remember that Saturn is in Libra until October 29, and whenever the moon and Saturn link up, your emotions may feel constricted, stymied. It's important to have an outlet for these feelings, and physical exercise is one option. Meditation is another. Even better, take a yoga class.

Friday, April 6 (Moon in Libra)   Today's full moon in Libra could bring news about a relationship, your finances, even about an artistic project. There may be more structure to the day than there ordinarily is during a full moon, and you have Saturn to thank for that. It forms a wide conjunction to this moon. You might, for instance, receive a check, the kind of structure we all anticipate!

Saturday, April 7 (Moon into Scorpio, 11:18 a.m.) Your siblings or other relatives may play a role in today's activities. Or perhaps someone in your community figures into the day's events. Regardless of who it is, you're prepared to help and be of service. There's an element of heightened sexuality and secrecy with this moon too.

Sunday, April 8 (Moon in Scorpio)   Intensity and secrecy are hallmarks today. You may be involved in something—a project or relationship—that you don't want others to know about. Equally possible is that someone is keeping secrets from you. It's a perfect day for research, investigation, and getting the real scoop on just about anything.

Monday, April 9 (Moon into Sagittarius, 11:13 a.m.) Today's fire-sign moon can work on you in several ways—a restlessness that's hard to pin down, a grasp of the larger picture, a need to travel. But it can also fire up your passions and get you involved in causes. You might, for instance, volunteer at a homeless shelter or an animal shelter. Or you might attend an antiwar demonstration.

Tuesday, April 10 (Moon in Sagittarius)   Pluto turns retrograde in Capricorn, in your solar fifth house, and remains that way until September 17. One possible ramification is that people you have known and loved in the past reappear in your life. Your ambition may not be quite as pronounced as it has been.

Wednesday, April 11 (Moon into Capricorn, 1:02 p.m.)
Romance and creativity may go hand in hand today.
Perhaps you and your partner are working on a creative
project together. Or one of you serves as the other's
muse. It's also a good day for just getting out and enjoying yourself. What a concept, right?

Thursday, April 12 (Moon in Capricorn)   With
Mercury now moving direct in Pisces, you and your
partner may be discussing issues in your relationship.
There's nothing contentious about the conversation. In
fact, you are both delighted to discover that what drew
you together to start with is still alive and well.

Friday, April 13 (Moon into Aquarius, 5:48 p.m.)
You're gearing up for a busy weekend and strive to
get your desk cleared off, obligations met. This air-sign
moon livens up your intellect and moves you away from
that constant, nagging voice of self-criticism. You are
a diamond that is already beautiful, Virgo. No need to
keep polishing and perfecting.

Saturday, April 14 (Moon in Aquarius)   Group activities are front and center today. The group can be a
family, friends, even strangers who share your interests
and passions. Or you may be attending a seminar or
workshop. Just be sure to have your business card handy.

Sunday, April 15 (Moon in Aquarius)   As the old
Grace Slick song says, "Feed your head." Today that
means books, art films, conversation with friends. It
could also mean an online community where stories are
shared, messages are posted, and friendships are started.
And yes, here in the U.S., it's also tax day!

Monday, April 16 (Moon into Pisces, 1:38 a.m.)
Mercury enters Aries, where it will be until May 9. You
experienced this same transit between March 2 and
12, before Mercury went retrograde, so you probably

252

know what to expect. But just to remind you, this transit brings discussions about taxes, insurance, and things that go bump in the night. It's a good time to consult an attorney about drawing up a will.

Tuesday, April 17 (Moon in Pisces)   With Venus still in Gemini and your career sector, professional matters should continue to run smoothly. You may be hobnobbing with bosses and the higher-ups at an office party or some other social gathering. You're planting seeds now for what will blossom during Jupiter's transit of your career area, which runs from June 11, 2012, to June 25, 2013.

Wednesday, April 18 (Moon into Aries, 12:00 p.m.) The moon joins Mercury and Uranus in Aries, a powerful combination that brings sudden, unexpected events. You could feel somewhat edgy and restless today due to this trio, and it's best to work it off by engaging in physical activity. Take a run. Go for a long walk. Do some yoga.

Thursday, April 19 (Moon in Aries)   Today could be a repeat of yesterday. The same energies dominate. If you don't have a regular exercise routine already, then start one. Sign up for a gym membership. Buy a block of yoga classes. If it's spring where you live, you'll want to be outside, so perhaps your exercise routine can include spirited walking.

Friday, April 20 (Moon in Aries)   With Saturn in your financial sector until October 5, you may be feeling a money pinch. The best way to mitigate it is to create and stick to a budget. Try to pay for everything in cash, so that you're more aware of what you buy and how much you pay for it. Leave your credit cards and debit card at home.

Saturday, April 21 (Moon into Taurus, 12:06 a.m.) Today's new moon in Taurus should be lovely for you.

You can expect new opportunities to surface in publishing, education, foreign travel. Your product and/or services may expand to overseas markets. You may have an opportunity to work for better pay. Neptune forms a beneficial angle to this new moon, suggesting your ideals are involved.

Sunday, April 22 (Moon in Taurus)   This earth-sign moon feels like home to you, Virgo. It brings emotional stability and a solid, intuitive base from which to live your day. You're able to finish what you start and exhibit great resoluteness and fortitude. You're also more stubborn than usual, which may confuse the people around you.

Monday, April 23 (Moon into Gemini, 1:06 p.m.) You start a blog, a Web site, a newsletter. Or all three. In some way, shape, or form, today is about communicating your ideas and wisdom. It's about spreading the word. If there's something about which you feel passionate—a topic, interest, cause—then that's your focus.

Tuesday, April 24 (Moon in Gemini)   Gossip and rumors swirl at work. Ignore all of it, and look for the facts on your own. Do your research. Balance what you discover factually with how you feel intuitively. Then make your decision. Always, always ignore the people who say that something can't be done the way you're envisioning.

Wednesday, April 25 (Moon in Gemini)   Emotionally fluid: that's you today. Your mood fluctuates between highs and lows and everything in between. Just roll with it. Tomorrow's moon in Cancer will be more to your liking.

Thursday, April 26 (Moon into Cancer, 1:43 a.m.) Intuitively you're right on. Today is all about how you feel and why. If you have a hunch, definitely follow it. If you experience resistance to an idea or course of action, then reach for more positive thoughts. Your mother or another nurturing female in your life has advice you should consider.

Friday, April 27 (Moon in Cancer)   You and your partner may meet with like-minded friends for a small get-together this evening. Or, if you're not in a committed relationship, you spend time with friends. Regardless of how things shake out, keep your options—and your social calendar—open for today.

Saturday, April 28 (Moon into Leo, 12:11 p.m.)   The Leo moon asks that you shine and perform beyond the call of duty. You rise to the occasion admirably and then turn your attention inward for some psychic house-cleaning. Remember that the Leo moon enables you to tie up loose ends and clear the deck, all in preparation for when the moon enters your sign.

Sunday, April 29 (Moon in Leo)   Down deep in your psyche is a private spot where you go to figure things out and work through issues, situations, relationships. You may do this through meditation, divination techniques, even through dreams. Any inner work you do today pays off in the long run.

Monday, April 30 (Moon into Virgo, 7:03 p.m.)   The moon enters your sign this evening. It's a relief, isn't it? Now you can really get on with the business of living, working, and loving, and feel good about everything you do.

MAY 2012

Tuesday, May 1 (Moon in Virgo)   You're in the groove, Virgo. Remember how this feels so that on days when you don't feel as terrific as you do now you can conjure the same emotions and transform your day. Your inner and outer worlds are in complete synch, and the usual self-nagging voice is barely a whisper in the back of your mind. Mars is still in your sign too, so even your physical energy and sexuality are in perfect alignment.

Wednesday, May 2 (Moon into Libra, 10:04 p.m.) Your artistic interests take over today. Whether your projects are professional or personal or both, this moon prompts a deeper awareness of color, texture, and message and how the three combine to create a pleasing product. You're after greater balance.

Thursday, May 3 (Moon in Libra) You may act as a negotiator or middle man today in a heated discussion or argument. You're able to see and defend both viewpoints. Your finances may be an area of focus too. Stay on top of financial statements. Know where your money is going and why.

Friday, May 4 (Moon into Scorpio, 10:20 p.m.) As you approach tomorrow's full moon in Scorpio, life may get a bit nuts. A lot of people may suddenly want/expect your attention or presence, and you're not in the mood for any of it. Your laserlike insight delivers the real scoop on what's going on.

Saturday, May 5 (Moon in Scorpio) The full moon in Scorpio brings news and/or insight into a relationship with a sibling or other relative. If you're looking for a neighborhood more amenable to what you and your family need and want, this full moon could help you find the right spot. Pluto forms a wide and beneficial angle to the full moon, suggesting a powerful confluence of energy that enables you to make the right choices.

Sunday, May 6 (Moon into Sagittarius, 9:40 p.m.) On May 15, Venus will turn retrograde in Gemini, in your career area. One possible ramification is that professional matters won't run as smoothly. Prepare for this before the retrograde begins by tying up loose ends, completing projects you've pushed aside, and making sure appliances in your work area are functioning correctly—fans, heaters, air conditioners, the comfort things!

Monday, May 7 (Moon in Sagittarius)   You could feel torn today between your professional and personal obligations. The trick is to make time for both areas of your life—not necessarily equal time, but quality time. Include family in your decisions, and tip off coworkers that you may have to keep an irregular schedule or ask your boss if you can work at home today.

Tuesday, May 8 (Moon into Capricorn, 10:01 p.m.)
Romance on your mind? Is your muse whispering in your ear? Are you ready to just get out and have some fun? All are possibilities with the moon in fellow earth sign Capricorn. But because it's Capricorn, you may feel quite ambitious today and tackle long-standing projects that have waited patiently for your return.

Wednesday, May 9 (Moon in Capricorn)   Mercury enters fellow earth sign Taurus, where it will be until May 24. Jupiter is still in Taurus too, so this terrific combination brings magnanimous feelings, some sort of intuitive expansion, and a sense that you're on the right track, in the right place at the right time. In addition, Pluto is in Capricorn, which confers personal power!

Thursday, May 10 (Moon in Capricorn)   With all of today's earth energy in your court, Virgo, it should be easy to make significant strides in any area of your life. So whether you're applying this energy in a relationship, on the job, or at home, keep in mind that today you can do no wrong!

Friday, May 11 (Moon into Aquarius, 1:04 a.m.)
You're primed for the weekend ahead. You may have a seminar to attend, a barbecue to go to, or some other social function that beckons. Whatever it is, the activity involves groups, and the conversations will turn your thoughts in new directions. Take notes and pictures.

Saturday, May 12 (Moon in Aquarius)   Armed with your camera and a notebook, off you go today into a new adventure. Whatever it is you're seeking will come your way through synchronicities—meaningful coincidences that point the way or provide guidance, warnings, and affirmation.

Sunday, May 13 (Moon into Pisces, 7:43 a.m.)   A softer you emerges. Your imagination today is expansive, and your intuition is so accurate that if you ignore it, you do so at your own peril. This moon, though, can bring difficulty in making decisions. Your head screams to go one way; your heart begs to go in another.

Monday, May 14 (Moon in Pisces)   There's plenty to celebrate. You and your partner may be taking your relationship to the next level—you move in together, get engaged, buy a home together. Just remember that Venus turns retrograde tomorrow, so get things out in the open now. Be up front and honest.

Tuesday, May 15 (Moon into Aries, 5:47 p.m.)   Venus turns retrograde in Gemini, in your career area, and stays that way until June 27. As stated above, it can cause bumps and bruises in a relationship, but can also create physical discomforts in your environment. If you buy a large-ticket item during this retrograde, it's possible to get some good deals. We once bought a car during a Venus retrograde, got a great deal on it, then traded it in a year later for nearly the same price we paid for it.

Wednesday, May 16 (Moon in Aries) The moon joins Uranus in restless, impatient Aries. Sudden, unexpected events could turn your day inside out quickly. You need to think on your feet, make rapid decisions, and not look back. The combination also confers passion, zeal, and unique ideas. Keep pen and paper at hand.

Thursday, May 17 (Moon in Aries) An entrepreneurial spirit rules the day. You may be seeking unusual solutions, and the search takes you into areas you may not have explored before. It's an adventure, Virgo; that's how you have to look at it. Taxes, insurance, and mortgages may be part of the day's concerns.

Friday, May 18 (Moon into Taurus, 6:04 a.m.) As you approach the solar eclipse in Gemini that will occur on the twentieth, be sure to have your priorities and desires in mind. This one happens in your career area, so spend some time today preparing a list of what you would like to manifest professionally. Today's earth-sign moon keeps you focused and on track.

Saturday, May 19 (Moon in Taurus) It's a good day to read up on exotic locales that you would like to visit. There's something of the nomad in you right now, so take a look at airfares and other expenses entailed in your virtual trip. Pick a time of year that's kind to your bank account! You may also sign up for a workshop or be looking at colleges and grad schools.

Sunday, May 20 (Moon into Gemini, 7:06 p.m.) Today's solar eclipse in Gemini in your career area should be filled with excitement, and it will usher in new professional opportunities. Uranus forms a wide but beneficial angle to the eclipse degree, suggesting an element of unpredictability. Be alert and ready to seize opportunities as they surface.

Monday, May 21 (Moon in Gemini)   Pitch your ideas, make your submissions, garner support for your ideas. This moon favors communication of all kinds. Blogging, making updates to your Web site, starting a newsletter, catching up on e-mail: take your pick, Virgo. One or all of the above are possibilities.

Tuesday, May 22 (Moon in Gemini)   You're brainstorming today with coworkers, family, friends. It may all be part of the new opportunities headed your way—or already at your doorstep. Next month Jupiter enters your career area, and you'll be treated to more than a year of luck and expansion. So get your priorities lined up now.

Wednesday, May 23 (Moon into Cancer, 7:32 a.m.) With the nurturing Cancer moon in play today, your compassion comes roaring to the forefront. Perhaps a friend or family member or even a stranger needs emotional support. You're right there, extending your hand. Virgo enjoys being of service to others.

Thursday, May 24 (Moon in Cancer)   Mercury enters Gemini and your career area, where it will be until June 7. So get ready for plenty of meetings, discussions, and communications about professional matters. If you've had a yen to write a book, now would be a good time to get started. The words roll out of you.

Friday, May 25 (Moon into Leo, 6:12 p.m.)   Shine on, Virgo. Strut your stuff and be proud of your accomplishments. Then get to work, and start paving the way toward new accomplishments and creations. You're preparing for the moon entering your sign on the twenty-eighth. That means tie up loose ends and clear the decks.

Saturday, May 26 (Moon in Leo)   Good friends, good food, good conversation. A small group gathers to celebrate the approach of summer and lazier days ahead. Remember to carve out time for enjoyments like this, Virgo. Even a worker bee like you needs periodic breaks.

Sunday, May 27 (Moon in Leo)   Synchronicities abound today, and each one of them has a message for you about something coming up or a path you're following. Decipher the message; listen to the voice of your intuition. But save major decisions until tomorrow when the moon enters your sign.

Monday, May 28 (Moon into Virgo, 2:07 a.m.) You're in the power seat. Mars is still in your sign, the moon enters your sign, and Pluto is in fellow earth sign Capricorn. This all amounts to greater practicality, efficiency, and making the intangible understandable to others. Tall order? Not for you.

Tuesday, May 29 (Moon in Virgo)   Life flows your way. With the moon and Mars both in your sign, there isn't much today that daunts you. Any challenges or obstacles that surface simply dissolve beneath your laser-like work ethic. You nail down details, connect all the dots, and are on your way!

Wednesday, May 30 (Moon into Libra, 6:46 a.m.) You may be looking over your bank accounts, trying to figure out how much you can afford for a summer vacation. The situation isn't bleak at all, Virgo. You can bring in more of what you want through the law of attraction. Take a few minutes daily to meditate and visualize.

Thursday, May 31 (Moon in Libra)   If your kids are now out of school for the summer, you may be doing a balancing act worthy of a high trapeze artist. Apply your usual organizational skills to family matters, and the summer should unfold with astonishing smoothness.

Friday, June 1 (Moon into Scorpio, 8:32 a.m.)
With Venus still retrograde in Gemini, you may be experiencing some snarls in relationships. But with today's Scorpio moon, you're able to understand these minor complications and rectify them. Things are about to accelerate big time on June 11, when Jupiter enters Gemini and your career area. So be on top of everything now, and don't waste time with regrets or recriminations.

Saturday, June 2 (Moon in Scorpio)   Intense emotions swirl today. Don't let it overwhelm you, though. Pour the feelings into a creative project or discussions with siblings and friends. This water-sign moon powers up your intuition and brings exactly the right information at the right time.

Sunday, June 3 (Moon into Sagittarius, 8:33 a.m.)
You and your partner may slip away for the day. It could be something as simple as a drive to a nearby town, a picnic in the countryside, or a visit to a museum. It depends, obviously, on your interests as individuals and as a couple. If your interests are vastly different, then try to do something that each of you enjoys.

Monday, June 4 (Moon in Sagittarius)   Two events mark today. Neptune turns retrograde in Pisces and won't go direct again until November 10. This motion brings inner scrutiny to a close partnership. Is the relationship meeting your needs and expectations? There's also a lunar eclipse in Sagittarius, which brings news that stirs up powerful and positive emotions.

Tuesday, June 5 (Moon into Capricorn, 8:32 a.m.)
The moon joins Pluto in Capricorn and your solar fifth house. This duo may bring heightened sexuality into a romantic relationship and perhaps some sort of power

play. But because these two planets form beneficial angles to your sun, you should be in the driver's seat.

Wednesday, June 6 (Moon in Capricorn)   Everything you approach in a spirit of fun and enjoyment attracts more to enjoy. It also lifts you out of any emotional negativity so that you are continually humming along in a very positive place. You're about to discover how this will translate on a daily basis in your life.

Thursday, June 7 (Moon into Aquarius, 10:18 a.m.) Mercury enters compatible water sign Cancer, where it will be until June 25. During this period, your intuitive ability is heightened, particularly in regard to loved ones. You may be connecting more frequently with friends and groups and spending more time with one of your parents.

Friday, June 8 (Moon in Aquarius)   Your emotions are somewhat detached today. You're more concerned about what's going on in the larger world—climate changes, natural disasters, hunger, orphaned children. You may volunteer for a charitable organization that supports your concerns.

Saturday, June 9 (Moon into Pisces, 3:23 p.m.)   It could be challenging to make firm decisions today. In fact, if you have to make a major decision, wait until the moon is in your sign or another earth sign. You'll feel more grounded emotionally and better equipped to see all sides of the issue.

Sunday, June 10 (Moon in Pisces)   Imagination and intuition are the hallmarks of this moon. So kick back and let your imagination wander the highways and byways of alternate worlds, other realities, and your own psyche. Your dreams are more accessible to you now, and it's easier to remember them.

Monday, June 11 (Moon in Pisces) Jupiter enters Gemini, where it will be until June 25, 2013. Read about this in depth in the Big Picture section for your sign. Be aware that the transit expands everything it touches, so it behooves you to know where Gemini falls in your natal chart. That area will experience luck and great expansion.

Tuesday, June 12 (Moon into Aries, 12:22 a.m.) Jupiter in Gemini helps you to take full advantage of today's moon in Aries. You're able to move forward with confidence in a relationship, on a project, or with some other matter that is important to you. You feel like an entrepreneur. Forge ahead, Virgo!

Wednesday, June 13 (Moon in Aries) Venus is still retrograde in Gemini until the twenty-seventh, so you won't get the full benefit of Jupiter's transit until after that date. But with your intuitive guidance system in place, thanks to Mercury in compatible water sign Cancer, you're on a trajectory toward success. Belief in yourself is key.

Thursday, June 14 (Moon into Taurus, 12:22 p.m.) From the afternoon onward through the next few days, your life feels as comfortable as your favorite pair of shoes. It's a good time to tackle things you've procrastinated about doing. You have the fortitude now to see these projects/situations to completion.

Friday, June 15 (Moon in Taurus) Planning the family summer vacation? Select a spot that will have something for everyone to enjoy. Have a figure in mind that you can afford for this vacation, and then determine your possible expenses and how long a trip you can take. You could be studying esoteric subjects today. If you're bound for college or grad school in the fall, start making preparations now.

Saturday, June 16 (Moon in Taurus)   You feel emotionally stable today, grounded, and life is moving along at a pace that suits you. In fact, the stars are lined up in your court, and with a bit of focus and not much effort you can make significant advances both professionally and personally. You more readily grasp the idea that you write the script of your life from the inside out.

Sunday, June 17 (Moon into Gemini, 1:24 a.m.)   The moon joins Jupiter and Venus retrograde in Gemini, in your career area. Your communication skills are greatly heightened today, so dive into that blog or Web site you started. Or perhaps your company is ready for an online newsletter. Take on the responsibility.

Monday, June 18 (Moon in Gemini)   It's a good day to network and reach out to clients through e-mail and phone. It's also a great day for sales, if that's your business. Today you can sell just about anything to anyone. Your gift of gab is one of your greatest assets, and with the moon, Jupiter, and Venus in Gemini—the other sign known for communication talent—you are at the top of your game.

Tuesday, June 19 (Moon into Cancer, 1:34 p.m.)   The moon joins Mercury in Cancer in your solar eleventh house. This duo brings a beautiful, intuitive flow to your conscious mind. Your impressions about people and situations are right on, and you probably don't feel any pressing need to validate these impressions with facts. You know what you know.

Wednesday, June 20 (Moon in Cancer)   Another intuitive day. In addition, friends are highlighted in the day's activities and concerns. It's possible that you and a group of close friends get together this evening or make plans to see each other over the weekend. Your place looks like the location!

Thursday, June 21 (Moon into Leo, 11:48 p.m.)   Saturn in Libra turns direct on June 25, so prepare yourself for this one, Virgo, by making sure you've got your finances in order. If you've been experiencing delays and setbacks with money, take heart. Once Saturn turns direct, things improve considerably. Set up a realistic budget, and stick to it.

Friday, June 22 (Moon in Leo)   You're busy behind the scenes, tying up loose ends, meeting obligations to others and yourself as well. Your dreams should be especially vivid now and filled with information about issues and concerns you may have. You can easily recall dreams too, since your personal unconscious is more accessible to you.

Saturday, June 23 (Moon in Leo)   You're reaching out to people today—not in person, but through e-mail, phone, your blog. It's where you shine—your words, the energy behind your words and thoughts. There's real substance in your belief system, and your eagerness and willingness to share it with others are much appreciated.

Sunday, June 24 (Moon into Virgo, 7:43 a.m.)   The moon enters your sign. For the next two days you're in tip-top shape, tending to details that others may overlook and tackling your work with the same diligence that you bring to your personal life. Worker bee, Virgo. That's what you are!

Monday, June 25 (Moon in Virgo)   Mercury enters Leo and your solar twelfth house, and Saturn turns direct in Libra. Mercury is in Leo until August 31 and turns retrograde on July 14. Read more about this transit in the Big Picture for your sign. While Mercury is moving direct, you're able to confront and resolve issues you've buried and to do it in a mindful, conscious way. Once Saturn turns direct in Libra, your relationships and finances should move forward again.

Tuesday, June 26 (Moon into Libra, 1:16 p.m.) The moon joins Saturn in Libra. Finances are on your mind, but so are friends and other relationships you enjoy. You begin to see a correlation between your emotions and what you experience. Any synchronicities you experience today are guideposts. Heed them.

Wednesday, June 27 (Moon in Libra) Venus turns direct in Gemini, and professional matters are suddenly moving in your favor again. In fact, projects or ideas that you implement between now and August 7 have the solid backing of Saturn, which confers structure. Any flirtation that begins during Venus's transit of Gemini should be quite lively intellectually.

Thursday, June 28 (Moon into Scorpio, 4:33 p.m.) Your communications and relationships with siblings and other relatives could be quite intense. It's a good time, though, to check out new neighborhoods in anticipation of a move and talk to people about these neighborhoods to find out what they like—or don't like—about living there.

Friday, June 29 (Moon in Scorpio) Research and investigation are favored. Your intuitive abilities deepen significantly during this transit, so don't shrug off hunches that you have. Neptune forms a strong angle to this moon, suggesting that your ideals play into everything you do and that inspiration is key to your success with creative ventures.

Saturday, June 30 (Moon into Sagittarius, 6:05 p.m.) The moon in Sagittarius brings your emotional focus to a partnership, foreign travel, publishing, and higher education. It's easier to grasp the big picture of a relationship. Your mood is buoyant.

Sunday, July 1 (Moon in Sagittarius)   You may be getting ready for out-of-town visitors over the July 4 holiday. Or perhaps you're headed out of town. Whichever it is, today is likely to be hectic. But you take it all in stride, just as you do with everything else in your life. As a mutable sign, Virgo, your adaptability is one of your great strengths.

Monday, July 2 (Moon into Capricorn, 6:52 p.m.)
Time for fun and enjoyment! While you're out and about doing all this stuff you enjoy, mull over your career goals. It's hard not to do that when the moon joins Pluto in Capricorn. You may even be prioritizing in your head for most of the day and tonight will sit down and write up notes. You're leading up to tomorrow's full moon in Capricorn.

Tuesday, July 3 (Moon in Capricorn)   Mars enters Libra and your solar second house, where it will be until August 23. This transit brings a lot of activity concerning your finances. You may be working longer hours to make ends meet, could take on a second job, or could land a nice raise. With today's full moon in Capricorn, there's news about a romance or a creative project. Pluto forms a close conjunction to this moon, suggesting power issues are part and parcel of the day.

Wednesday, July 4 (Moon into Aquarius, 8:26 p.m.)
Happy Independence Day, USA. With the moon in visionary Aquarius, you'll undoubtedly have something special and outrageous planned for today. In some way it relates to your daily work schedule or the way you maintain your health from day to day. Perhaps you're testing out new and delectable recipes?

Thursday, July 5 (Moon in Aquarius)   You may try a new nutritional or vitamin program—not because you need to lose weight, but to energize yourself. If it's now summer where you live, then include a long walk in your regular exercise routine. It's not just good for your body, it also calms your mind and brings your creative muse out of hiding.

Friday, July 6 (Moon in Aquarius)   You may be hustling to finish up your work before the weekend. Enlist the aid of others; don't hesitate to delegate. If you're involved in a group that supports your passions and interests, today is a great day to meet with them. Ideas will abound.

Saturday, July 7 (Moon into Pisces, 12:29 a.m.) Your partner or spouse is front and center today. The two of you may want to get away together for a trip to a nearby town. Exploration is key to the day's energy, and it doesn't matter if it's physical exploration or the exploration of ideas and concepts.

Sunday, July 8 (Moon in Pisces)   Your imagination soars and takes you places you've never been before. You may want to keep a recorder and a notepad handy so you can jot down ideas, random thoughts. Dive into your creativity, and see where it leads you.

Monday, July 9 (Moon into Aries, 8:14 a.m.)   The entrepreneurial spirit seizes you, and you run with several different ideas just to see where they'll go. One possibility? You come up with an innovative way to invest your money. Or perhaps you join a growing movement in the country and move your funds to a community bank.

Tuesday, July 10 (Moon in Aries)   You deal with mortgages and loans today, with taxes and insurance. In other words, you run up against bureaucrats and may not be at your best. Don't be impatient or short-tempered. Just try to take it all in stride and know that this too shall pass!

Wednesday, July 11 (Moon into Taurus, 7:30 p.m.)
Today's moon in fellow earth sign Taurus leaves you feeling much more peaceful than you did yesterday. You feel more resolute and determined to do things your way, at your pace. Life can't be rushed and neither can you. So kick back and go with the flow, Virgo, and don't make apologies to anyone for how you are.

Thursday, July 12 (Moon in Taurus)   Your beliefs take center stage. You don't hesitate to explain what you believe and why, but you should avoid outright arguments and dissension. You won't ever change anyone's mind through arguing. Practice and example are more convincing.

Friday, July 13 (Moon in Taurus)   Uranus turns retrograde in Aries and remains that way until December 13. The bottom line with this movement is that mortgages and loans could be more difficult to obtain. Or you obtain them in unusual ways. With Jupiter now in your career area, more options are opening up. The most difficult part for you is deciding which option to take. Mercury turns retrograde tomorrow, and by now you know the drill on this one: back up computer files, finalize travel plans, be prepared to revise, rewrite, and revisit.

Saturday, July 14 (Moon into Gemini, 8:27 a.m.)
Mercury turns retrograde in Leo, in your solar twelfth house, and remains there until August 8. Old issues and relationships from the past may surface now. Your dreams are more accessible to you, and you should be able to glean information and insights from them. Read about this retrograde under the Big Picture section for your sign.

Sunday, July 15 (Moon in Gemini)   With the moon joining Jupiter in your career area, you're primed for new endeavors today. If you have a dusty manuscript locked away in a drawer somewhere, then now is the time to take it out and go through it. If you think it can be salvaged, then set aside time daily to work on it.

Monday, July 16 (Moon into Cancer, 8:32 p.m.) Who or what are you nurturing today? You may be nurturing memories of the past and become steeped in nostalgia. A certain scent might bring back a torrent of memories, for example, or the sight of a familiar object or even a photo. What in the past would you change if you could?

Tuesday, July 17 (Moon in Cancer) Your friends rally today. Perhaps you're involved in a brainstorming session for a new project, are planning some sort of social event, or are traveling with a group. Regardless of how this shakes out for you, you're aware of how deeply you appreciate the people in your life. You have a deep intuitive connection to others.

Wednesday, July 18 (Moon in Cancer) Things are happening today and no wonder. You're moving toward tomorrow's new moon in Cancer, so it's possible new opportunities are already cropping up. On other fronts, you may be obsessing about your finances, which only attracts more of the same. Best to offer appreciation for what you have and to do that continually throughout the day.

Thursday, July 19 (Moon into Leo, 6:14 a.m.) The new moon in Cancer that occurs shortly after midnight should usher in new opportunities with friends and groups and also in your domestic scene. You might, for example, sell your home and move or move one of your parents to a different location. Or you may have an opportunity to nurture and develop your intuitive abilities.

Friday, July 20 (Moon in Leo) Delve into your own psyche, and deal with issues that you've disowned over

271

the years. The point with this moon is to clear the decks and tie up loose ends and obligations so that when the moon enters your sign tomorrow, you'll be ready to take advantage of the wonderful energy.

Saturday, July 21 (Moon into Virgo, 1:25 p.m.) With the moon entering your sign early this afternoon, you're in good shape to move forward with your various plans, projects, and relationships. Even though Mercury is retrograde right now, you can review what you've been doing and figure out how to do things differently.

Sunday, July 22 (Moon in Virgo) With Venus now in direct motion in your career area, you can apply today's lunar energy to professional matters and trust that all is well. Sometimes the only thing you lack is a little faith that you're on the right path, that you're doing the right things. Nurture that faith today.

Monday, July 23 (Moon into Libra, 6:39 p.m.) The moon joins Saturn in Libra. Today's balancing act involves money and a relationship and not necessarily in that order! If you have a teenager, then the balance that is needed could involve your child's spending habits. Or perhaps your spending habits!

Tuesday, July 24 (Moon in Libra) Your values come into play in some way. Perhaps it's simply that you have to define what's important to you and why. If you can figure this out, then you're able to prioritize your day (and your life) and make more efficient use of your time. With this moon, you may be feeling more flirtatious than usual and more willing to strike up conversations with strangers.

Wednesday, July 25 (Moon into Scorpio, 10:30 p.m.) Despite the intense emotions and secrecy that usually surround this moon, it speaks to you in the archetypal language of the soul—dreams, synchronicity, hunches.

You may have more contact with neighbors and your community today or with siblings. It could be that something is brewing in your neighborhood, and you should stay on top of it.

Thursday, July 26 (Moon in Scorpio)   Today you may be more aware of how your moods and emotions attract certain experiences. In fact, take a look around your environment. Everything you see is a manifestation of a belief that you hold. It's something you attracted into your life. If you don't like what you see, then change your beliefs, and your experiences will change.

Friday, July 27 (Moon in Scorpio)   Mercury turns direct on August 8; until then stick to what you know. Rather than start anything new, follow the three rules for this retrograde: revise, review, rewrite. You need some time to chill, anyway. You've been pushing yourself too hard. You're going to need all your energy for the three lunations that take place next month.

Saturday, July 28 (Moon into Sagittarius, 1:18 a.m.) Fitting that the Sadge moon comes around on a weekend, when you're more likely to be at home. This moon highlights your domestic environment—and perhaps your restless need to be traveling. The contradiction isn't a problem for you. You may simply decide to load up the kids, your partner, and the family pets and head elsewhere for the weekend.

Sunday, July 29 (Moon in Sagittarius)   If you have a manuscript that you would like to see published, wait until after Mercury turns direct on August 8 to submit it. In fact, give it a few days beyond the eighth, so Mercury has a chance to settle in. Then send it out into the world backed with positive thoughts and appreciation.

Monday, July 30 (Moon into Capricorn, 3:30 a.m.) You're a workaholic today, an ideal way to start the week. Be sure to have your list of priorities so that you can dive into whatever you're doing with an efficient use of your time and energy. At some point in the day, though, be sure to save time for fun and pleasure. Balance, Virgo. Balance.

Tuesday, July 31 (Moon in Capricorn)   If you have children, then they figure into the day's events every day, but today they require more attention, support, and love. Or *you* require that from them. Well, maybe "require" is the wrong word. Hope? Need? Spend time with them. Take them to a bookstore or movie, something all of you enjoy.

AUGUST 2012

Wednesday, August 1 (Moon into Aquarius, 5:56 a.m.) Today's full moon in Aquarius is the first of three lunations this month. This full moon should bring news about your daily work. Thanks to an exact and beneficial angle from Jupiter, the news looks positive! This full moon could also bring insights about your health—how to maintain it, how to read your body's signals more accurately.

Thursday, August 2 (Moon in Aquarius)   Your ideas may not be to everyone's taste, but they're certainly cutting-edge stuff. The big challenge is how to translate these ideas into something tangible, grounded. Wait until the moon is in your sign. Your inner and outer worlds will be in agreement, and you'll know exactly how to connect the dots.

Friday, August 3 (Moon into Pisces, 9:58 a.m.)   A partnership is highlighted. Perhaps you and your business partner have the same basic ideas about your products/service, but are differing on the fine points. Spend some time brainstorming about your business plan, your collective goals.

Saturday, August 4 (Moon in Pisces)   Intuitively, you're right on the money. So whatever hunches you have, follow them. Don't play mind games with yourself, wondering if it's your imagination at work. Just heed that small intuitive voice, and see where it leads you.

Sunday, August 5 (Moon into Aries, 4:59 p.m.)   The moon joins Uranus in Aries, which makes for an interesting and exciting day with its share of surprises. Some possibilities? You make significant strides on a creative project, you experience a breakthrough in your understanding of some metaphysical concept, or—on a mundane level—you get a break on taxes or insurance.

Monday, August 6 (Moon in Aries)   You're a powerhouse of energy today, impatient to get things moving and done, and you're insistent that you can go it alone. You would do better to delegate some responsibility to others, so be sure the others are people you trust to do the job the way you think it should be done.

Tuesday, August 7 (Moon in Aries)   Venus enters compatible water sign Cancer, where it will be until September 6. During this period, it's possible that a friendship turns to romance. Or perhaps you meet a romantic interest through friends or through a group to which you belong. Try not to get involved, though, until after Mercury turns direct tomorrow.

Wednesday, August 8 (Moon into Taurus, 3:28 a.m.) Today's earth-sign moon is made to order for you. You feel resolute, determined, and perfectly equipped to defend your beliefs if you need to. In addition, Mercury turns direct again, in Leo, your solar twelfth house. Since Mercury rules your sun sign, its movement is important for you. It will be in Leo until August 31. Get ready!

Thursday, August 9 (Moon in Taurus)   Dreaming about foreign shores? Exotic ports? Then do your research today, and figure out a location, how much the trip might cost, all the particulars. Be sure that the place you pick reflects your deeper interests and passions. In other words, if you want to study ancient civilizations, then Greece might be the ticket.

Friday, August 10 (Moon into Gemini, 4:12 p.m.) The moon joins Jupiter in Gemini in your career area. Between now and June 25, 2013, these Gemini-moon days enable you to move forward professionally. Your career potential and choices are expanding, and the people you meet are helpful in this regard. So make these days count, Virgo!

Saturday, August 11 (Moon in Gemini) Even though it's the weekend, you may have your nose to the grindstone. Whether you're beginning a project, in the middle of it, or completing it, you bring that same meticulous mind-set and attention to detail. This evening, you and your partner—or you and friends—may head out on the town.

Sunday, August 12 (Moon in Gemini) Despite the fact that work calls to you today, take time off to read, browse a bookstore, catch a movie. In other words, keep time open to enjoy yourself. None of us functions well without relaxation and fun! This is especially true for you, industrious Virgo.

Monday, August 13 (Moon into Cancer, 4:29 a.m.) Power issues could surface with a friend. Try not to be confrontational, even if you feel you're right. You don't want to wreck the friendship, and besides, opinions and beliefs are rarely changed through confrontation. Nurture yourself as you do others.

Tuesday, August 14 (Moon in Cancer) Today you may be nurturing a parent or other family member. Perhaps they need additional emotional support at this time. Or perhaps it's just time to build up or invigorate the relationship. With Saturn still in Libra and your solar second house of finances, it's a good time to review your budget.

Wednesday, August 15 (Moon into Leo, 2:06 p.m.) As you approach the new moon in Leo on the seventeenth, prepare by listing the opportunities you would like to manifest in your life. New job? New relationship? New home? Back your desires with emotion. If you haven't read *The Vortex* by Esther and Jerry Hicks, head over to the bookstore and pick up a copy. The techniques will be useful as you approach the new moon.

Thursday, August 16 (Moon in Leo) With today's moon forming a beneficial angle to Saturn, it's a good day to discover how you actually feel about money. How much importance do you attach to it? Are you being paid what you feel your skills and services are worth? The Leo moon also forms a beneficial angle to Uranus in Aries, so unusual ideas and emotions are par for today.

Friday, August 17 (Moon into Virgo, 8:34 p.m.) The new moon in Leo brings opportunities to show off your skills and talents. With Saturn forming an exact and beneficial angle to this moon, you enjoy a serious venue for exhibiting your abilities. Jupiter also forms a beneficial though wide angle to this new moon, indicating that the opportunities that surface expand your life in some way. Then this evening the best part: the moon enters your sign again.

Saturday, August 18 (Moon in Virgo) The next two days are power days. The moon is in your sign, and everything in your life seems to hum along more smoothly and evenly. So whether you're doing stuff around your home, have gone into work, or are simply enjoying the weekend, you feel self-confident, optimistic, perhaps even content.

Sunday, August 19 (Moon in Virgo)   If you have places to go and people to see today, you're in the driver's seat and calling the shots. You're also very much in the flow of things, so it's likely you'll experience synchronicity today. Meaningful coincidences can be signposts or warnings and offer guidance and affirmations. Decipher the message.

Monday, August 20 (Moon into Libra, 12:46 a.m.) Aesthetics are high on your list. Whether it's beautiful art or jewelry, poetry or wonderful music, you gravitate toward things and people that speak to the artist in you. If you feel the urge to splurge on a large-ticket item, be sure you have the cash in the bank. Otherwise you may feel a crunch next month when the credit-card bill comes due.

Tuesday, August 21 (Moon in Libra)   On the twenty-third, Mars will be in Libra. Tomorrow the moon moves into Scorpio, a water sign compatible with your earth-sign sun. So today take stock of your finances. Are you in better shape now than you were a month ago? Six months ago? If not, how can you rectify the situation? If your income has increased, how do you feel about it?

Wednesday, August 22 (Moon into Scorpio, 3:54 a.m.) The Scorpio moon pumps up your communication abilities, but not in any sort of frivolous way. You're delving into deep waters today—metaphysics, your own psyche, other people's motives and beliefs. You now grasp that the mechanics of fear on any level are detrimental to your well-being and prosperity.

Thursday, August 23 (Moon in Scorpio)   Mars enters Scorpio and joins the moon in your third house. Contact with siblings and other relatives could be intense, not necessarily in a negative way. You're digging for information and won't stop until you find what you're looking for. The Mars transit lasts until October

278

6 and brings a lot of physical energy to your daily life. Make good use of it!

Friday, August 24 (Moon into Sagittarius, 6:50 a.m.)
Mulling over the larger picture of your life? Looking at the woods instead of the trees? Good. Then you're right in tune with the Sagittarius moon. Spend a few minutes today looking at different areas of your life in this way—for the big picture.

Saturday, August 25 (Moon in Sagittarius)   Party time! The festivities may be at your place, and if so, keep the crowd small. You'll be glad you did tomorrow morning. If you have natal planets in fire signs, then this moon probably suits you, firing up your passions and causes. If your natal chart is dominated by planets in elements other than fire, you can still use the Sadge-moon energy to grasp the larger picture of your personal and domestic environment.

Sunday, August 26 (Moon into Capricorn, 9:59 a.m.)
Whenever the moon joins Pluto in Capricorn in your solar fifth house, any of a number of patterns may manifest themselves. Power issues between you and a romantic interest may crop up. Or your partnership is a powerhouse of sexuality, enjoyment, compatibility. Whatever you do for fun and pleasure and your creative endeavors can change you at the most fundamental levels.

Monday, August 27 (Moon in Capricorn)   Whenever Capricorn is involved in a transit, ambition is highlighted. You may be revising your professional goals. Perhaps you're in search of a career path that's more enjoyable or that involves more of what you enjoy. Do you need additional skills for this career? If so, start researching what you need and how to get it.

Tuesday, August 28 (Moon into Aquarius, 1:39 p.m.)
To maintain your daily health, you may be experiment-

ing with various exercise regimens and nutritional programs or perhaps trying acupuncture, meditation, yoga, or other alternative therapies. But regardless of what you try, the bottom line may be what you think, feel, and believe is more important.

Wednesday, August 29 (Moon in Aquarius)   As the days move into fall, you can feel the shift in the air, in the way people interact with each other, in how your body feels. Take a few minutes today to express your appreciation for what you have and for what you are going to have. Take stock of how your summer went, and imagine how the last four months of the year will unfold. No, the world isn't going to end, not on December 21, regardless of what the Mayan Calendar or the doomsayers are telling you.

Thursday, August 30 (Moon into Pisces, 6:32 p.m.) The moon enters your opposite sign, and what fun this should be, leading up to the full moon in that sign tomorrow. For today, though, with the moon in Pisces you and your partner should plan something special for the weekend. Something romantic, imaginative, maybe even a tad exotic!

Friday, August 31 (Moon in Pisces)   Mercury enters your sign, where it will be until September 16, and there's a full moon in Pisces. Mercury first: what a treat. Your mind and your ego now work in tandem, one feeding and encouraging the other. Since Mercury is your ruler, your communication abilities shine. The full moon enjoys a wide conjunction with Neptune, and that suggests that today you idealize love.

SEPTEMBER 2012

Saturday, September 1 (Moon in Pisces)   Here's that Pisces moon once again, with that imagination as

280

huge as a continent and that great intuitive flow that you can tap into. You and your partner may be following hunches and synchronicities today that lead you out of town or perhaps across the country. You could be searching for something you haven't even defined yet. Enjoy the journey, wherever it leads. It's a long weekend, and you have time to explore.

Sunday, September 2 (Moon into Aries, 1:38 a.m.)
The odd combination of today's energy—the Aries moon traveling in tandem with Uranus, Mars in Scorpio—suggests that you may feel somewhat frustrated or impatient. You really want to uncover the truth, but can't seem to focus enough to get there. You're like a four-year-old on a long car ride: *Are we there yet?*

Monday, September 3 (Moon in Aries)   Pushing too far, too fast, taking too many risks: it's the tale of Icarus, who flew too close to the sun on wings made of wax. That could be the texture of your day. So instead of capitalizing on this energy, change the possibilities before you even get out of bed. Be mindful of how you would like your day to unfold. Visualize yourself moving at a more measured pace; be clear about what you would like to experience.

Tuesday, September 4 (Moon into Taurus, 11:42 a.m.)
The wonderful Taurus moon is your best friend today. It keeps you grounded, stubborn when you should be stubborn, sensuous when you should be sensuous. It also enables you to feel your way through your belief system. Rather than think about it with left-brain logic, you intuit your way through it.

Wednesday, September 5 (Moon in Taurus)   If you're considering college, grad school, law school, or some other form of higher education, now is the time to get your priorities straight. Obtain applications, take the necessary standardized tests, do your research.

Thursday, September 6 (Moon in Taurus) Venus
enters Leo and your solar twelfth house, where it will
be until October 3. During this transit, a secret romantic
liaison is possible. The only thing you have to consider
about this relationship is: why is it secret? It won't be
for long, at any rate. Once Venus enters your sign in
early October, you may be telling the world about this
relationship.

Friday, September 7 (Moon into Gemini, 12:11 a.m.)
Think about it. That's the mantra for Gemini. But because it's the moon in this sign, your "thinking" hums
along at a deeper intuitive level where language is in
symbols. So let these intuitive symbols speak to you. Use
them to find your way into your next project, your next
career.

Saturday, September 8 (Moon in Gemini) So here
you are again, with the Gemini moon coaxing you forward, onward, using your ability to adapt to a fluid situation and to do it at a moment's notice. Camouflage is
your middle name today. Keep your plans to yourself;
reveal only what is necessary.

Sunday, September 9 (Moon into Cancer, 12:50 p.m.)
The Cancer moon brings softness and nostalgia to your
day. What is it that you're remembering? What triggered it? You may be looking at how you nurture others
and yourself and may decide you're lacking something.
That's just your inner critic speaking, Virgo. Don't be so
hard on yourself.

Monday, September 10 (Moon in Cancer) If you
can find a middle ground today, you'll feel better generally about everything. Your friends are important to
you, and today, as usual, they are helpful and supportive.
With Mars forming a beneficial angle to this moon and
your sun, your physical energy is abundant.

Tuesday, September 11 (Moon into Leo, 11:01 p.m.)
Late this evening, Jupiter and today's moon form a beneficial angle to each other, so expect some sort of expansion to your inner life. Perhaps your dreams are more accessible to you now, unfolding like solid stories with plots, characters, a moral. Or maybe your meditation practice is yielding insights into your own psyche.

Wednesday, September 12 (Moon in Leo)　Yesterday's introspection continues, but in a more measured way. You're able to use yesterday's insights to make decisions today. Your inner housecleaning prepares the way for the new moon in your sign on the fifteenth, the start of a new chapter this month.

Thursday, September 13 (Moon in Leo)　Sometimes the best-laid plans don't quite make it, but it isn't your fault. You may have to tweak your plan to accommodate certain people who aren't crazy about it. Compromise is something you usually do well, but wait until the new moon in your sign before you do anything.

Friday, September 14 (Moon into Virgo, 5:31 a.m.)
The moon enters your sign, and things are looking up, for sure! If you've got various ongoing projects—at work, at home—try to complete them. Tomorrow is the new moon in your sign, which comes around just once a year and sets the tone for the next twelve months. Be ready for it by knowing what experiences and situations you would like to have in your life.

Saturday, September 15 (Moon in Virgo)　Today's new moon in Virgo enjoys a close conjunction with your ruler, Mercury. Expect new opportunities to surface in communication and travel, with kids, and in your daily life. The opportunities could involve writing, blogging, starting a newsletter, a study group of some kind, more contact and interaction with people generally in your day-to-day life.

Sunday, September 16 (Moon into Libra, 8:55 a.m.)
Mercury enters Libra and your solar second house and will be there until October 5. This transit brings discussions and a lot of contemplation about relationships, balance, and money. It's also possible that you sell something you've written—article, short story, novel, screenplay.

Monday, September 17 (Moon in Libra) Pluto turns direct in Capricorn, a nice plus for your career, love life, creativity, and whatever you do for fun and pleasure. If things have been stalled in any of these areas, the blockade will start breaking up shortly. Once Saturn moves into Scorpio in early October, it will be making a beneficial angle to your sun, and life should get considerably easier.

Tuesday, September 18 (Moon into Scorpio, 10:46 a.m.) Your mood today lends itself to research and investigation. Consider renting *The Man from Earth,* a thought-provoking film that examines the nature of reality and man's place in it. For your reading list, include *The Nature of Personal Reality* by Jane Roberts and *The Power of Now* by Eckhart Tolle.

Wednesday, September 19 (Moon in Scorpio) What's the line between secrecy and privacy? Today you may discover the difference and just how thin that line is. The issue, whatever it is, resolves itself by day's end, but your discovery is an important one and enables you to make a decision.

Thursday, September 20 (Moon into Sagittarius, 12:34 p.m.) Your domestic and personal environments may conflict with professional responsibilities. If you work out of your house, this conflict may be more pronounced, and you probably should set aside specific hours for work and post a Do Not Disturb sign on your door when you're in your office.

Friday, September 21 (Moon in Sagittarius)   If your life feels sort of nutty and chaotic right now, don't fret about it. Just go with the flow. By tomorrow afternoon, just in time for the weekend, you'll be in a much better place within yourself, and it will be easier to put things in perspective.

Saturday, September 22 (Moon into Capricorn, 3:21 p.m.)   Even if this moon sometimes makes you feel more like a hard nose, it serves its purpose in that it grounds you and your ideas. It's especially favorable for creative work because you're better able to make the abstract comprehensible.

Sunday, September 23 (Moon in Capricorn)   Set up your priorities for the week ahead in the various areas of your life. You're feeling organized today, so this should be a cinch and give you a blueprint to work with when you're feeling scattered and unfocused. If you want, expand the list to include specific jobs you want to complete.

Monday, September 24 (Moon into Aquarius, 7:33 p.m.)   With the moon in visionary Aquarius, you're in rare form today, able to think way outside the box, where you find the solutions to a challenge or issue. This moon forms a beneficial angle to your career area and bolsters your communication abilities. You may do group work of some kind today.

Tuesday, September 25 (Moon in Aquarius)   Practicing gratitude moves you closer to what you desire. If someone pays you a compliment, if you get help from a stranger, say thank you. In fact, go through your day looking for something and someone to appreciate. Your ideas are bountiful, and there are people around you who just can't wait to hear them.

Wednesday, September 26 (Moon in Aquarius)   With the full moon in Aries coming up on the twenty-ninth, life may start feeling a little crazy. Just take your time, set your own pace, and don't allow other people's deadlines and issues to affect you. You know better than anyone how much you can take on at any one time.

Thursday, September 27 (Moon into Pisces, 1:25 a.m.)
Your partner—business or personal—has ideas about how the relationship should work. You have your own ideas about this issue. Somehow the two of you have to arrive at a compromise that suits you both. The differences between your respective ideas may be small, but they're important.

Friday, September 28 (Moon in Pisces)   Think of your life as a treasure hunt. What's the treasure? Does it matter? The journey is what counts. With the moon in Pisces, your heart yearns to go one way, your head demands to go in another direction. You may not resolve this today, but again, it's the journey that teaches you what you need to learn.

Saturday, September 29 (Moon into Aries, 9:15 a.m.)
Today's full moon in Aries brings high energy and lots of movement and activity. Expect the unexpected; Uranus forms a nearly perfect conjunction with this moon. New people who enter your life now are apt to be idiosyncratic, perhaps even geniuses. Power issues could surface—with authority figures like a parent, a boss, a cop.

Sunday, September 30 (Moon in Aries)   If you're still reeling from yesterday's full moon, then today is when you kick back and relax. Even if everything inside of you is demanding that you do something, that you push yourself to extremes in some way, resist it. Really, you deserve a break.

OCTOBER 2012

Monday, October 1 (Moon into Taurus, 7:27 p.m.)
In a few days, Venus enters your sign, and the current
of life will really turn in your favor. So prepare for it
today by making a list of what you desire. Or create a
poster board with photos and pictures of what you want,
and post it in a spot that you'll see frequently. Back your
desires with emotion. The more powerful the emotion,
the more likely it is that your desire will manifest itself.

Tuesday, October 2 (Moon in Taurus)   You're very
determined today to start or finish something. You want
to do this your own way, proceeding at your own pace,
which is fine. Just don't step on anyone else's toes. Someone in your environment may be somewhat territorial.

Wednesday, October 3 (Moon in Taurus)   One of
the most romantic and creative periods all year begins
for you today, when Venus enters your sign. This transit
lasts until October 28 . . . 25 beautiful days! If you're not
involved when this transit starts, you probably will be
when it ends. If not, it won't matter because you'll be
having too much fun! Read more about this transit in
the Big Picture section for your sign.

Thursday, October 4 (Moon into Gemini, 7:47 a.m.)
The moon joins Jupiter in Gemini, a combination that
feeds your emotions and your mind. As a result, you
may blow things out of proportion today. Anything that
is good seems very good; anything negative seems very
negative. But this duo increases your communication
abilities and may bring involvement with publishing and
higher education.

Friday, October 5 (Moon in Gemini)   Mercury
and Saturn enter Scorpio. The Saturn transit lasts for
two and a half years and should be helpful to you since
it's forming a beneficial angle to your sun. It will help

to bring stronger structures into your life and will strengthen existing ones. Read more about this transit in the Big Picture section for your sign. Mercury's transit through Scorpio lasts until October 29 and brings a nice intuitive flow to your daily life. It favors research, investigation.

Saturday, October 6 (Moon into Cancer, 8:46 p.m.) Mars enters Sagittarius, where it will be until November 16. This transit brings a lot of activity into your home and domestic life. You may be refurbishing your home in some way, kids may be coming and going at all hours, your parents could visit for a few days or perhaps they're moving and you help out. If you have fire-sign natal planets, the transit shouldn't be a problem. If you don't have natal planets in fire signs, then this transit is your booster rocket, Virgo, urging you to get things done.

Sunday, October 7 (Moon in Cancer) Nurturing and being nurtured are the day's themes. Whether you're among friends or family, strangers or coworkers, your approach is softer, gentler, more intuitive. You sense the ebb and flow of events and relationships in your life. You can't slow things down or speed them up, but you can alter your perception of time and movement.

Monday, October 8 (Moon in Cancer) If you're feeling nostalgic about the past today, just go with the emotions. Don't resist them. Let them flow through you, and as they do, release the feelings. Remember that your point of power is the present. It's from this moment that you create your life.

Tuesday, October 9 (Moon into Leo, 7:55 a.m.) You have opportunities to get things done today— projects on which you've procrastinated, cleaning the garage or attic or even your closets. The external cleaning reflects what you're doing internally, getting rid of attitudes and beliefs that no longer serve your best interest. The universe loves symbolic gestures.

Wednesday, October 10 (Moon in Leo)   Your dreams and information and guidance that come through them are more accessible to you now. If you have trouble deciphering what the dreams are telling you, try to put them into the context of a story. A good way to do this is to begin at the end of the dream and try to work your way back through it.

Thursday, October 11 (Moon into Virgo, 3:24 p.m.) The stars are stacked in your favor. With Venus and the moon in your sign, Pluto in fellow earth sign Capricorn, and both Mars and Mercury in compatible water sign Scorpio, romance and creativity are highlighted and so is your ability to communicate. It's the sort of day, Virgo, when you can sell just about anything to anyone. Product, idea, opinion: sell away!

Friday, October 12 (Moon in Virgo)   You and a loved one are preparing for something fun this weekend. Whether it's an overnight trip or a party, a joint creative project or attending a school function with one of your kids, the key word here is enjoyment. All too often, we get swept up in our responsibilities, jobs, and ourselves and forget how to laugh.

Saturday, October 13 (Moon into Libra, 7:02 p.m.) Now that Saturn has moved out of Libra, you may find that your finances are improving. Or perhaps the budget you set up earlier in the year is yielding results, i.e., more savings. A raise or bonus is also possible, Virgo. So try not to splurge on big-ticket items until the increased income comes through. Better yet, wait until Christmas!

Sunday, October 14 (Moon in Libra)   You're feeling flirtatious, and this holds true regardless of your relationship status. Just be careful that you don't hurt anyone's feelings. What is flirtatious for you may be perceived as overtures by someone else. You may want to clarify your intentions in your own mind.

Monday, October 15 (Moon into Scorpio, 8:07 p.m.)
Today's new moon in Libra at 8:02 A.M. should usher in new opportunities with relationships and finances and in the arts. The financial opportunities can range from a raise or promotion to a new job that pays more than you make now. If you're involved in the arts, then this new moon could bring a new opportunity to flex your creative ability. Jupiter forms a beneficial angle to this new moon, indicating that the opportunity expands your life in a positive way.

Tuesday, October 16 (Moon in Scorpio) The moon joins Saturn and Mercury in Scorpio, your solar third house. Intense discussions and conversations ensue today with siblings or neighbors. It may be connected to something going on in your neighborhood or even in the larger community. The combination of planets favors research, maybe something you're writing? Or perhaps in preparation for a speech you're going to give?

Wednesday, October 17 (Moon into Sagittarius, 8:26 p.m.) You're all fired up today. It could be in anticipation of a trip you're going to take, a relationship, something going on at work or in your domestic environment. It's okay if others aren't into your causes and interests. You don't mind going it alone.

Thursday, October 18 (Moon in Sagittarius) There are certain things you understand more clearly than other people. You're able to recognize patterns—in behavior, motives, even the way shells are spread on a beach. It's part of what makes you a master at divination.

Friday, October 19 (Moon into Capricorn, 9:42 p.m.)
With the moon in a fellow earth sign, you're infinitely

more comfortable in your own skin. In fact, you feel so at home with yourself today that your self-confidence soars, and the nagging voice of your inner critic is blissfully silent! Remember how this feels so that when that critic is picking you or someone else apart you can change course quickly.

Saturday, October 20 (Moon in Capricorn) Your love life is pleasant at the moment, so why rock the boat? You and your partner understand each other (or should!), and you're compatible. Yes, you may be feeling antsy, looking around for greener pastures, but don't leap into another relationship just yet.

Sunday, October 21 (Moon in Capricorn) Your muse is up close and personal. Take advantage of it. Spend the day working on a creative endeavor that really speaks to you at a profound level. If your creative work is what you do in your free time, and you would like to make it your full-time job, then now is the time to figure out how to bring about that situation.

Monday, October 22 (Moon into Aquarius, 1:03 a.m.) When the moon enters an air sign, you feel the distinct change, especially if you don't have a lot of air-sign planets in your natal chart. Suddenly you look at the world and yourself in a different light, from a more mental than an emotional perspective. The Aquarius moon brings emotional detachment, something you may need today.

Tuesday, October 23 (Moon in Aquarius) Some of the friends you make through daily work are like family to you. Ask yourself what it is about these people that feels so comfortable. If you can define it, it will reveal quite a bit about your own needs and desires. Self-knowledge, as all Virgos know, is vital for your well-being.

Wednesday, October 24 (Moon into Pisces, 7:01 a.m.)
A softer you comes out when the moon is in Pisces or
Cancer. It's because emotions move through you like
a gentle river, clearing away psychic clutter. Without
the clutter, you're able to see exactly where you need
to be and why. You're able to define what makes you
happy. When you can define that quality, then you can
reach out for more of the experiences that create your
happiness.

Thursday, October 25 (Moon in Pisces)   You and
your partner may be discussing what you expect from
your relationship, where you hope it may go. Chances
are you won't make any definitive decisions about
changing things, but it's always positive to clear the air
and talk about your respective expectations.

Friday, October 26 (Moon into Aries, 3:32 p.m.)   With
both the moon and Uranus in Aries, your mood is wild,
excitable, daring, perhaps a little reckless. That mood is
likely to persist throughout the weekend. Great for par-
tying, socializing. Just be sure that you don't speed while
driving. On other fronts today, there could be activity
involving taxes and insurance.

Saturday, October 27 (Moon in Aries)   If you're
walking on the wild side today—and you may be—then
reach for the stars, reach for your wildest dreams, Virgo,
and believe that it can happen. Tomorrow, Venus leaves
your sign, so put Venus's energy to use today in a love
relationship, creative project, or something else that is
near and dear to your heart.

Sunday, October 28 (Moon in Aries)   Venus enters
Libra and your solar second house. This transit lasts until November 21 and should bring some nice surprises to
your finances. Perhaps you get a raise. Perhaps someone
gives you an expensive gift. Or, just as likely, you may
buy an expensive item for yourself. Whether it's art, jew-

elry, an antique book, or the car you've dreamed about, look at it as an investment.

Monday, October 29 (Moon into Taurus, 2:16 a.m.) Mercury enters Sagittarius, and there's a full moon in fellow earth sign Taurus. The Mercury transit lasts until December 31 and should bring about a lot of activity at home—people coming and going, discussions, visitors. Between November 6 and 26, it's retrograde. Read more about that in the Big Picture section for your sign. The Taurus full moon brings news about a trip abroad, higher education, publishing. Thanks to a strong angle from Neptune, it also stirs up your ideals.

Tuesday, October 30 (Moon in Taurus) If you're the parent of a young child, then you may be getting ready for Halloween—decorations in the yard, the right costume. You may also be thinking about the last two months of 2012. What all have you achieved this year? Did you keep your new year's resolutions? What would you change if you could? Are you happy with where you are, right this instant?

Wednesday, October 31 (Moon into Gemini, 2:41 p.m.) Happy Halloween! Your thoughts are on work today, your career, professional matters. But even worker bees like you need a break. So kick back this evening with friends, chill, and get ready for November!

NOVEMBER 2012

Thursday, November 1 (Moon in Gemini) If it's cold now where you live, and you can feel the approach of winter, you may want to schedule some time in a warmer climate. Ask for the time off now. How does mid-February look? That's when the winter deep freeze is usually wearing away at your soul, and you have a bad case of the blahs!

Friday, November 2 (Moon in Gemini)   Finish up whatever you've been working on this week so that the weekend ahead is free and clear. With daylight saving time ending on the fourth, the days are about to get darker earlier, and you'll want to be spending time with friends and/or family who brighten your mood. On other fronts, if you haven't started your blog yet, do so today.

Saturday, November 3 (Moon into Cancer, 3:43 a.m.) The Cancer moon is that softer energy that comforts and nurtures you. There's a deep intuitive flow to events and situations today, and when you're in that flow, you're in your psychic groove. Remember how it feels so that on days when you're feeling out of synch, you can find this inner place again.

Sunday, November 4—Daylight Saving Time Ends (Moon in Cancer)   You're enjoying your Sunday and may not even notice that it gets darker earlier. If you've managed to maintain yesterday's flow, then anything you do today should have a strong creative component. So whether you're painting, writing, snapping photos, refurbishing a room in your home, or just hanging out with friends, you're feeling very good about life.

Monday, November 5 (Moon into Leo, 3:40 p.m.)   If you're seeking approval and acceptance from someone or from a group, you may want to step back and ask yourself why someone else's approval is important to you. Chances are you'll discover self-approval makes more sense. After all, if you love and approve of yourself, then it's likely that others approve of you and your actions too.

Tuesday, November 6 (Moon in Leo)   Mercury turns retrograde in Sagittarius and remains retrograde until November 26. This transit can mess up your vacation plans and your Thanksgiving travel plans. That said, it may also bring old friends and former lovers back into your life! Read more about this retrograde in the Big Picture section for your sign.

Wednesday, November 7 (Moon in Leo)   Tomorrow the moon enters your sign, a power day. Get ready for it by exploring your desires. How would you like your life to be? Let your imagination run wild with this one. Your inner critic immediately wants to toss up reasons why your desires won't work. Put tape over your critic's mouth, and shove him or her into a basement!

Thursday, November 8 (Moon into Virgo, 12:36 a.m.)
Your power day! Your inner and outer worlds meld perfectly today. Whatever angst you sometimes feel is blissfully absent. You know the kind of angst we're talking about—that you're not quite up to snuff, that you're an imperfect being, that you're not doing the right thing—you know this drill, right?

Friday, November 9 (Moon in Virgo)   Your attention to details saves the day. You're the great connector, the one who sees exactly how the trees line up in the forest! Supporters join your cause, your project, your mission, whatever it is that you're tackling. On a personal front, you feel quite content with life right now. Isn't that the way life should be all the time?

Saturday, November 10 (Moon into Libra, 5:36 a.m.)
Neptune turns direct in Pisces, your opposite sign. Your ideals and those of your partner become even more important in the dynamics of your relationship. This is true whether the partnership is romantic or strictly business. Neptune's retrograde periods aren't as obvious as those of Mercury, but it's still preferable to have this planet functioning at optimum capacity.

Sunday, November 11 (Moon in Libra)   Your values are highlighted. There could be an event or situation today that drives home what you value and why. You may even discover that what you thought you valued most isn't all that important. For instance, if you've believed for years that money is what you value most, you'll begin to discover that money is actually pretty far down the list.

Monday, November 12 (Moon into Scorpio, 7:11 a.m.) There are days that favor moving ahead and days when it's best to lie low. This one is the former. Just be sure to do your research, collect your facts, and listen to your intuition. If that sounds contradictory, it really isn't. The way the Scorpio moon collects facts is to follow intuitive leads.

Tuesday, November 13 (Moon in Scorpio) Today's solar eclipse in Scorpio should usher in new opportunities in your daily life that thrill you. It's a great time to heal rifts with siblings or other relatives, to look for a neighborhood that would suit you and your family, or to delve into that dusty manuscript that may be sitting in a desk drawer. New opportunities in communication and travel are also possible.

Wednesday, November 14 (Moon into Sagittarius, 6:53 a.m.) Mercury has now retrograded back into Scorpio, so there could be a slight shift in the general mood of people around you and in your own mood. But with the moon entering gregarious Sagittarius, you're ready for a get-together with friends. Party time?

Thursday, November 15 (Moon in Sagittarius) Mars and the moon in Sagittarius travel together for one more day. Make good use of this energy to get things done at home and tend to home-improvement projects that you've put off. You may be fired up about a particular project or plan and should save some time in your busy day to tend to it.

Friday, November 16 (Moon into Capricorn, 6:36 a.m.) Mars enters Capricorn and your solar fifth house, where it will be until December 25. This transit galvanizes your love life, your creativity, and everything you do for fun and pleasure. It also highlights your sexuality. If you're not involved when this transit begins, you may be before it ends.

Saturday, November 17 (Moon in Capricorn) Another day when Mars, the moon, and Pluto travel together. By now, you've undoubtedly figured out how Pluto's transit through Capricorn is affecting romance, creativity, fun, and pleasure in your life. One possibility you may not have considered is that you start a family. The fifth house represents children.

Sunday, November 18 (Moon into Aquarius, 8:11 a.m.) Today's moon forms a beneficial angle to your career area and to Jupiter. This moon should help you to define your professional goals for the coming year. If you feel that your career hasn't expanded as rapidly as you hoped or that you aren't in the profession that's right for you, all of that can change before next June, when Jupiter leaves your career area.

Monday, November 19 (Moon in Aquarius) Cutting-edge ideas and how to implement them: that's your challenge for today. You've got the ideas, but may not understand the nuts and bolts of the last part of the equation. A little research on the Internet or through talking to experts in the field may shed light on this.

Tuesday, November 20 (Moon into Pisces, 12:55 p.m.) The moon joins Neptune in direct motion in your solar seventh house. Romance is in the air. So plan something special with the one you love. Maybe a local restaurant has a Tuesday night deal, and the restaurant is perfect for couples—cozy, dimly lit, with fantastic food and wine. Or, if you're a great cook, then plan a meal at your place. You get the idea. Set the mood.

Wednesday, November 21 (Moon in Pisces)   Venus enters Scorpio and your solar third house, where it will be until December 15. During this period, your daily life should unfold pleasantly, without too many bumps and glitches. This transit also suggests that any relationship that begins is apt to be deeply psychic, sexual, and intense. Your romantic interest could live in your own neighborhood or be someone you meet through a neighbor or siblings.

Thursday, November 22 (Moon into Aries, 9:12 p.m.) The moon joins Uranus in your solar eighth house. The combination of planets can lead to some unusual psychic experiences. You might, for instance, see a ghost. Or you may have a strong hunch to take a different route home from work and meet the lover of your dreams. Or perhaps you have a vivid dream tonight that suddenly plays out in real life tomorrow. Happy Thanksgiving!

Friday, November 23 (Moon in Aries)   Your passions are running fast and furiously. If you're in a romantic relationship, this could mean that you experience jealousy about something that's going on. Or perhaps your sexuality is heightened. You may feel that your partner isn't paying enough attention to you, so you become indignant and refuse to speak to the person for several days.

Saturday, November 24 (Moon in Aries)   You may have to deal with mundane things today—banks and mortgages, taxes, insurance items. You may be looking for tax write-offs too. Don't forget contributions to your 401K, IRA, or similar account. Unless you're up to date on tax laws, you may want to consult with an expert.

Sunday, November 25 (Moon into Taurus, 8:18 a.m.) Finally. Another earth-sign-moon day. This one should help you to get prepared for the Christmas holidays next month. Wait until after Mercury turns direct tomorrow before making travel plans for your December holidays. But it won't hurt to touch base with family and friends now to find out what they're planning.

Monday, November 26 (Moon in Taurus)   Mercury turns direct in Scorpio, a major plus for any traveling you'll be doing over the Christmas holidays. Too bad it hadn't turned direct in time for Thanksgiving travel! You'll notice the change first in your daily life, when the simplest tasks occur without glitches or changes. Since it's another Taurus-moon day, consider planning a menu for the week ahead. Enlist the help of your kids, if you have them, or a partner.

Tuesday, November 27 (Moon into Gemini, 8:59 p.m.) Take stock today of where the year has taken you and what you have achieved professionally and personally. Think about the year that's coming up. What would you like to experience in 2013? What would you like to do, become, achieve?

Wednesday, November 28 (Moon in Gemini)   Today's lunar eclipse in Gemini brings news about a communication project, professional matters, a peer or boss, a coworker. Thanks to a beneficial angle from Jupiter, the news looks positive. Time to celebrate your good fortune!

Thursday, November 29 (Moon in Gemini)   The gift of gab is yours today. Use it well and wisely. If you're in sales, you're riding the tide of yesterday's lunar eclipse and should do remarkably well. Now that Mercury is moving direct, start planning for the December holidays and New Year's Eve.

Friday, November 30 (Moon into Cancer, 9:56 a.m.) Leave your social calendar open. Tonight and the rest of the weekend will be busy. Friends have you on their radar, and your inbox is filling up with invitations, suggestions, stuff to do, and places to go. It's a good way to end the month.

DECEMBER 2012

Saturday, December 1 (Moon in Cancer)   Another soft and fuzzy day. Things may not be real clear to you in a left-brain sense, but intuitively it all makes sense. You're in a creative flow that enables you to go along with whatever is happening around you. No resistance. Remember how this feels so that on days when you seem to resist one thing after another, you can put a stop to that fruitless pattern.

Sunday, December 2 (Moon into Leo, 9:58 p.m.) Once the moon enters Leo tonight, you should have a very good next few days. The Leo moon forms a beneficial angle to Mars in Sagittarius. The combination heightens your emotional pitch so that some things may get blown out of proportion. Just be careful to think before you speak. You don't want to say something you can't take back that might be hurtful to another.

Monday, December 3 (Moon in Leo)   The emotional roller coaster continues. But today you figure out how to keep the pitch at a level you can use to get things done. In addition to the beneficial angle that Mars makes to this moon, Uranus is also forming a beneficial angle. That means nothing is predictable, and sudden, unexpected events are the norm.

Tuesday, December 4 (Moon in Leo)   Tomorrow the moon enters your sign, so it's time to do your internal housecleaning. Make a symbolic gesture by cleaning out a closet, garage, attic, or basement, and as you do that, think of the psychic garbage you're tossing out. Imagine

300

tying the garbage into a neat little bag and dropping it in the trash can.

Wednesday, December 5 (Moon into Virgo, 7:53 a.m.) Today and tomorrow are power days. So dive into whatever you want, Virgo, and go to town on it. You may be surprised by how much you can accomplish in any area where you place your attention and focus. Mindful presence is the key to success in all endeavors today.

Thursday, December 6 (Moon in Virgo)   Connect the dots, all of them. Don't leave anything out of the equation. Whether you're applying this ability of yours to a relationship or a job, a situation or an idea, you bring the same energy to it. As a mutable earth sign, one of your great strengths is adaptability. So at the end of the day, if you have to adapt to an unexpected turn of events, you do so at a moment's notice.

Friday, December 7 (Moon into Libra, 2:37 p.m.) You may get help today from an unexpected source. It could come from an individual, from something you run across online, or perhaps from your own inner wisdom. You may have to find a greater balance in your finances. If you haven't kept to your budget very well this year, then set that goal for 2013.

Saturday, December 8 (Moon in Libra)   Right about now, you're probably hearing a lot about how the Mayan Calendar ends on December 21. Doomsayers are undoubtedly predicting the end of the world, others may be saying that space brothers are going to arrive, and still others . . . well, you'll hear every nutty idea this month. Ignore all of it. The only things you control are your own emotions, thoughts, desires.

Sunday, December 9 (Moon into Scorpio, 5:52 p.m.) The moon joins Saturn in Scorpio. This duo favors solidifying plans, whatever they may be. So take a look at your holiday plans. If you're leaving town, get your itinerary set up. If you're sticking close to home and visitors are coming to your place, figure out what you need to do and when. Saturn helps with all these preparations and keeps you organized.

Monday, December 10 (Moon in Scorpio)   Mercury enters Sagittarius, where it will be until December 31. This transit, in other words, takes you through Christmas and certainly galvanizes all activities in your domestic environment. If you're staying home, that means your days will be hectic. If you're going to be traveling, then Mercury's transit through Sadge certainly brings excitement and a restlessness for new experiences.

Tuesday, December 11 (Moon into Sagittarius, 6:22 p.m.)   The moon and Mercury together in Sadge: your conscious mind and your emotions are in synch. Your Virgo sun may balk at just how chummy these two planets are, but you're able to adapt to the fluid situation and use the Sadge energy to your advantage. How? Look for the big picture, engage in some sort of physical activity, socialize, gather ideas.

Wednesday, December 12 (Moon in Sagittarius)   Do something you've never done before. Take a risk. Be wild. Let your hair down. Don't think about consequences, don't allow your inner critic to squeal about danger, what your mother would think, or anything else. *Just do it.*

Thursday, December 13 (Moon into Capricorn, 5:43 p.m.)   Uranus turns direct in Aries, a welcome change that coincides with a new moon in Sagittarius that occurs at 3:42 A.M. This new moon ushers in opportunities in publishing, higher education, travel, and your domestic environment. Some possibilities? You may have a chance to travel abroad, could find an editor/publisher for your novel, get into the college or grad school of your choice, move. This afternoon the moon enters fellow earth sign Capricorn, and you feel comfortable in your own skin again.

Friday, December 14 (Moon in Capricorn)   If reincarnation is a topic that interests you, then you may treat yourself to a past-life regression. Today, after all, is about enjoyment—the moon in your solar fifth house—so enter into this as you would any adventure. Schedule the regression when the moon is in your sign, so that you don't have any emotional conflict about the experience. Make it a Christmas gift to yourself.

Saturday, December 15 (Moon into Aquarius, 5:53 p.m.)   Venus enters Sagittarius, joining Mercury in your solar fourth house. This transit, which lasts until January 2013, promises that your domestic life will be a hotbed of romance. You may also discover romance on the road, while traveling to foreign locales. That's the Sadge part of the equation.

Sunday, December 16 (Moon in Aquarius)   Venus and today's moon form a beneficial angle to each other, suggesting the possibility of a workplace flirtation developing into something more. Or perhaps you and your present partner embark on a creative endeavor together, and it's the beginning of a business partnership.

Monday, December 17 (Moon into Pisces, 8:48 p.m.) The moon once again joins Neptune in your solar seventh house. Given all the astrological energies today, this duo can manifest itself in one of several ways. You may get sucked into someone's sob story. In this instance, you may play the role of victim or sucker. Or you feel deeply inspired, and you and your partner reach new spiritual heights in your relationship. Another possibility is that you're completely blinded to a partner's true nature.

Tuesday, December 18 (Moon in Pisces)   Done your holiday shopping yet? If you're the type who waits until the last possible minute (like a week before Christmas!), then you'd best hit the mall today. It's too late to order online and expect things to arrive before the new year. Do it all in one fell swoop, but try to make the presents personal.

Wednesday, December 19 (Moon in Pisces)   As we close in on December 21, the media hysteria could be deafening. Best to ignore it and just do your own thing. Also, reread the early sections of the book that discuss December 21, 2012. Think: paradigm shift, not end of world! With the moon and Neptune in Pisces, it's way too easy to buy into the end-of-the-world scenario. Imagination and all that!

Thursday, December 20 (Moon into Aries, 3:44 a.m.) The countdown to the new year—and to December 21—begins. It's likely that the December 21 hype is akin to the millennium fever that occurred at the turn of this century. The survivalists have laid in food and supplies, the religious fanatics are all over cable news, predicting the end of the known universe, and the politics of fear run rampant. Be true to yourself and your belief system, whatever it is, but don't surrender to the hype.

Friday, December 21 (Moon in Aries)   So here we are. How're things in your universe today? Chances are, you're preparing for the holidays, caught up in the plans of family and friends who may be visiting. Just for fun, track the news on TV and online and witness just how nuts the collective can be. Have UFOs landed on the White House lawn? Has the planet tilted on its axis? Has the sun fallen from the sky? Laugh and enjoy your day.

Saturday, December 22 (Moon into Taurus, 2:26 p.m.) This lunar energy helps you to organize and keeps you grounded and yet at the same time urges you to reach for the exotic, the unknown, the mystical. You may be feeling a certain urge to get out of your routine and hit the road. Even if you don't go very far, the movement, the journey, is what matters. Be sure to bring your camera.

Sunday, December 23 (Moon in Taurus)   Now that everyone knows the world didn't end, you're ready for your next adventure. The Taurus moon brings a resolute determination to explore the unexplored, to unearth the mystical, the strange, the curious. On a mundane level, if you haven't finished your holiday shopping, you'd better hustle. *Tempus fugit!*

Monday, December 24 (Moon in Taurus)   Christmas Eve. Depending on how you and your family celebrate Christmas, perhaps tonight is the opening gifts ritual. Or the dinner ritual. Or the church ritual. Or all three. However you celebrate, be genuine about it, and at the very least offer thanks and appreciation for what you have.

Tuesday, December 25 (Moon into Gemini, 3:14 a.m.) Merry Christmas! The moon enters Gemini and the career sector of your chart. But work is undoubtedly the farthest thing from your mind, so use this energy to communicate. Discuss over dinner. Brainstorm with family and friends. With Mars entering Aquarius today, unusual ideas flow quickly. Capture those ideas by jotting them down. Later you'll be glad you did.

Wednesday, December 26 (Moon in Gemini)   With just six days left in the year, it's time to figure out your professional goals for 2013. What are your new year's resolutions in this regard? Are you happy with where you are now in your career? What would you change? Define the obvious; find the magical.

Thursday, December 27 (Moon into Cancer, 4:08 p.m.)
During this hectic holiday season, be sure to nurture yourself. Maintain your exercise regimen. Keep up your nutritional program. Add herbs and vitamins as needed. If it's cold where you are, perhaps additional doses of vitamin C and antioxidants are called for. Research what your body may need.

Friday, December 28 (Moon in Cancer)   It's the last full moon of the year, and it falls in Cancer, a water sign compatible with your earth-sign sun. Uranus forms a challenging angle to this full moon, so opportunities that surface do so suddenly, unexpectedly, and may be in your face and insistent that you make a decision. Don't rush anything. Take your time to mull over the various options.

Saturday, December 29 (Moon in Cancer)   You're still feeling the impact of yesterday's full moon. Today you could meet someone through a group to which you belong or through a friend. The individual really captures your attention. So now you have to ask yourself what you're actually looking for in a partner. A buddy? A sexual partner? A soul mate? The answer could surprise you.

Sunday, December 30 (Moon into Leo, 3:47 a.m.)
It's clear the decks time. You're getting ready for 2013, and it looks as if the moon will be in your sign very early in January. That means it will be your power day, Virgo. Do your psychic cleansing now so that you start 2013 with a clean slate.

Monday, December 31 (Moon in Leo)   What a strange night for Mercury to enter Capricorn. This sign is usually associated with ambition, career. But tonight you're celebrating the fact that a new leaf is turned, it's the dawn of a new year. And hey, the world didn't end, right?

HAPPY NEW YEAR!

Lunar Nodes Ephemeris

Locate your date of birth, find the sign of your North Node, then read the description in chapter 11.

07-04-1930 NN Taurus
12-29-1931 NN Aries
06-25-1933 NN Pisces
03-09-1935 NN Aquarius
09-14-1936 NN Capricorn
03-04-1938 NN Sagittarius
09-11-1939 NN Scorpio
05-23-1941 NN Libra
11-19-1942 NN Virgo
05-13-1944 NN Leo
12-01-1945 NN Cancer
12-10-1945 NN Cancer
12-14-1945 NN Cancer
07-31-1947 NN Gemini
01-22-1949 NN Taurus
07-26-1950 NN Aries
03-29-1952 NN Pisces
10-10-1953 NN Aquarius
04-02-1955 NN Capricorn
10-04-1956 NN Sagittarius
06-16-1958 NN Scorpio
12-15-1959 NN Libra
06-08-1961 NN Virgo
12-21-1962 NN Leo
08-25-1964 NN Cancer
02-18-1966 NN Gemini

08-20-1967 NN Taurus
04-20-1969 NN Aries
11-04-1970 NN Pisces
04-27-1972 NN Aquarius
10-27-1973 NN Capricorn
07-11-1975 NN Sagittarius
01-08-1977 NN Scorpio
07-04-1978 NN Libra
01-11-1980 NN Virgo
09-23-1981 NN Leo
03-16-1983 NN Cancer
09-13-1984 NN Gemini
04-01-1986 NN Taurus
04-14-1986 NN Taurus
04-22-1986 NN Taurus
11-30-1987 NN Aries
05-24-1989 NN Pisces
11-19-1990 NN Aquarius
08-03-1992 NN Capricorn
02-01-1994 NN Sagittarius
08-01-1995 NN Scorpio
01-25-1997 NN Libra
10-19-1998 NN Virgo
04-12-2000 NN Leo
10-11-2001 NN Cancer
04-11-2003 NN Gemini
12-24-2004 NN Taurus
06-19-2006 NN Aries
12-15-2007 NN Pisces
08-22-2009 NN Aquarius
02-28-2011 NN Capricorn

SYDNEY OMARR

Born on August 5, 1926, in Philadelphia, Pennsylvania, **Sydney Omarr** was the only person ever given full-time duty in the U.S. Army as an astrologer. He is regarded as the most erudite astrologer of the twentieth century and the best known, through his syndicated column and his radio and television programs (he was Merv Griffin's "resident astrologer"). Omarr has been called the most "knowledgeable astrologer since Evangeline Adams." His forecasts of Nixon's downfall, the end of World War II in mid-August of 1945, the assassination of John F. Kennedy, Roosevelt's election to a fourth term and his death in office . . . these and many others are on the record and quoted enough to be considered "legendary."

ABOUT THE SERIES

This is one of a series of twelve *Sydney Omarr® Day-by-Day Astrological Guides* for the signs of 2012. For questions and comments about the book, go to www.tjmacgregor.com.